Lecture Notes in Computer Science

Edited by G. Goos, J. Hartmanis, and J. van Leeuwen

Springer
Berlin
Heidelberg
New York
Barcelona
Hong Kong
London
Milan
Paris
Tokyo

Tomas Sander (Ed.)

Security and Privacy in Digital Rights Management

ACM CCS-8 Workshop DRM 2001
Philadelphia, PA, USA, November 5, 2001
Revised Papers

 Springer

Series Editors

Gerhard Goos, Karlsruhe University, Germany
Juris Hartmanis, Cornell University, NY, USA
Jan van Leeuwen, Utrecht University, The Netherlands

Volume Editor

Tomas Sander
InterTrust STAR Lab. - New Jersey
821 Alexander Rd., Princeton, NJ 08540-6303, USA
E-mail: sander@intertrust.com

Cataloging-in-Publication Data applied for

Die Deutsche Bibliothek - CIP-Einheitsaufnahme

Security and privacy in digital rights management : revised papers / ACM
CCS-8 Workshop DRM 2001, Philadelphia, PA, USA, November 5, 2001.
Thomas Sander (ed.). - Berlin ; Heidelberg ; New York ; Barcelona ; Hong Kong ;
London ; Milan ; Paris ; Tokyo : Springer, 2002
    (Lecture notes in computer science ; Vol. 2320)
    ISBN 3-540-43677-4

CR Subject Classification (1998): E.3, C.2, D.2.0, D.4.6, K.6.5, F.3.2, H.5, J.1, K.4.1,
K.4.4, K.5

ISSN 0302-9743
ISBN 3-540-43677-4 Springer-Verlag Berlin Heidelberg New York

Springer-Verlag Berlin Heidelberg New York
a member of BertelsmannSpringer Science+Business Media GmbH

http://www.springer.de

© Springer-Verlag Berlin Heidelberg 2002
Printed in Germany

Typesetting: Camera-ready by author, data conversion by DA-TeX Gerd Blumenstein
Printed on acid-free paper   SPIN 10846660   06/3142   5 4 3 2 1 0

Preface

The ACM Workshop on Security and Privacy in Digital Rights Management is the first scientific workshop with refereed proceedings devoted solely to this topic. The workshop was held in conjunction with the Eighth ACM Conference on Computer and Communications Security (CCS-8) in Philadelphia, USA on November 5, 2001.

Digital Rights Management technology is meant to provide end-to-end solutions for the digital distribution of electronic goods. Sound security and privacy features are among the key requirements for such systems.

Fifty papers were submitted to the workshop, quite a success for a first-time workshop. From these 50 submissions, the program committee selected 15 papers for presentation at the workshop. They cover a broad area of relevant techniques, including cryptography, system architecture, and cryptanalysis of existing DRM systems. Three accepted papers are about software tamper resistance, an area about which few scientific articles have been published before. Another paper addresses renewability of security measures. Renewability is another important security technique for DRM systems, and I hope we will see more publications about this in the future. I am particularly glad that three papers cover economic and legal aspects of digital distribution of electronic goods. Technical security measures do not exist in a vacuum and their effectiveness interacts in a number of ways with the environment for legal enforcement. Deploying security and anti-piracy measures adequately requires furthermore a good understanding of the business models that they are designed to support.

We felt there was a need for a workshop devoted to DRM in order to create an interdisciplinary forum for the exchange of ideas from a number of relevant areas. The lively discussions at the workshop suggest that we were not mistaken.

During the conference pre-proceedings were made available. Final versions were prepared by the authors shortly after the workshop and have been included in this volume without further review.

It is a great pleasure for me to thank everyone whose help and contribution made the workshop a success. The 17 program committee members did a great job in reviewing and selecting the papers within a tight schedule. Mike Reiter was the General Chair of our host conference CCS-8 and took very good care of all the organizational aspects of the workshop. I would like to thank Microsoft Research for access to their committee software for the review process. Mike Freedman helped with running the committee software. I would further like to thank the ACM CCS-8 conference organizers and our sponsoring organization, the ACM, for being such great hosts. Special thanks go to Stuart Haber, who gave an invited talk introducing and surveying modern DRM technology.

As this goes to press the jury is still out about the practical effectiveness of security measures in DRM systems. Much more real-world data and experience are needed. Fortunately we will see the first mass deployments in 2002, and thus we may reasonably hope to gain some insights from these deployments for future workshops focusing on DRM.

February 2001   Tomas Sander

Conference Organizers

Table of Contents

Cryptanalysis

Economics, Legal Aspects

Discouraging Software Piracy
Using Software Aging

Markus Jakobsson[1] and Michael K. Reiter[2]

[1] RSA Labs
Bedford, MA, USA
mjakobsson@rsasecurity.com
[2] Carnegie Mellon University
Pittsburgh, PA, USA
reiter@cmu.edu

Abstract. Most people consider frequent software updates a nuisance. However, we show how this common phenomenon can be turned into a feature that protects against software piracy. We define a protocol for "drop-in" upgrades of software that renders a large class of software piracy more traceable. A novel feature of our approach is a *software aging* technique by which we force the updates to occur, or else the software becomes decreasingly useful over time.

1 Introduction

According to a recent study [ ], the computer industry loses $11 billion annually to piracy, with 40 percent of all software programs pirated. Software piracy is a crime that traditional legal and technical methods to a large extent fail to prevent, much due to the low cost of the crime and the inherent impossibility of preventing data copying. Still, and as we show in this paper, there are practical methods that can be employed to discourage software piracy by making it less economically viable. The threat that we address here is that in which a pirate obtains, potentially alters, and then distributes copies of a piece of software in order to make a profit. We do *not* consider the situation in which several mutually trusting and coordinating users buy a piece of software together, although this is also a major concern to the software industry. We also do not consider piracy that is performed "for the fame of it", but focus on the problem in which pirated software is distributed for a profit.

Our protection method relies on periodic updates of software. Traditionally, and independently of our proposal, users want to have their software updated, typically in order to fix known bugs, to add security patches, to add new functionality, and to keep their software compatible with other programs. We consider how these two seemingly independent issues, i.e., piracy protection and software updates, can be addressed at the same time, giving us an improved system as a result. We also introduce a novel method, *software aging*, for increasing the dependence on updates.

T. Sander (Ed.): DRM 2001, LNCS 2320, pp. 1–12, 2002.

Our software updating methods discourage piracy by benefiting legitimate users while inflicting damage on illegitimate users. This differentiation of service creates a situation in which illegitimate users—in order to avoid that their software becomes incompatible to that of their surroundings—are forced to rely on the pirate for updates. This increases the operating costs for the pirate, and forces the pirate to keep in touch with its customers (which in turn increases the risk of discovery by authorities). At the same time, it increases the amount of trust the buyer of pirated software needs to place on the pirate (namely that he will provide updates). This decreases the value of the pirated software to its buyer, due to the risk that it may become incompatible if the updating service is not kept running. It is interesting to note that the customers of the pirate do not necessarily benefit from the pirate being successful; namely, the risks of the pirate's discovery increase with the number of customers the pirate needs to update. (This is in contrast to the typical economy of large operations.)

In addition to inflicting the above disadvantage on pirates, our methods can be used to shorten the life of *pirate* software below its current life span. Clearly, necessary and frequent updates further lowers the value of pirated software and further aggravates piracy by increasing the necessary updating frequency. (We note that this must be done with the convenience of the legitimate user in mind, as much as the inconvenience of his illegitimate counterpart, in order not to alter the perception of the software for the legitimate users.)

Altogether, we believe our techniques will infringe upon the economical viability of piracy by raising the operating costs for the pirate, and lowering the resale value of his merchandise. At the same time, the costs of maintaining the updates are kept low for the distributor, assuming that the updates are performed using an on-line protocol. This is a reasonable approach given that most computer users also are modem owners.

We note that our methods work even under the pessimistic assumption that the pirate is able to remove or alter any pieces of code and data that are used to detect or prevent piracy, such as code-embedded watermarks, verification of CPU identities, and similar. Also, in addition to defending against piracy, our suggested model makes software rentals easier to administer (simply by charging for the updates as opposed to providing these for free).

Outline: We begin by introducing our model in section 2, followed by a discussion of our general goals and methods in section 3. Then, we review related work in section 4, followed by a more precise description of our solution. One part of our method is the updating protocol we suggest in section 5; another part is our suggested methods to speed up "aging" of software (section 6). We conclude in section 7 by stating and arguing the properties of our solution.

2   Model and Requirements

We consider a model with the following participants:

- **Distributor.** The distributor sells software, keeps a list of registered users, and maintains a service for software updates for legitimate users. The goal of the distributor is to maximize his profit, and to discourage pirate versions of his software from being used.
- **Legitimate users.** Legitimate users purchase software from the distributor, and obtain updates from the same. The legitimate users want the piracy protection to be transparent as far as possible, in the sense that it should cause a minimum of negative side effects (such as delays and increases of file sizes). In other words, in terms of the features offered to the users, the legitimate users want their software to be as close as possible to the *ideal* of the software (where we use the word "ideal" as done by Plato).
- **Pirate.** The pirate obtains the software sold by the distributor, and redistributes (potentially altered) copies of the software for a charge. We make the pessimistic assumption that the pirate has access to the source code of the software he wants to redistribute, and that he is capable of altering (and compiling) this in order to remove any protection mechanisms. The pirate wants to maximize his profit and minimize the risks of discovery/prosecution.
- **Illegitimate users.** Illegitimate users obtain software from the pirate. Just like the legitimate user, the illegitimate user wants the software he uses to be as close as possible to the ideal of the software, again in terms of the functionality offered to the user. Additionally, illegitimate users want to maximize their profit (by buying software at a "piracy discount") and minimize the risks of failure. We assume that illegitimate users generally do not cooperate with one another, nor permit their pirate software copies to serve updates to other pirate copies (e.g., lest they be implicated as pirates themselves).[1] Rather, we assume that illegitimate users interact only with the pirate for the purposes of obtaining software.

3   Approach

Goals. We want to force the pirate to be responsible for regularly updating its customers' software. We consider the link between pirate and customer as the cost (in terms of risks of discovery) to the pirate, as opposed to the bandwidth between them once a connection is made. Requiring a link therefore requires either that the pirate can be contacted by its customer in some manner (preferably electronically in order for the illegitimate user not to be inconvenienced) or that the pirate can contact his customers[2] (again, preferably electronically). Here, the selection of the "meeting place" (which may be a public bulletin board) may be fixed over time and the same for all users; unique for each user and changing according to some pseudo-random pattern; or somewhere between these two extremes. In either case, we have that the need for communication increases the

---

[1] Experience with anonymous file sharing systems such as Gnutella suggests that this position is overwhelmingly the norm [1].

[2] We note that the latter contact method allows the pirate to move around, at the cost of forcing illegitimate users to register their location.

risks for legal action against the pirate, as it would allow "infiltrators" to discover the pirate and take action to trace him. This threat increases the risk of the pirated software to its users, as these will be made to rely on updates from a pirate that may either disappear to avoid tracing or be successfully traced and taken out of business.

Method for forcing interaction. We achieve our goals by letting the distributor supply software updates to registered, legitimate users. If an illegitimate user were to contact the distributor for an update, he would have to give a registration number. In case it is invalid, the distributor may supply a "random update", thereby efficiently corrupting the operation of the pirate software. In case it is valid, it allows the distributor to partially trace the criminal (from software distribution lists). He may also supply a random update in case he has already updated the software for the given user in this time period (i.e., another clone of it).

Therefore, a rational pirate would have to alter the portion of the software that requests updates in a way that it either contacts the pirate (which would hardwire a contract address for the pirate in every piece of pirate software sold) or that awaits an update from the pirate. If this is not done, then illegitimate users will be refused updates, which will lower the value of the pirated software to them, and therefore also the possible profit to the pirate.

Means for communication. The software distributor supplies updates by either the legitimate users contacting the distributor, or vice versa. Then, after contact has been established, some identification scheme is run, and the update is transmitted from the distributor to the user. The pirate has the same type of communication channel available. In addition, we assume that he may use (potentially anonymous) bulletin boards as a communication channel.

Limitations. In this paper we consider only programs that generate files or messages that may need to be interpreted by other instances of the same program; hereafter, all such outputs are referred to as "files". Numerous programs are of this form, include word processors, spreadsheet packages, and networked games. We do not consider software that works in perfect isolation, such as single-player games for a PC. However, our methods can be extended to any program by a hierarchical approach in which the operating system requires updates[3], and the operating system requires all programs it runs to be updated.

---

[3] On the surface it may appear sufficient that the operating system requires the programs it runs to be updated, but that it does not have to be updated itself. This, however, would allow a pirate to circumvent the protection by disabling the portion of the operating system that forces the programs it runs to be updated. On the other hand, in order for the attacker to avoid this from happening in a situation where the operating system has to be updated is to supply illegitimate users with operating system updates.

Conflict resolution. In the above, we have only considered what happens in the common case. There are two special cases of interest:

- **Synchronization problems.** It is not unlikely that sometimes, the connection between a user and the distributor is interrupted during a transfer. Whereas the typical approach to this in a standard setting is to execute the same sequence of steps again (with the same input and random strings), we note that such an approach is inadequate here. The reason is that this would allow a pirate to clone software that "hangs up" after having received the update, allowing another clone to claim that the connection was interrupted right *before* the last step. On the other hand, legitimate users must not be denied updates, creating an interesting new kind of fairness/synchronization problem.
- **Repentant illegitimate user.** It may be of interest to allow illegitimate users to become legitimate (by paying some fee closely corresponding to the costs of acquiring the software to begin with). By doing this, the pirate is used by the distributor much like an advertiser handing out samples that work for a limited time period. This corresponds functionally to selling the software using an on-line protocol, although it may require less information to be transferred. We will not elaborate on this scenario.

Method for forcing frequent updates. Typically, updates to software are currently done on roughly an annual basis, as there is not much need for more frequent updates, and as the cost and inconvenience of more frequent updates is substantial (using currently employed updating methods). As the success of our protection mechanism depends on the frequency with which updates are necessary, we wish to increase the frequency. We may, for example, want weekly or bi-weekly updates to be (automatically) made.

Note that it is not sufficient to force *legitimate* users to perform these updates. (In fact, it is the *illegitimate* users we want to force to make updates.) It appears that the only way to force illegitimate users to perform updates is to make these necessary for smooth operation. We consider a method in which files output by the software contain a version-dependent number that affects how the file should be interpreted when read or written. In order for software of illegitimate users to be compatible with that of legitimate users—or more specifically, for it to be able to interpret files received from legitimate users—the illegitimate software must be (roughly) as up-to-date as the legitimate user's software that created the file. To enforce this, the software contains a short secret that, together with the version number of the software, allows interpretation of files that are older or as old as the software (where age is measured in terms of version number). We propose a method achieving this goal, while smoothly allowing new software versions to interpret both old and new files.

We note that the functional changes embodied in updates must not be possible for an attacker to predict, since then the pirate could implement these updates directly and thus avoid that the illegitimate users are forced to request updates. Similarly, it must be infeasible for an isolated program (i.e., that of the illegitimate user) to *determine* the functional updates (e.g., by observing files from properly updated pieces of software). Our solution offers these properties.

4   Related Work

Requiring registration (see, e.g., [ ]) is a common method of protecting against piracy. However, this only protects software that has not been manipulated by a pirate, and therefore aims more toward preventing copying between friends than "professional piracy". Here we show that interaction allows to defend against a stronger type of adversary.

There are two classes of commercial products that work according to similar principles as our solution, as they use interaction to control piracy. One such product [ ] allows registered users—but only these—to access a large repository of clipart. It is likely that it is verified that the access frequencies for each user remain at a reasonable level, thereby discouraging massive cloning of the accessing software. Another commercial service [ ] first gives users a free virus detecting program, with a few free updates, after which the updating service only becomes available per subscription.

Our scheme is also to some degree related to the problem of fair exchange of signatures (see, e.g., [ ]). Recall that we aim to obtain security of our scheme via software updates. However, for each updating period, only *one* update should be sent per software identifier (each corresponding to one sold software package). It is possible that the transmission is interrupted during an update; that one of the parties willfully terminates before the completion of the protocol; or that one party claims to have been disconnected, while he was not. It is impossible for the protocol participants to distinguish between accidentally dropped connections and intentionally dropped connections, and impossible to determine whether the transmission was interrupted before or after a certain transcript was received. This causes a situation resembling that in exchange of signatures (that one entity may interrupt the transmission in order to obtain some benefit). Our approach to address this problem, though, is significantly different from that used for exchange of signatures, as there is a very different adversarial model, and due to the inherent asymmetry of the desired exchange in our setting.

A similar situation to that described above can also occur during the withdrawal protocol for e-cash schemes. There, the solution is to repeat transcripts *identically* to avoid extraction of a higher number of valid coins by a cheater; in our setting, however, it is better to *change* the format of the transcripts for "re-connecting" updates. This is done in a way that disrupts independent clones from getting updates, while not complicating the re-transmission for legitimate users, whether connecting or re-connecting.

5   Updating Method

Initialization. The distributor $\mathcal{D}$ assigns an identifier to each piece of software he sells. This could be done either by incorporating this identity in the software, or as is often done, as a paper document from which the user copies the identity at the time of installation. Identifiers are chosen by drawing (without repetition) random elements from a sparse space.

Updating Protocol. At predetermined intervals, the user $\mathcal{U}$ updates his software portfolio by sending in a list of program identifiers to the distributor $\mathcal{D}$. $\mathcal{D}$ verifies that these are valid identifiers, and that they have not been used for updates during the current time period.[4] Then, for each piece of software that is determined to correspond to a valid update request (i.e., a legitimate user), $\mathcal{D}$ sends out a correct update of this program. If the request is found not to be valid (i.e., if there is no such identifier registered, or if the maximum number of updates have already been performed for this time interval; both correspond to an illegitimate user) then $\mathcal{D}$ may either refuse an update, or may send a "random update". What constitutes a "correct update" or "random update" is determined by our software aging mechanism and thus will be described in Section 6. Intuitively, however, a correct update, once applied to the user's software, makes this software functionally current with other updated copies of the software (i.e., files produced by one can be read by the other) and partially backwards compatible with out-of-date versions (i.e., it can read files produced by out-of-date software, but out-of-date software cannot read files it produces). A "random update", once applied to the user's software, renders that software ineffective in reading any files created by other (current or out-of-date) copies of the program.

Remarks. In the above, we consider a setting with only one distributor. This trivially generalizes to any number of distributors, who may then either operate independently, or cooperate in updating user software. Also, we did not address the communication protocol. Assuming a public communication channel, we would use some form of encryption for sending the transcripts. For this, some form of symmetric encryption method may be employed. (The user identifier as used so far is a shared secret key for identification purposes, and may be augmented with a portion used for encryption.)

Conflict Resolution. If the transmission is interrupted during an update, the user has to request another update. In order for the distributor not to mistake such a repeated request for a separate request made by a clone, we suggest a variety of methods, potentially used in combination with each other:

– **Failure counter.** If both parties record in a local counter the number of failed attempts by this user, and if the user transmits this at the beginning of the update protocol, this allows the distributor to distinguish between a repeated transmission and an independent transmission by a clone. (Recall that illegitimate users are assumed to not cooperate with each other.)

---

[4] If the distributor grants multiple licenses to one site, then the updating may either be performed in a coordinated manner, or the distributor will allow a number of updates corresponding to the number of licenses.

- **Random nonces.** The distributor may send a random nonce to the user during his first move of a multi-move interactive protocol; this nonce has to be transmitted by the user during the next connection (or re-connection). Here, the distributor will know that the user received a nonce if the distributor receives a (potentially implicit) acknowledgement from the user. Otherwise, he will accept both the current and last nonce during the next (re-)connection.
- **Extra updates.** The distributor may allow a low number of (say five) repeated identifiers to get updates, thereby efficiently preventing against large-scale piracy still, but without introducing problems related to interrupted transmission (since it is unlikely that an update will fail more than five times).
- **Human involvement.** The distributor may require the user to call a toll-free number to "roll back" the state after a failed updating attempt. Here, the distributor may verify from whom the call is made, etc., before the roll-back is allowed. Moreover, if updates are sufficiently frequent, the inconvenience imposed on illegitimate users by this mechanism would already decrease the pirated software's value.

Pirate Tracing. For each update request that is recorded as being initiated by an illegitimate user, the distributor determines to what cluster of illegal copies the copy belongs. This is indexed by the identifier of the user software, and other available information. Similar methods are used for pirate software recovered by other means. This allows the distributor to determine (with some accuracy) the extent and source of the problem.

Avoiding Anonymous Pirates. In order to restrict the pirate to an approach in which he needs to be in direct contact with each customer for each update, it is important to limit the usefulness of bulletin boards, and in particular, anonymous bulletin boards. We note that if bulletin boards are used, the pirated software must initiate the update (as the bulletin board will not). Therefore, the software must carry with itself a description of where to look and for what, starting with what bulletin boards to search. If law enforcement or a representative of the software distributor gets access to a piece of pirate software, they can perform the same search. If an update is found on a bulletin board, the corresponding administrator can be pressured by legal means to remove the entry, and if submitted anonymously, to aid a trace.

6   Software Aging

So far, we have only been concerned with how to make updates, and not how to force the user to do these. To a certain extent, users will want to (and have to) update software due to naturally occurring changes of the same. However, since it is beneficial for us if frequent updates were necessary (as this makes life more difficult for the pirate), we have an interest in making the software *age*, i.e., decrease the time periods between necessary updates. Although this is contrary to the interests of users in a traditional setting, we suggest that it does not cause difficulties in our setting, where updates are made automatically, and without human user involvement.

Additionally, if we allow a certain flexibility in terms of what phase a user is in (e.g., any one out of the three most recent time periods) then we avoid synchronization problems and potential difficulties due to failure of getting updates (e.g., while traveling). If such a flexible timing is adapted (we address how to do this below) then we may also allow updates to be performed in an overlapping fashion (i.e., not all users need to update during the same short interval of time).

Aging. Our solution is for the software to encrypt all files[5] it outputs using a symmetric key common to all copies of that version of the software. Each file also is labeled with the time interval in which it was last modified (in plaintext), which indicates the key with which encryption was performed.

In order to avoid having to refresh all files when a key update is performed, and in order to avoid storing all old keys, we propose a method in which old keys can be computed from new keys (but not vice versa). More specifically, let $K_t = f(K_{t+1})$, where t denotes a time interval, $t + 1$ denotes the next time interval, and f is a public one-way function that is infeasible to invert for the pirate. The distributor either has a trap-door key allowing him to invert the function f, or starts with a value K_T from which all "earlier" values down to an initial value K_0 are computed.[6] A "correct update" sent to a legitimate user at the transition from interval t to $t + 1$ includes K_{t+1}, which the legitimate user uses to replace his old key. The correct update may also include patches to the software to add new features, fix newly-discovered security problems, etc. A "random update" sent to a detected illegitimate user would contain a random number in place of K_{t+1}. It may also include patches to the software that actively corrupts the software, so that it will no longer execute. Note that even if the illegitimate user detects the random update and prevents it from being applied to his software, the utility of his software will continue to degrade because it cannot read files output by later versions (and thus encrypted by K_{t+1} or some later key).

Remarks. For the software aging method we propose, any type of encryption scheme may be employed as a building block. For maximum efficiency, we propose using a symmetric cipher, such as DES [ ]. We note that this is safe even if DES is not considered to be safe in a general setting. The reason is that we only need to protect against individual users from being able to decrypt messages or establish the key from seen messages. We do not need to prevent a more powerful

---

[5] A practical alternative is to only encrypt *portions* of the file, such as vital formatting-related portions or compression tables.

[6] Here, a value T exceeding the anticipated number of update periods is selected. For example, assuming that no piece of software has a life exceeding one hundred years, and assuming weekly updates, this corresponds to $T = 5200$.

adversary, such as the pirate himself, as if he determines the decryption key, he would have to distribute it to all his customers anyway (which is, by the cost and risk of doing this, a factor we base the security of our system on). We use the encryption scheme in a somewhat unusual way, in that we distribute *the same* encryption/decryption key to all legitimate users (allowing these to correctly interpret each other's files). Again, this is not a security flaw, even though it will be very easy for the pirate to get the keys (he may even *be* one of the legitimate users, and so, receive the key automatically). The reason for this is to force the illegitimate users to receive the key via updates from the pirate, if they cannot compute it themselves. Therefore, this unusual use of encryption does not negatively affect the security of our solution.

We further note that f does not have to remain infeasible to invert over the life of the software, but only require "too much" computational effort to invert for it to be convenient to do every time period by the illegitimate users. Should, however, an attack become known, allowing fast inversion of the function, then a new function has to be selected and employed. All software needs then to be updated to "refresh" all files of the old format, which can be performed by an intermediary version with knowledge of both the old key and the new key, and the corresponding one-way functions.

Allowing for flexible updates. In order to make new files readable to a software version that is not updated to the same version, the following method may be employed: Instead of using the most recently distributed key K_t for writing files in time interval t, the software may instead use $K_{t-\delta}$, where δ reflects the updating frequency necessary for a piece of software to be able to read new files from legitimate users. For example, we may set $\delta = 2$, allowing programs to be two updates "behind".

7   Claims

Our scheme hinders a pirate in that it forces him to frequently distribute updates to his clients. At the same time the piracy protection scheme is transparent to legitimate users (under reasonable assumptions) in that they will not be inconvenienced by the protection methods. We will now state these properties more carefully.

We assume that the pirate does not collude with honest users. If some user performs updates for another user, we consider the first user to be part of the pirate organization. Recall that δ determines the frequency of updates needed to ensure that a legitimate user's software remains compatible. Let $I_1, \ldots, I_N$ be N illegitimate users of the software in question. Let n be the number of updates the distributor allows to one and the same software clone (where we typically have $n = 1$), and finally, let c be the number of software packages the pirate has legally purchased from the distributor.

Let us assume that it is infeasible for the adversary to compute the trap-door of f (if there is one). We also assume that it is impractical for an illegitimate user to invert f, or to determine the encryption key for a given time period from transcripts in his possession.

Claim 1: In order for the software of the illegitimate users to work without a significant degradation of functionality at any time, and given the above assumptions, the pirate needs to update at least $N - cn\delta$ of the users $I_1 \ldots I_N$, and at least every δ time intervals on average.

Correctness Argument for Claim 1:
By assumption, the pirate has distributed N copies of the (potentially altered) software. Assume that these users are not interacting with each other or with the pirate (after a first interaction in which they receive the software from the pirate). It is necessary for each user to get a software update at least every δ time intervals. For each legitimate software package sold, the distributor is willing to perform at most δn updates in this time period. Since honest users by assumption do not collaborate with the illegitimate users, the illegitimate users can get a maximum of $c\delta n$ updates for the c licenses the pirate purchased (if any). This leaves $N - c\delta n$ illegitimate users without updates for at least δ consecutive time intervals, considering only updates from the distributor.

By assumption, it is not feasible (neither for the pirate nor the illegitimate users) to invert f, and so, it is not possible to determine new keys from old ones by inverting f. Note that none of the trap-door information (if any) is made part of the transcripts (such as files communicated), and so, access to such transcripts cannot make the inversion easier. Finally, since we have assumed that it is *impractical* for the illegitimate user to determine the current key from transcripts (using standard methods for cryptanalysis in order to extract the key), we have now exhausted the number of ways in which a user can obtain an updated key. The only possibilities that remain are for these users not to get updates as often as needed, or to get updates from the pirate. □

Remark: Note that software that was updated $\delta + i$ time periods ago only fails to read files that were written in the last i time intervals – this allows us to expand on this argument in terms of the "quality of service" of the illegitimate users. Thus, a more general version of the above argument can be used to show the minimum number of licenses for a minimum quality of service. However, here, we have only considered "full" quality of service, corresponding to pirated software that works *identically* to the corresponding legitimate software.

Claim 2: The software of a legitimate user will work without significant degradation of functionality at any time as long as the user manages to connect to the distributor at least every δ time periods.

Correctness Argument for Claim 2:
Legitimate users are eligible to receive updates each time interval. We assume that the periodic interaction can be performed with a frequency of at least δ time intervals (i.e., that the legitimate user can connect with this frequency, and that the update protocol is not consistently interrupted after which no recovery action is taken). As long as they succeed in receiving updates every δ time intervals,

they will have a key that can be used to decrypt files written by legitimate users who have just updated their software, and therefore have the most recent keys available. Older files can always be read since it is possible to compute an old key from a new in polynomial time, given the chaining property of keys. □

Acknowledgments

Many thanks to Eran Gabber and Fabian Monrose for helpful discussions.

References

1. E. Adar and B. A. Huberman. Free riding on Gnutella. *First Monday*, October 2000. http://www.firstmonday.dk/issues/issue5_10/adar/index.html. 3
2. N. Asokan, V. Shoup, and M. Waidner. Optimistic protocols for fair exchange. In *Proc. ACM Conference on Computer and Communications Security*, pages 6–17, 1996. 6
3. The Business Software Alliance. www.bsa.org. 1
4. McAfee Secure Cast / Active Shield. www.McAfee.com. 6
5. Microsoft Clip Art Gallery Live. cgl.microsoft.com/clipgallerylive. 6
6. NBS FIPS Pub 46-1. Data Encryption Standard, U. S. Department of Commerce, 1988. 9
7. Sheriff Software Development Kit. www.sheriff-software.com. 6

New Iterative Geometric Methods
for Robust Perceptual Image Hashing

M. Kıvanç Mıhçak[1] and Ramarathnam Venkatesan[2]

[1] Beckman Institute and ECE Department, University of Illinois
Urbana-Champaign, Urbana, IL, 61801
mihcak@ifp.uiuc.edu
[2] Microsoft Research
Redmond, WA, 98052
venkie@microsoft.com

Abstract. We propose a novel and robust hashing paradigm that uses iterative geometric techniques and relies on observations that main geometric features within an image would approximately stay invariant under small perturbations. A key goal of this algorithm is to produce sufficiently randomized outputs which are unpredictable, thereby yielding properties akin to cryptographic MACs. This is a key component for robust multimedia identification and watermarking (for synchronization as well as content dependent key generation). Our algorithm withstands standard benchmark (e.g Stirmark) attacks provided they do not cause severe perceptually significant distortions. As verified by our detailed experiments, the approach is relatively media independent and works for audio as well.

1 Introduction

An image hashing function $H_K(.)$ takes an image I as input and computes a short vector $h = H_K(I)$ which is a random value (indexed by the secret key K) in some large set. The hash value is required to be invariant under small changes to I that are perceptually insignificant, whereas on perceptually distinct inputs the hash values need to be approximately independent (and thus different with high probability). Such a function will be useful in identification of images in databases, with I possibly undergoing small non-malicious changes (such as compression and format changes, common signal processing algorithms, scanning, or watermarking). If h is binary, one may use the standard searching and sorting methods for database applications. In this case, if the database has size n, the search would take $\log n$ steps rather than n [ ]. This task is considerably harder if one is to weather malicious attacks (e.g. by a pirate) to I that intentionally aim to foil identifying the image.

Robust image hashing algorithms can be used in multimedia protection applications, namely watermarking and authentication. From a security viewpoint, using the same key for many images will introduce a weakness, since an attacker may recover the single secret given a large number of images all watermarked

T. Sander (Ed.): DRM 2001, LNCS 2320, pp. 13–21, 2002.

with the same key as each image may leak some information about the key. Instead, for each I, using an image dependent key $s = H_K(I)$ (with K secret) would avoid this problem. If the hash value is invariant under watermarking and small attacks, the decoder may compute s if K is known. Another use is of synchronization in a stream where one searches for some specific position, skipping all intentional insertions and deletions. Thus, one may watermark a video stream and can synchronize against de-synch attacks. In particular hash values could be used as pointers that indicate the location of the watermark. Such an approach would also provide extra computational efficiency when the size of the input stream to be watermarked is huge. These issues were also discussed in [,] and form the basis of our approach in [ ]. For the problem of image watermarking, the hash values of different regions could be used to gain robustness against *Stirmark* type de-synch attacks [ ].

Note that conventional cryptographic hashing algorithms, such as MD5 and SHA-1 would not be applicable in the aforementioned multimedia applications, since changing even one bit of the input will change the outputs dramatically [ ].

2   Problem Definition and Notation

We first outline the traditional approach to the hashing problem. Hash functions, that are quite useful in various cryptographic, compiler, database search applications, map long binary strings to short binary strings. The requirements are uniform distribution on the output data and pairwise independence (i.e. given any pair of outputs of the hash function, that should be independent of each other). These requirements suffice to maximize the probability that a pair of distinct inputs results in distinct hash values. In particular it can be shown that collision probability of the output is minimized if the output distribution is uniform.

Clearly, we need similar minimization of collision probabilities in the case of image hashing. Furthermore, the constraint, that the output of the hash function should be invariant under small perceptually insignificant modifications (unintentional or malicious), forces us to follow an entirely new approach. This is clearly not a well–defined notion; we will say that two images are "perceptually same" if a human eye cannot distinguish them. However, in general some applications would need to tolerate a wider set of modifications; if two images are approximately the same for all practical purposes, despite the fact that the changes are visible, we wish to produce the same hash value for these two inputs. A similar approach was taken in [ ].

Let $\mathbf{X}$ denote a particular image, $\hat{\mathbf{X}}$ denote a modified version of this image which is "perceptually similar to $\mathbf{X}$ for all practical purposes". Let $\mathbf{Y}$ denote an image that is "perceptually different" from $\mathbf{X}$. Let L be the final length of the hash, and let $H_K(.)$ represent a hashing function that uses the secret key K. We use a normalized Hamming distance $D(.,.)$ for comparing two hash values which is the ratio of the usual Hamming distance and the size of the inputs. Our criteria can be stated as:

1. **Randomization:** $\Pr[H_K(\mathbf{X}) = \alpha] \approx \frac{1}{2^L}, \quad \forall \alpha \in \{0,1\}^L.$
2. **Pairwise independence for perceptually different inputs:**
   $\Pr[H_K(\mathbf{X}) = \alpha | H_K(\mathbf{Y}) = \beta] \approx \Pr[H_K(\mathbf{X}) = \alpha], \quad \forall \alpha, \beta \in \{0,1\}^L.$
3. **Invariance under perceptual similarity:**
   $\Pr\left[H_K(\mathbf{X}) = H_K\left(\hat{\mathbf{X}}\right)\right] \approx 1.$

Hence, in addition to uniform distribution on the hash values, we want to have $D\left(H_K(\mathbf{X}), H_K\left(\hat{\mathbf{X}}\right)\right) = 0, \quad D(H_K(\mathbf{X}), H_K(\mathbf{Y})) > 0$ for all possible different images $\mathbf{X}, \mathbf{Y}$ and for all possible acceptable modified versions of $\mathbf{X}$, represented by $\hat{\mathbf{X}}$. In order to simplify the problem, we propose to divide it into 2 stages:

1. **Intermediate hash value:** At the end of the first stage, we aim to obtain hash values that are of length M, where $M \gg L$ and have the following separation property:

$$D\left(H_K(\mathbf{X}), H_K\left(\hat{\mathbf{X}}\right)\right) < T_1, D(H_K(\mathbf{X}), H_K(\mathbf{Y})) > T_2, \qquad (1)$$

   where $0 < T_1 < T_2 < 0.5$.
2. **Final hash value:** Given the intermediate hash, we aim to use randomized lattice vector quantization to get the final hash which has the properties mentioned in the previous paragraph.

In this paper, we focus on producing intermediate hash values. We experimentally showed that our algorithm achieves (1) for an extensive range of attacks and different inputs. A solution has been proposed for the second stage of the problem in [ ]. The ongoing research targets more efficient solutions and using hash functions in watermarking applications.

3   Proposed Algorithms

We propose two algorithms, Algorithm A and Algorithm B. We present Algorithm A first as it is simpler and deterministic, and forms the backbone of the main and second algorithm which uses randomization to increase the output entropy and enhance robustness properties.

3.1   Algorithm A

Our task may be viewed as irreversible compression that dramatically shrinks the input while keeping the essence of the input image. We employ discrete wavelet transformation (DWT) since it compactly captures significant image characteristics via time and frequency localization. Next we pick up the significant regions by thresholding. In order to gain robustness against modifications, we propose a simple iterative filtering technique that minimizes the presence of "geometrically weak components" and enhance the "geometrically strong components" by means of *region growing*. A region which has isolated significant components (geometrically weak) is a good candidate to be erased via modifications, whereas a region which has massive clusters of significant components (geometrically strong) would probably remain though the location might be perturbed a little and the shape of the cluster could be varied slightly. The novelty of this procedure is that we rely on the convergence of a *self-correcting* iterative procedure. The number of potential limits for the set of all meaningful images is large enough since the output is based on the geometric structure of the input image. Due to the self-correcting nature of the algorithm, we conjecture that the output of the proposed iterative filtering scheme is a stable attractive point for the region of most possible slight modifications.

Let $\mathbf{X}$ represent the input image, L be the number of levels DWT that is applied. Let $W(x)$ be the normalized Hamming weight of any binary input x which is the ratio of the usual Hamming weight and the size of the input. For a given 2-dimensional matrix $\mathbf{A}$, let $A(i, j)$ represent the (i, j)-th entry of $\mathbf{A}$. Next, we define *order-statistics filtering* $S_{[m,n],p}(.)$: Given a 2-dimensional input $\mathbf{A}$, $S_{[m,n],p}(\mathbf{A}) = \mathbf{B}$ where $\forall i, j$, $B(i, j)$ is equal to the p-th element of the sorted set of $\{A(i', j')\}$, where $i' \in \{i - m, i - m + 1, \ldots, i + m\}$ and $j' \in \{j - n, j - n + 1, \ldots, j + n\}$ (sorting is done in ascending order); here we term $S_{[m,n],p}(.)$ as the order-statistics filter. Note that we require $1 \leq p \leq (2m+1)(2n+1)$ and for $p = (2m+1)(2n+1)/2$ order-statistics filtering is equivalent to 2-dimensional median filtering with a window of size $(2m+1) \times (2n+1)$. During geometric region growing, we also use linear shift invariant filtering via 2-dimensional FIR filter f, which has low pass characteristics and achieves spatial localization. Now, we present the step-by-step description of the algorithm.

1. Find the DWT of $\mathbf{X}$ up to level L. Let $\mathbf{X}_A$ be the resulting DC subband.
2. Perform the following *thresholding* operation on $\mathbf{X}_A$ to produce the binary map $\mathbf{M}$:
$$M(i, j) = \begin{cases} 1 \text{ if } X_A(i, j) \geq T \\ 0 \text{ otherwise} \end{cases}.$$
   T is chosen such that the $W(\mathbf{M}) \approx q$ where $0 < q < 1$ is an algorithm parameter.
3. (Geometric region growing) Let $\mathbf{M}_1 = \mathbf{M}$, $ctr = 1$.
   3.1 (Order-statistics filtering on $\mathbf{M}_1$)
      $\mathbf{M}_2 := S_{[m,n],p}(\mathbf{M}_1)$ where m, n and p are algorithm parameters.
   3.2 Apply 2-dimensional linear shift-invariant filtering on $\mathbf{M}_3$ via filter f where $M_3(i, j) = A M_2(i, j)$; f and A are algorithm parameters. Let the output be $\mathbf{M}_4$.
   3.3 Apply a thresholding operation on $\mathbf{M}_4$. This operation is similar to the one explained in step 2. Let $\mathbf{M}_5$ be the output, such that $W(\mathbf{M}_5) \approx q$.
   3.4 If $ctr \geq C$, terminate the iteration and go to step 4. If this is not the case, find $D(\mathbf{M}_5, \mathbf{M}_1)$; if it is less than ϵ terminate the iteration and go to step 4; if not, set $\mathbf{M}_1 = \mathbf{M}_5$, $ctr = ctr + 1$ and go to step 3.1.
4. $H(\mathbf{X}) = \mathbf{M}_5$.

Remarks:

A . We rely on our experimental observations that isolated significant components are not robust. The non–linear filtering applied in step 3.1 eliminates such "spike-like" components. On the other hand, around big masses of significant data, steps 3.2& 3.3 introduce artificial "blurred tolerance regions" to gain stability (in shape and size) against small modifications. We observed that in general attacks split, distort, bend, stretch, and translate the smaller masses more than the larger ones, and our iterative and convergent algorithm introduces a self-correcting mechanism. We hope to formally model and analyze our algorithm in this aspect, namely the conjecture that there exists a stable fix point modulo small distortions. It is important that there are such fix points, and indeed for a given image there should be ample supply of them, one for almost every secret random key K. However it is not important exactly how these fix points visually relate to the given input and indeed we exploit this aspect.

B. Our approach is generic, allowing the use of any transform, that achieves robustness and compactly captures the image characteristics. For instance, the shift-invariant and shape-preserving "complex wavelets" [ ] and any overcomplete wavelet representations or wavelet packets are good candidates.

C. We contrast with *Image halftoning* algorithms that also produce a binary version of the input image, but where visual quality and similarity of the output is paramount (see remark **A.**). Indeed our outputs have very little resemblance to the input. It is natural to ask if one may adapt some tools of halftoning (e.g. dithering matrices or error diffusion techniques), but meeting the robustness requirements may be non-trivial.

D. The use of randomness (derived from the secret key) is important not only for robustness and security against malicious attacks, but also for scalability (i.e. ability to work with large data sets without too many collisions of hash values). As noted earlier, the goals are to achieve almost uniform distribution of hash values in a large set and that the hash values of distinct inputs be (almost) pairwise independent. The aim is to minimize the collision probability in a rigorous sense.

Algorithm A uses no secret key and hence there is no pseudo–randomness involved (that is why we use $H(.)$ instead of $H_K(.)$ in this section). This motivates our next Algorithm B.

3.2   Algorithm B

Randomizing algorithm A while preserving its good properties turns out to be a delicate problem and we first propose to apply algorithm A on randomly chosen regions of an image (or its suitable transform). We use random rectangles for this purpose.

Let N be the number of rectangles; let R_i be the i-th rectangle and let w_i and h_i be the width and the height of R_i respectively, where $i \in \{1, 2, \ldots, N\}$.

Let $\mathbf{X}_i$ be the "sub-image" that is formed by taking the portion of $\mathbf{X}$ that is in R_i, $i \leq N$. The secret key K will be used as the seed of the random number generator that will be employed for randomizing all steps below. We now describe Algorithm B.

1. For each i, find randomly positioned rectangle R_i such that $w_s \leq w_i \leq w_l$ and $h_s \leq h_i \leq h_l$ where w_s, w_l, h_s and h_l are algorithm parameters.
2. Apply Algorithm A on all X_i; the outputs are $H(X_i)$, $i \leq N$.
3. Convert each matrix $H(X_i)$ into a 1-dimensional vector $\hat{H}_i$ by randomly ordering it. Concatenate $\left\{\hat{H}_i\right\}$, $i \leq N$ to produce $\hat{H}$.
4. (Random Projection of $\hat{H}$) Let $\hat{M}$ be the length of $\hat{H}$. Randomly choose a set $\{i_1, i_2, \ldots, i_M\} \subseteq \left\{1, 2, \ldots, \hat{M}\right\}$. Then $H_K(\mathbf{X}) := \left[\hat{H}(i_1), \ldots, \hat{H}(i_M)\right]$.

Note that if N is sufficiently large and $\{R_i\}$ are sufficiently big, the geometric robustness properties of Algorithm A hold for Algorithm B. The further advantage is the decrease in the probability of collision and the increase in the robustness against adverserial attacks due to randomization, but at the expense of extra complexity, since Algorithm A is applied on each sub-image individually.

4   Experimental Results

We applied 3–level DWT using Daubechies, length–8 filters. For parameters of Algorithm A, we used $m = n = 5$ with $p = 13$, $f(i,j) = 1/9$, $i, j \in \{1, 2, 3\}$, $A = 255$, $C = 20$, $\epsilon = 0.01$ and $q = 0.5$. It can be shown that $q = 0.5$ maximizes the separation between $H(\mathbf{X}, \mathbf{Y})$ and $H\left(\mathbf{X}, \hat{\mathbf{X}}\right)$. For parameters of Algorithm B, we used $w_s = h_s = 192$. $w_l = h_l = 320$ and $N = 100$. Prior to applying both algorithms, we resize the input image to 512×512 via bicubic interpolation. For colored images, we take intensity plane since most of the energy of the image is concentrated on this plane.

We did tests for several different images, each of which was subject to 20–30 different attacks. The results of 3 of test images are shown here for illustrative purposes. The performances were observed to be approximately the same for both algorithms and on average a similar behavior was observed for all test images for a fixed attack. The attacks considered were AWGN (additive white Gaussian noise), histogram equalization, non-linear attacks on the distribution of image samples and all *Stirmark* attacks[ ]. A clear separation between the hash values of different images and perceptually similar images has been observed (we choose $T_1 = 0.25$ and $T_2 = 0.35$). Some of the sample results are shown in Table 1. Except for rotation attacks larger than 5 percent, cropping attacks larger than 10 percent, the goal stated in (1) has been achieved. As expected, the performances for both algorithms is approximately the same since we are working on sufficiently many rectangles that cover approximately the whole image. We believe that for various applications, including using hashing within watermarking, large rotation and cropping attacks can be handled via a simple search algorithm. Algorithm B would in particular be useful against malicious attacks due to the presence of the secret key. Fig. 1 show one of the test images "Lena" and its 3 different attack versions which are obtained using the Stirmark software. Fig. 2 shows the results of algorithm A at different stages for the image Lena and these attacked version. More extensive experimental results on larger data sets are going to presented in the final version.

Table 1. Normalized Hamming distances between the hash values of original and attacked images using Algorithm A

Attacks	Baboon	Goldhill	Lena
AWGN, $\sigma=40$	0.03	0.04	0.03
Hist. equalization	0.01	0.02	0.02
3×3 Gaussian filt.	0.00	0.01	0.00
3×3 Sharpen. filt.	0.05	0.01	0.01
JPEG, QF=10	0.01	0.02	0.01
4×4 median filt.	0.04	0.04	0.04
Scaling, 50 percent	0.01	0.01	0.01
Shearing, 5 percent	0.13	0.12	0.11
Rotation, 1 degree	0.06	0.06	0.05
Rotation, 2 degrees	0.09	0.08	0.08
Rotation, 5 degrees	0.21	0.17	0.21
Cropping, 2 percent	0.07	0.06	0.04
Cropping, 5 percent	0.12	0.10	0.10
Cropping, 10 percent	0.20	0.16	0.19
Random bending	0.07	0.05	0.04

5   Conclusions and Future Work

We propose novel image hashing algorithms that use perceptually significant components of images via iterative filtering methods. We rely on empirically observed facts that in case of attacks which produce perceptually similar images, big masses of significant data in the transformation domain would be retained though perturbed, whereas isolated significant data are more likely to be erased. Our approach is media insensitive and can be applied to other sources [ ]. In all the experiments we have conducted, we observed robustness under *Stirmark* attacks except for large rotation and cropping and that distances between the hash values of perceptually similar images are clearly separated from the distances between different images. We intend to use randomized lattice vector quantization algorithms on intermediate hash to produce the final hash. For video watermarking applications see [ ].

Original image

JPEG attack, QF=10

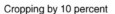

Cropping by 10 percent

Rotation by 5 degrees and scaling

Fig. 1. Top left: original image Lena, top right: attacked version by JPEG compression with quality factor 10, bottom left: attacked version by cropping by 10 percent, bottom right: attacked version by rotation by 5 degrees and scaling

References

1. D. E. Knuth, *The Art of Computer Programming*, Addison–Wesley, 1998. 13
2. R. Venkatesan, S.-M. Koon, M. Jakubowski and P. Moulin, "Robust image hashing," *Proc. IEEE ICIP*, Vancouver, Canada, September 2000. 14, 15
3. M. K. Mıhçak and R. Venkatesan, "A Perceptual Audio Hashing Algorithm," *preprint*, 2000. 14, 19
4. F. A. P. Petitcolas and R. J. Anderson, "Evaluation of copyright marking systems," *Proceedings of IEEE Multimedia Systems'99*, vol. 1, pp. 574–579, 7–11 June 1999, Florence, Italy. 14, 18
5. M. K. Mıhçak and R. Venkatesan, "Video Watermarking Using Image Hashing," *preprint*, 2000. 14, 19

Fig. 2. The outcomes of different steps of Algorithm A for lena image and its 3 different attacked versions. The first column shows the results of the original image, the second column shows the results after JPEG attack with the quality factor 10 percent, the third column shows the results after cropping attack by 10 percent, the fourth column shows the results after rotation by 5 degrees and scaling. The first row shows the resulting image after step 2; the second, third and fourth rows show the resulting images after steps 3,4 and 5 respectively at the first iteration. The bottom row show the intermediate hash that is obtained after convergence of the iterative filtering algorithm

6. A. J. Menezes, P. C. van Oorschot and S. A. Vanstone, *Handbook of applied cryptography*, CRC Press, Boca Raton, FL, 1997. 14
7. N. G. Kingsbury, "Complex wavelets for shift invariant analysis and filtering of signals," *submitted to Journal of Applied Computation and Harmonic Analysis*, June 2000. 17

On Crafty Pirates and Foxy Tracers

Aggelos Kiayias[1] and Moti Yung[2]

[1] Graduate Center
CUNY, NY USA
akiayias@gc.cuny.edu
[2] CertCo, NY USA
moti@cs.columbia.edu

Abstract. Piracy in digital content distribution systems is usually identified as the illegal reception of the material by an unauthorized (pirate)
device. A well known method for discouraging piracy in this setting is
the usage of a traitor tracing scheme that enables the recovery of the
identities of the subscribers who collaborated in the construction of the
pirate decoder (the traitors). An important type of tracing which we deal
with here is "black-box traitor tracing" which reveals the traitors' identity using only black-box access to the pirate decoder. The only existing
general scheme which is successful in general black-box traitor tracing
was introduced by Chor Fiat and Naor. Still, this scheme employs a pirate decoder model that despite its generality it is not intended to apply
to all settings. In particular it is assumed that (1) the pirate decoder is
"resettable", i.e. the tracer is allowed to reset the pirate decoder to its
initial state after each trial (but in many settings this is not possible: the
pirate decoder is "history-recording"), and that (2) the pirate decoder is
"available", i.e. it does not employ an internal reactive mechanism that,
say, disables the tracing process (such as shutting down) — we will call
such reactive decoders "abrupt."
In this work we discuss pirate-decoders of various types which we categorize according to their capabilities: resettable vs. history recording, and
available vs. abrupt. These (crafty) pirate decoders of "enhanced capabilities" (compared to the model of Chor et al.) appear in many plausible
piracy scenarios. We then present new (foxy) black-box traitor tracing
schemes which cope with such pirate decoders. We present a generic black
box traitor tracing technique against any abrupt/resettable decoder. This
generic tracing method can be implemented readily in a linear ciphertext
size traitor tracing scheme. By employing a new relaxation technique,
which we call list-tracing, we describe a traitor tracing scheme with sublinear ciphertext size that is successful against abrupt/resettable pirate
decoders. Finally, we present the first black-box traitor-tracing scheme
and techniques that are successful against abrupt/history-recording pirate decoders (in the multimedia transmission setting).

1 Introduction

Consider the distribution of scrambled data to a set of subscribers who pay for
services, for example in a Cable-TV network. The Internet is currently providing

T. Sander (Ed.): DRM 2001, LNCS 2320, pp. 22–39, 2002.
© Springer-Verlag Berlin Heidelberg 2002

a new venue for such applications to flourish and expand; undoubtedly in the next few years such networks will be established in Web-based environments. A well known shortcoming of such digital content distribution systems is the fact that pirate devices that receive the scrambled content can be constructed and even distributed to thousands of users via the Internet.

Hiding the decoding mechanism from the subscriber is of course a solution but it is difficult to enforce since: (1) Software-based subscriber decoders are desirable due to the need to cut-down costs on the part of the distributor and so that decoders can be downloaded over the Internet. Using program obfuscation to hide the subscriber key at present does not appear to be a reliable solution in the cryptographic sense (see [ ]); further (2) even if subscriber decoders are in hardware, the secrecy of the descrambling key from a "nosy" subscriber is relative, since tamper-resistance comes at a cost (see [ ]). This setting puts forth the following important problem: assuming the subscriber decoders are "open" and as a result the subscribers' descrambling keys are readily available, is it possible to eliminate (or discourage) piracy? In this case subscribers, using their personal key information, may collude to generate pirate decoders that are able to receive the scrambled data without paying. Chor et al. in [ ] introduced and discussed a solution to this problem. The distributor is using an encryption scheme that allows *traitor-tracing*, i.e. there is a procedure that given the information contained in the pirate decoder can trace back to one of the legitimate subscriber keys that was used in its construction. This reveals the identity of a subscriber that participated in the process of the pirate-decoder construction (henceforth called a "traitor"). In such a system piracy would be reduced due to the fear of exposure.

In many settings it is very important for the traitor tracing procedure to be *black-box*. This allows tracing to work successfully using merely black-box access to the pirate decoder. Black-box traitor tracing reduces tracing costs significantly as there is no need to "reverse-engineer" the pirate-decoder (something that can be infeasible in many cases) and even allows tracing to be performed remotely without the physical availability of the pirate decoder. For example, feeding signals to a device remotely and observing the reaction or the display of the output (on a T.V. screen, say) may be the only way a tracer can access a device, in which case black-box tracing is the only possible way to trace. The techniques of [ ] (see also [ ]) apply to the black-box setting as well, provided that the tracer has the capability to *reset* the pirate decoder to its initial state and the decoder is "available" – a concept we formalize below.

Let us next briefly overview the previous work on Traitor Tracing. As mentioned above, the concept was introduced in [,], with the presentation of a generic TTS. Explicit constructions based on combinatorial designs were given in [ ]. A useful variation of the [ ] scheme is presented in [ ]. Public key TTSs were presented in [,]. These two schemes were shown to be inadequate in the black-box traitor tracing setting when the pirate construction is general and has a superlogarithmic (in the number of users) number of traitor keys at its disposal [ ]. In [ ] a useful method of deterring piracy called "self-enforcement" was discussed in the context of traitor tracing schemes together with user-key revocation techniques. We note that in most settings (here as well) it is assumed that the tracing authority is trusted. The case when the authority is not trusted is considered in [17,18,19]. An "on-line" approach to preventing piracy in Pay-TV like systems, called "Dynamic Traitor Tracing," is taken in [9,20,3]. Further combinatorial constructions of traitor tracing schemes in combination with revocation methods (cf. broadcast encryption) were discussed in [10,14].

Given that the area is relatively young and there are only a few works dedicated to it, there are many issues yet to be studied and many new properties to be desired from traitor tracing schemes. There are several parameters that are involved such as the *key-size* (denoted by u), the *ciphertext-size* (denoted by v), and the *maximum traitor collusion size* allowed by the tracing technique (denoted by t). Seen as functions in the number of subscribers n, the ideal would be that key-size and ciphertext size are constant whereas the maximum traitor collusion size allowed is large, close to n. The greatest problem perhaps is achieving the highest possible t while keeping the ciphertext size v and key size u as small as possible since v is directly related to the cost of data distribution, and u is related to the cost of the user decoder. We note here that although constructing a linear ciphertext size Traitor Tracing Scheme (TTS) is straightforward, it is not equally straightforward to prove that such a scheme has black-box tracing capability.

This paper concentrates on introducing new *black-box* traitor tracing schemes against pirate decoders of various (enhanced) capabilities. To facilitate our exposition we will categorize pirate decoders according to two basic characteristics: their memory capabilities (resettable vs. history-recording) and the usage of self-protection reactive mechanisms that abort/react to the detection of the tracing process (available vs. abrupt). We will not limit the process by which the traitors produce the pirate device or the resources/techniques that they may apply. Our results (which are the three traitor tracing mechanisms mentioned in the abstract) are presented in section 2.5 after the proper background regarding pirate-decoder types is introduced.

Organization.

First in section 2, we give the necessary background which explains in more details the above enhanced capabilities of pirate decoders and explain our results in light of this background. Then, in section 3.1 we describe formally our model of digital content distribution called a Multicast Encryption Scheme, and we define non-black-box traitor tracing. In sections 3.3 and 3.4 we formalize the concepts of black-box traitor tracing and coloring, and we describe the modeling for the various types of pirate decoders. In section 4 we present our generic black-box traitor tracing technique against abrupt/resettable pirate decoders. A new relaxed form of tracing that we call "List-tracing" and allows more efficient constructions is discussed in section 5. Finally the black-box traitor tracing scheme against abrupt/history-recording pirate decoders is presented in section 6.

2 Background: Decoder Types and Our Results

Next, we will describe the various categories of decoders we consider and then we will review earlier works and our results in light of the categorization.

2.1 Resettable vs. History Recording Pirate Decoders

Resettable decoders can be reset to their initial state by the tracer after each descrambling. This gives the tracer the advantage of making independent tests during the tracing process, something that prevents the decoder from using previous querying information submitted by the tracer in order to decide its present action.

Resettable pirate decoders constitute a natural model for black-box traitor tracing since they can be encountered in a number of settings, mainly:

- Software pirate decoders. If the tracer possesses a software pirate decoder, evidently we can assume that such a decoder is resettable, since the tracer may restart the decoder at each trial using a previously stored copy.
- A hardware pirate decoder can also be considered resettable if the tracer can flood its internal memory with data so that history recording between two probings is eliminated.

Most previous work in black-box traitor tracing assumed the resettable pirate-decoder model. In contrast, a *History Recording* pirate decoder "remembers" the previous queries made by the tracer and because the tracing procedure is public the history recording capability can be used by the decoder to evade tracing. History-Recording pirate decoders can also be encountered in a number of settings such as:

- A software pirate decoder that is only remotely accessible by the tracer, e.g. the decoder runs in some server connected to the Internet and the tracer may only probe it remotely.
- Hardware pirate decoders in general.

2.2 Available vs. Abrupt Pirate Decoders

Abrupt pirate decoders are those devices that may take some counter-actions against the tracing process which can be "defensive" or "aggressive" in their nature. More specifically, by a "defensive" action we refer to a "shutting down" mechanism, a process by which the pirate decoder erases all internal key information, thus making tracing impossible (and rendering itself useless at the same time). Such defensive actions are mechanisms that can be implemented successfully only in hardware devices. On the other hand, an "aggressive action" (more suitable for software decoders) could be crashing the host system, or releasing a virus. This is particularly important in the case of an installable pirate-decoder: even though the tracer is capable of resetting the decoder to its initial state (by using a previously stored copy) this does not prohibit the pirate-decoder of taking some "aggressive" counter-action to tracing, such as releasing a virus to its working environment. Such aggressive counter-actions may not entirely prohibit tracing but they can substantially increase its cost as well as its negative consequences.

In both cases (software aggressive counter-actions or hardware shutting-down mechanisms) we will assume that the tracer wants to avoid the occurrence of any such reaction and if such reaction is triggered it is immediately detectable by the tracer. On the other hand the pirate decoder does not want such a mechanism to be triggered during normal operation. Since it is not possible to force the pirate decoder not to use such reaction mechanisms if they are available, what needs to be shown is that there are systems where the usage of such mechanisms is detrimental to the pirate decoder itself (i.e. the triggering of the mechanism leaks some information about the traitor keys or it significantly interferes with the decoder's data-reception capabilities).

An "available" pirate decoder is a device (software or hardware) that does not possess such a reaction mechanism.

2.3   Types of Pirate Decoders

Depending on the capabilities of a given pirate decoder we will categorize it to a certain type according to the diagram of figure 1.

Note that the four types are hierarchical: a black-box traitor tracing scheme successful against decoders of a certain type is also successful against decoders of a "smaller" type (where smaller is defined by the partial order revealed by the arrows in figure 1).

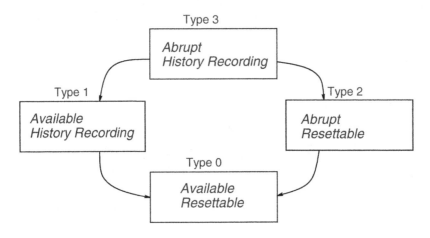

Fig. 1. Types of Pirate Decoders

These plausible "crafty" pirate decoder models have not been investigated thoroughly in the literature and as they appear in many practical settings, new black-box traitor tracing techniques are required.

2.4   Previous Work and Motivation in Light of the Decoder Types

A type-0 black-box traitor tracing scheme was presented in [,]. This system (and its variants) is the only existing scheme that is capable of tracing general type-0 pirate decoders in a black-box fashion. In [ ], a type-0 scheme of a restricted nature was introduced under the name "single-key pirates": the pirate-decoder uses a single key for decryption *without* any other side computation (note though that this single key could be the combination of many users' keys). Nevertheless such a scheme is too restrictive (as pointed out in the same paper) since there is no guarantee that a decoder will be constructed in this fashion. In the same paper, a weaker mode of black-box traitor tracing was presented: "black-box confirmation." In this setting the tracer has a set of suspects and wants to confirm that the actual traitors that constructed the pirate decoder are indeed included in the set of suspects. Black-box confirmation can be used for black-box traitor tracing by trying all possible subsets but this results in an inefficient (exponential-time) procedure. In [ ] it was shown that it is impossible for non-trivial schemes of the type of [,] to support efficient black-box traitor tracing procedures against general type-0 decoders if the number of traitors is superlogarithmic in the number of users.

A different mode of black box traitor tracing was considered in [ ]: minimal access black box tracing: for any query to the pirate decoder, the tracer does not obtain the plaintext but merely whether the pirate-decoder can decrypt the ciphertext and "play" it (e.g. the case of a pirate cable-box incorporating a TV-set). This is in contrast with "full access black box tracing" where the tracer obtains the actual data returned by the pirate decoder.

In [ ] a restricted type-2 *prevention* method was briefly noted: if a pirate-decoder shuts-down whenever an invalid ciphertext is broadcasted (which may indicate tracing as we will see), then the authority may disperse invalid ciphertexts in normal operation so that these decoders shut-down and therefore become useless. In such a system, type-2 decoders can be "reduced" to type-0 decoders, since shutting down renders them useless. Although Pfitzmann's comment provides a simple yet powerful method for disabling abrupt decoders that shut down it does not solve the problem completely. This approach raises the issue of how the decoders used by the lawful subscribers should deal with invalid ciphertexts since shutting down is a double-edge sword. Any method that would allow a lawful decoder to ignore the invalid (possibly malicious) ciphertexts, can be taken advantage of by a pirate-decoder and used to avoid shutting down when it is not needed. As a result this approach is not very stable in general. It is of great interest to see if it possible to allow black-box traitor tracing of abrupt decoders without affecting the normal operation of the system.

2.5   Our Results

We present three different designs for black-box traitor tracing schemes that are successful against pirate decoders of various types. The black-box traitor tracing methods for type-2 and type-3 pirate decoders that we present are, as far as we know, the first of their kind in the literature. Our designs combine new ideas with the known tracing methods for the basic decoders to achieve the new capabilities. Specifically:

- We first present a generic black-box traitor tracing technique against type-2 pirate decoders. A direct implementation of our technique yields a linear ciphertext size traitor tracing scheme of type-2 black-box traceability.
- By a new relaxation idea which allows some level of uncertainty in the tracer's part and results in an output of a list of suspects some of which are guaranteed to be traitors, we construct a "list-tracing" scheme with sub-linear ciphertext size that is successful against pirate decoders of type-2. The tracing procedure, (building on ideas from [ ]) exhibits a trade-off between the size of the suspect list and the size of the ciphertexts. In the case of linear ciphertext size the scheme reveals at least one traitor with overwhelming probability. By allowing the suspect list to be larger it is possible to lower the ciphertext size. Our results on type-2 traceability also hold in the minimal access model introduced in [ ].
- Finally, extending the above with watermarking and ambiguous decryption ideas, we present the first traitor tracing scheme successful against history-recording decoders (i.e. type-3 pirate decoders) in the context of multimedia transmission (as it was dealt with in [,]). In our method (which is based on the [ ]-scheme) the walking black-box traitor tracing argument of [ ] is substituted by "watermarking the walking space in parallel" resulting in a new method that defeats the history-recording capabilities of the pirate-decoder.

3   Preliminaries

3.1   Multicast Encryption Schemes

Any traitor tracing scheme is based on an underlying encryption mechanism called a Multicast Encryption Scheme (MES) [ ]. In this section we overview this primitive.

Let $\mathcal{U} := \{1, \ldots, n\}$ be the set of users, and $\mathcal{M}, \mathcal{C}$ and $\mathcal{D}$ denote the message-space, ciphertext-space and user-key space respectively. Without loss of generality we assume that each of these spaces contains objects of the same size. If the elements of $\mathcal{M}$ have size w, thought of as a security parameter, we assume that the elements of $\mathcal{C}, \mathcal{D}$ have size $wv(n)$ and $wk(n)$ respectively. The functions $v(n), k(n)$ express the expansion factor of $\mathcal{C}$ and $\mathcal{D}$ respectively based on the number of users n. A Multicast Encryption Scheme (MES) is a triple (G, E, D) with the following properties:

- Key Generation. G is a probabilistic algorithm that on input 1^w and 1^n, G produces a pair (e, K) with $K \subseteq \mathcal{D}$, $|K| = n$; the encryption key of the system is e whereas the elements of K constitute the user-keys that are distributed to the users.
- Encryption. E is a probabilistic algorithm that on input $m \in \mathcal{M}$ and e it outputs an element $c \in \mathcal{C}$: $c \leftarrow E(1^w, m, e)$. Note that the encryption function is *not* thought to be a surjection over $\mathcal{C}$ and in fact this point is crucial for black-box traitor tracing. In other words the space $\mathcal{C}$ includes elements that do not correspond to "valid" encryptions of messages in $\mathcal{M}$.
- Decryption. D is a deterministic algorithm that given $c \leftarrow E(1^w, m, e)$ and a user-key $d \in K$ so that $(e, K) \leftarrow G$, it returns m. Note that D can also be generalized to be a probabilistic algorithm.

A MES can be either public or secret key. It is easy to adapt the standard notions of semantic security or chosen-ciphertext security for MESs. Let $\mathcal{F}$ be the set of constructible non-decreasing functions of $(\mathbb{N} \to \mathbb{N})$, such that if $f \in \mathcal{F}$ it holds that $f(n) \leq n$ for all $n \in \mathbb{N}$. We may occasionally suppress the "(n)" when referring to a member of $\mathcal{F}$. To facilitate traitor tracing, [ ] pointed out that some additional security requirements have to be imposed on the MES that involve the population of subscribers; in the following let $t \in \mathcal{F}$:

Impossibility of Keyless Decryption. The knowledge of a user-key (or a combination thereof) is necessary for decryption.

Key-User Correspondence. Any collusion of up to t users is incapable of producing a user-key of some other user. This property has also been referred to in other contexts as the "frameproof" property. It guarantees that a user is liable (passively or actively) when its key is being used for decryption.

Non-Ambiguity of Collusions. It should be infeasible for any two disjoint collusions of up to t users to produce a common key in $\mathcal{D}$ that can be used for decryption.

For a more formal treatment the reader is referred to [ ]. A MES that satisfies the above properties will be called "a MES suitable for collusions of up to t users." The existence of a traitor tracing algorithm transforms a suitable MES into a traitor-tracing scheme:

Definition 1. Traitor Tracing Scheme (non-black-box). *Given $t, f, v \in \mathcal{F}$, a MES suitable for collusions of up to $t(n)$ users with ciphertext expansion factor $v(n)$ is called a $\langle t(n), f(n), v(n) \rangle$-Traitor Tracing Scheme (TTS) if there exists a probabilistic polynomial time algorithm B (tracing algorithm) s.t. for any set $T \subseteq K \leftarrow G(1^w, 1^n)$, with $|T| \leq t(n)$ and any probabilistic polynomial time algorithm A that given T and all public information outputs an element of $\mathcal{D}$, it holds:* $\mathbf{Prob}[t \in T : t \leftarrow B(d, K), d \leftarrow A(T)] \geq 1/f(n)$.

Note that because of key-user correspondence, the recovery of t is equivalent to exposing a traitor. In the non-black-box setting it is assumed that the decoder is "open" and because of the impossibility of keyless decryption a decryption key is available to the tracer. Black-Box Traitor Tracing Schemes are discussed in subsection 3.4.

3.2   The Straightforward Scheme

The straightforward way to produce a TTS is the following: user i has a pair of secret/public keys for some semantically secure encryption scheme f_i, e.g. El-Gamal encryption (note that symmetric encryption can also be used). The distributor of the message M, produces the vector-ciphertext $\langle f_1(M), \ldots, f_n(M) \rangle$. Each user receiving the ciphertext applies its own private key and obtains M. Under the (plausible) assumption that the keys of the different instances of the encryption scheme are not *composable* i.e. a collusion of users can decrypt a vector-ciphertext only by applying one of the assigned secret user keys, we can easily show that:

Proposition 1. *The MES described above is a $\langle n, 1, \Theta(n) \rangle$-TTS.*

Obviously this scheme is inefficient as its ciphertext is proportional to the population size. As a result the goal of any TTS design is to achieve sublinear ciphertext size and obviously the ideal would be the construction of an $\langle n, 1, \Theta(1) \rangle$-TTS. The straightforward scheme can serve as a measure of efficiency for other more elaborate constructions. Note that when using asymptotic notation to express the order of the functions t, f, v we will suppress the dependency on the security parameter w.

3.3   Colorings

The following formalism, introduced in [ ], is a useful tool in describing the interaction between the tracer and the pirate decoder. For some Multicast Encryption Scheme fix $(e, K) \leftarrow G(1^w, 1^n)$. A *coloring* of the user population is a partition $\{C_i\}_i$ of $\mathcal{U}$. Given some $s \in \mathcal{C}$, we define the following relation of the set of user keys K: $d \equiv d'$ iff $D(1^w, d, s) = D(1^w, d', s)$ (if D is probabilistic the definition can be amended accordingly). It is easy to see that $\equiv$ is an equivalence relation. By the property of key-user correspondence it is immediate that the equivalence classes of $\equiv$ for some $s \in \mathcal{C}$ define a coloring over the user population. In this case we say that s induces a coloring over the user population $\mathcal{U}$.

If $c \leftarrow E(1^w, m, e)$ for some $m \in \mathcal{M}$ then it holds that for all $d, d' \in K$, $D(1^w, d, c) = D(1^w, d', c)$ (by the definition of the encryption/decryption functions) therefore there is only one equivalence class, i.e. all users are colored by the same color. Let $\mathcal{X}_1$ be the subset of $\mathcal{C}$ s.t. $\forall s \in \mathcal{X}_1, d, d' \in K : D(1^w, d, s) = D(1^w, d', s)$. Obviously the ciphertexts generated by E constitute a subset of $\mathcal{X}_1$.

We say that a MES can induce a family of colorings $\{\{C_i^{(j)}\}_i\}_j$ if there is an algorithm that given 1^j can produce $s \in \mathcal{C}$ that induces the coloring $\{C_i^{(j)}\}_i$ over the user population.

Given some $s \in \mathcal{C}$, the set $L_s := \{D(1^w, d, s) \mid d \in K\}$ is called the set of color labels that correspond to s. If s is a encryption of some message under E, the set L_s is a singleton that contains only the appropriate decryption of s. In general the number of elements of L_s will be equal to the number of different equivalence classes in the coloring induced by s. Note that a decryption algorithm of some sort may not necessarily return one of the "color labels". For example, this can happen if the decryption algorithm operates with some "compound" decryption key – that has been derived from combining more than one user keys).

For a given set of users $U \subseteq \mathcal{U}$ and a coloring $\{C_i\}_i$ we denote by $\{C_i\}_i \downarrow U$ the projection of the partition of the coloring over the set U, i.e. the partition of U defined by $\{C_i \cap U\}_i$.

The above properties were sufficient for the "negative" results (impossibility of non-trivial black-box traitor tracing schemes) of [11]. Here we are interested in "positive" results and as a result additional properties of the underlying MES are required in order to describe black-box traitor tracing techniques using the coloring terminology. In particular the underlying MES should satisfy:

- (i) **probabilistic encryption of tracing plaintexts**: if a certain coloring is inducible in the MES then it can be induced by exponentially many ciphertexts.
- (ii) **no shortcut ciphertext-validity checks**: ciphertexts do not have any inherent validity structure checkable in polynomial-time by any group of users (nevertheless coalitions of users may apply their keys individually to check whether a ciphertext is valid).

These conditions are quite natural and are satisfied by all MESs proposed so far (nevertheless one can produce artificial MES instantiations that fail them).

3.4   Black-Box Traitor Tracing Schemes

The algorithm employed by the pirate decoder will be denoted by $\mathcal{B}$. The input of $\mathcal{B}$ is an element $s \in \mathcal{C}$ (and will be called a "query"), and if s is a valid encryption the output of $\mathcal{B}$ is necessarily the proper decryption of s as dictated by the decryption algorithm D. In other words $\mathcal{B}$, thought of as a probabilistic polynomial-time Turing machine, incorporates a correct decoding algorithm. Due to the impossibility of keyless decryption, $\mathcal{B}$ incorporates some of the user keys or some combined form thereof, i.e. if e is the encryption key, $\mathcal{B}$ "contains" some element(s) of $\mathcal{D}$ suitable for inverting the encryption procedure E. As these elements were generated using some user keys without loss of generality we assume that $\mathcal{B}$ incorporates a set of user keys denoted by $\mathcal{T}$ (the "traitor" keys).

As a result and in the terminology of the previous section if all traitor keys are colored in the same way the pirate decoder $\mathcal{B}$ is bound to return the single color label that the traitor keys decrypt (by the "no shortcut ciphertext-validity checks" property). If $\mathcal{B}$, on the other hand, finds that something is wrong with the encryption it may take measures to protect itself depending on its type: a type-0,1 decoder can e.g. return a predetermined random output, and a type-2,3 (abrupt) decoder can additionally use its reaction mechanism (e.g. shut-down).

We formalize the additional capabilities of pirate decoders as follows:

- History recording pirate decoders $\mathcal{B}$ take as input, apart from the element s, a polynomial number of previous queries made to the decoder, for some predetermined polynomial function. This formalizes the notion of history-recording as it allows $\mathcal{B}$ to take actions according to the transcript of the communication between tracer and decoder. Note that a history-recording $\mathcal{B}$ is not bound to decrypt properly even if it is given a valid ciphertext provided that there is some invalid ciphertext in the previous queries.

- Abrupt pirate decoders use a polynomial-time deterministic predicate React with domain the set of all possible partitions of the set $\mathcal{T}$. Given some string $s \in \mathcal{C}$ let $\{C_i\}_i$ be the coloring induced by s over the user population; the pirate decoder computes the value of $\text{React}(\{C_i\}_i \downarrow \mathcal{T})$ and if true it activates its reaction mechanism. In a history-recording abrupt pirate decoder React may take as additional input the sequence of previous projections. Note that the limitation of React to a deterministic predicate is done for brevity and our results can be easily extended to the general probabilistic case. When the predicate React becomes true the tracing process terminates "abruptly." Note that $\text{React}(\{\mathcal{T}\}) = \text{False}$ (which corresponds to the case when all traitors are assigned the same color, e.g. in normal operation).

The tracer algorithm $\mathcal{R}$ is a probabilistic polynomial-time Turing machine that has oracle access to the pirate decoder $\mathcal{B}$. $\mathcal{R}$, if successful, returns (at least) one of the elements of $\mathcal{T}$ which in turn (due to key-user correspondence) reveals the identity of a traitor user. A list-tracer on the other hand returns a set of users that is guaranteed to contain one of the traitor users. More formally:

Definition 2. *If $t, f \in \mathcal{F}$, we say that a probabilistic poly-time Turing machine $\mathcal{R}$ is a*
(i) $\langle t(n), f(n) \rangle$-tracer if for any $\mathcal{T} \subseteq \mathcal{U}$ s.t. $|\mathcal{T}| \leq t(n)$ and for any pirate-decoder algorithm $\mathcal{B}$ containing the keys of $\mathcal{T}$, $\mathcal{R}^{\mathcal{B}}$, outputs a user with non-negligible probability in n, who is a traitor with probability at least $1/f(n)$.
(ii) $\langle t(n), f(n) \rangle$-list-tracer if for any $\mathcal{T} \subseteq \mathcal{U}$ s.t. $|\mathcal{T}| \leq t(n)$ and for any pirate-decoder algorithm $\mathcal{B}$ that was created using the keys of $\mathcal{T}$, $\mathcal{R}^{\mathcal{B}}$, outputs a list of users with non-negligible probability in n, such that the size of the list is at most $f(n)$, and is guaranteed to contain at least one traitor.

The function f is called the *uncertainty* of the tracer. It is clear that for any MES it is straightforward how to obtain a tracer with $\Theta(n)$ uncertainty: merely output any user at random (similarly a trivial list-tracer merely outputs the list of all users). The other extreme is a tracer with uncertainty 1, that no matter what is the user population size it returns a traitor always. If tracing has negligible probability of error $\sigma(n)$ (a function $\sigma(n)$ is called negligible if for all $c > 0$ there is a n_0 so that $\forall n \geq n_0$ $\sigma(n) < n^{-c}$) then the uncertainty is "slightly larger than 1" i.e. $(1 - \sigma(n))^{-1}$. A list-tracer is a strengthened tracer that can produce a list of suspects that can be used by the authority in an investigation. It is straightforward that any $\langle t(n), f(n) \rangle$-list-tracer can be transformed to a $\langle t(n), f(n) \rangle$-tracer but the opposite does not hold necessarily.

It should be clear from all the above that the queries submitted by the tracer to the decoder algorithm $\mathcal{B}$ should not be all drawn from the set $\mathcal{X}_1$ (i.e. those that induce the trivial coloring over the user population) as this cannot distinguish between different sets of traitors. In many cases the specific queries $s \in \mathcal{C}$ used by the tracer algorithm are not important and its description can be done in terms of the colorings that the tracer wants to induce over the user population. This allows a more abstract description of the tracing process that brings us to the next definition:

Definition 3. *For some $t, f, v \in \mathcal{F}$, a $\langle t(n), f(n), v(n) \rangle$-Black-Box Traitor Tracing Scheme (BBTTS), is a MES suitable for collusions of up to $t(n)$ users with ciphertext expansion factor $v(n)$ such that there is an $\langle t(n), f(n) \rangle$-tracer so that all colorings used by the tracer can be induced in the MES.*

Depending on the type of pirate decoders a BBTTS is successful, we will signify that the BBTTS is of type-i (list-)traceability, with $i \in \{0, 1, 2, 3\}$. By the relations between the different types it is easy to establish relations such as a BBTTS of type-3 traceability is also of type-0,1,2 traceability and so on (see figure 1).

4 Hybrid Colorings: Generic Black-Box Traceability of Abrupt/Resettable Pirate Decoders

In this section we present a generic technique against any resettable pirate decoder that can be abrupt. It is based on the capability of the underlying MES to produce a family of colorings which we call "Hybrid Colorings" (see figure 2). Hybrid Colorings: Consider the following collection of $n + 1$ partitions of the set of users: $\{\{C_1^{(n,r)}, C_2^{(n,r)}\}\}_{r=0,\dots,n}$ with,

$$C_1^{(n,r)} = \{1, \dots, r\} \qquad C_2^{(n,r)} = \{r+1, \dots, n\}$$

Theorem 1. *If a MES can induce the Hybrid Colorings, is suitable for collusions of up to $t(n)$ users, and has ciphertext expansion factor $v(n)$ then it is a $\langle n, (1 - \sigma(n))^{-1}, v(n) \rangle$-BBTTS of type-0,2 traceability, where $\sigma(n)$ is negligible.*

Proof. Let $s_0, s_1, \dots, s_n \in \mathcal{C}$ be some ciphertexts that induce the hybrid colorings. It holds that $s_0, s_n \in \mathcal{X}_1$, i.e. they induce a single color over the user population. Denote the color induced by s_0 as "0" and the color induced by s_n as "1".

Consider the following experiment E_r: the tracer generates an $s_r \in \mathcal{C}$ that induces the r-th hybrid coloring, i.e. users $\{1, \dots, r\}$ are colored by "0" and users $\{r+1, \dots, n\}$ are colored by "1". The tracer queries the pirate decoder and records its answer in terms of 0 and 1.

Denote by α_r the probability the decoder returns 1 in experiment E_r. It follows that $\alpha_0 = 0$ and $\alpha_n = 1$, and as a result $\alpha_n - \alpha_0 = 1$.

Suppose now that user j is not a traitor: it holds that the pirate-decoder can distinguish between the coloring induced by s_{j-1} and the coloring induced by s_j only with negligible probability (this is because the key of the j-th user is not

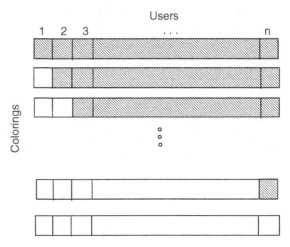

Fig. 2. Hybrid Colorings

among the keys used by the pirate-decoder). As a result it holds that $|\alpha_{j-1} - \alpha_j|$ is negligible in n. Since $\alpha_n - \alpha_0 = 1$ by the triangular inequality it follows that there is an $i_0 \in \{1, \ldots, n\}$ so that $\alpha_{i_0} - \alpha_{i_0-1} \geq 1/n$. It follows that user i_0 has to be a traitor.

The tracer repeats each experiment E_r independently a times for each $r \in \{0, \ldots, n\}$. Let N_r denote the random variable that expresses the number of 1's that were returned by the decoder during the a independent trials of experiment E_r. It follows that the expected difference between the random variable N_{i_0} and the random variable N_{i_0-1} is at least a/n. To facilitate the recovery of i_0 we have to make sure that the observed values of the variables N_r are sufficiently close to their expected values $\mu_r := \alpha_r \cdot a$. Using the Chernoff bound: $\mathbf{Prob}[|N_r - \mu_r| \geq \lambda] \leq 2e^{-2\lambda^2/a}$, it follows that $\mathbf{Prob}[|N_r - \mu_r| \geq a/6n] \leq 2e^{-a/18n^2}$ which is negligible in n provided that $a \geq n^2(\log n)^2$. It follows that with overwhelming probability (i) the difference between the observed value of N_{i_0} and the observed value of N_{i_0-1} is at least $\frac{2}{3}a/n$ and (ii) if i is not a traitor, the distance between the observed value of N_i and the observed value of N_{i-1} is at most $\frac{1}{2}a/n$ (this is due to the fact that $|\alpha_i - \alpha_{i-1}| := \sigma'(n)$ is negligible in n: as a result the expected value of $|N_i - N_{i-1}|$ is $a \cdot \sigma'(n)$ which is smaller than $\frac{1}{6}a/n$ for large enough n). This suggests the following method for computing i_0: collect all observed values N_j^O making $n^2(\log n)^2$ trials for each j, for $j = 0, \ldots, n$ and then i_0 will be the value so that $N_{i_0}^O - N_{i_0-1}^O \geq \frac{2}{3}n(\log n)^2$. This procedure has negligible probability of error.

Suppose now that the pirate decoder reacts at some step of the above procedure. If user j is not a traitor it follows that the colorings induced by s_j and s_{j-1} are identical according to the view of the pirate decoder: specifically $\{C_1^{n,j-1}, C_2^{n,j-1}\} \downarrow \mathcal{T} = \{C_1^{n,j}, C_2^{n,j}\} \downarrow \mathcal{T}$ and as a result $\mathrm{React}(\{C_1^{n,j-1}, C_2^{n,j-1}\} \downarrow \mathcal{T}) = \mathrm{React}(\{C_1^{n,j}, C_2^{n,j}\} \downarrow \mathcal{T})$. It follows that if the pirate-decoder reacts when given s_{i_1}, user i_1 is a traitor with negligible probability of error.   □

From the above proof it follows easily that,

Corollary 1. *The tracing procedure using the Hybrid Colorings has time complexity $\mathcal{O}(n^3 \log^2 n)$, and reveals a traitor with negligible probability of error.*

Hybrid Colorings can be used in the straightforward TTS of 3.2 in order to obtain a $\langle n, (1 - \sigma(n))^{-1}, \Theta(n) \rangle$-BBTTS that can trace any type-0 or type-2 decoder, where $\sigma(n)$ is negligible in n. We point here that it is not clear how to derive a sublinear TTS that can induce the hybrid colorings. Note that a history recording pirate decoder can defeat the Hybrid Colorings strategy as follows: upon detecting tracing, the decoder might continue to work by giving the color-label "0" for a random number of trials and then start returning the color-label "1". This with great probability will result in framing an innocent user. We note here that the technique of hybrid colorings was discovered independently for type-0 decoders in [ ] who also pointed at the difficulty of obtaining TTSs with sublinear ciphertext size that induce the hybrid colorings. In the next section we give a partial solution to this problem by introducing a new relaxation technique.

5   List-Tracing of Abrupt/Resettable Pirate Decoders with Sublinear Ciphertext Size

As pointed in the previous section it is not clear how to derive a sublinear ciphertext size MES that can induce the hybrid colorings. In this section we will show how to use the MES of [ ] and a new relaxation technique that yields a generic BBTTS of type-0,2 list-traceability with sublinear ciphertext size.
Description. ([ ]) Assume that $n \leq h(n)^{m(n)}$ for some functions $h, m \in \mathcal{F}$. A set of $m \cdot h$ keys are selected (we write m, h instead of $m(n), h(n)$ for simplicity), for some symmetric encryption scheme (note: public-key encryption can also be used). The keys are indexed by $K_{j,l}$, $j = 1, \ldots, m$ and $l = 1, \ldots, h$. For each j, each user is assigned one of the keys $\{K_{j,1}, \ldots, K_{j,h}\}$ at random. Consequently each user is assigned an m-tuple of keys, or one key from each row of the matrix $(K_{j,l})$. In order to encrypt M we break it into m random "shares": $M = M_1 + \ldots + M_m$ and then each M_j is encrypted under all keys $\{K_{j,1}, \ldots, K_{j,h}\}$ (note that modular arithmetic is assumed in the plaintext space). Since each user has one key for each j upon receiving the ciphertext (of length mh) it can obtain all shares of M and therefore compute it.
Tracing Type-2 Decoders. The tracing process proceeds as follows: a row $j_0 \in \{1, \ldots, m\}$ is chosen at random. For $i = 0, \ldots, h$ the tracer prepares an encryption of a plaintext M so that the first i positions of the j_0-th row are changed to random values. There will be an $i_0 \in \{1, \ldots, h\}$ s.t. the pirate decoder will either react (aborting tracing) or stop returning M (as in the type-0 tracing technique of [ ]); the tracer then concludes that there is at least one traitor in the subset of users using the key K_{j_0,i_0}. This yields a list of suspect users that

includes at least one traitor with very high probability. The size of this list is approximately n/h which corresponds to the number of users that are assigned a certain key $K_{j,i}$ (recall that each user is assigned a key from row j uniformly at random).

Proposition 2. *If $n \leq h(n)^{m(n)}$, the variant of the [ ]-MES described above is a $\langle n, n/h(n), \Theta(m(n)h(n)) \rangle$-BBTTS of type-2 list-traceability.*

Proof. Suppose the tracing algorithm selects row j_0. Let s_i be the ciphertext that has the first i positions of the j_0-th row randomized (where i ranges to $0, \ldots, h$). The coloring induced by s_i induces $i + 1$ classes as follows: $\{C_1^i, C_2^i, \ldots, C_i^i, C^i\}$ where C_v^i includes all users that are assigned the key $K_{j_0,v}$ with $v = 1, \ldots, i$ and $C^i = \{1, \ldots, n\} - \cup_{v=1}^i C_v^i$; note that $|C_v^i| = n/h$ approximately. Suppose that no traitor has the key $K_{j_0,i}$. It follows that $\{C_1^i, C_2^i, \ldots, C_i^i, C^i\} \downarrow \mathcal{T} = \{C_1^{i-1}, C_2^{i-1}, \ldots, C_{i-1}^{i-1}, C^{i-1}\} \downarrow \mathcal{T}$. As a result if the pirate-decoder reacts when given ciphertext s_{i_1} it follows immediately that $C_{i_1}^{i_1}$ includes a traitor (with very high probability).

On the other hand if the pirate-decoder never reacts tracing proceeds as described by [ ]. Below we give a short description in our terminology: first note that, there will be an s_i inducing a coloring $\{C_1^i, C_2^i, \ldots, C_i^i, C^i\}$ so that all traitors will be assigned a color different than C^i (i.e. $C^i \cap \mathcal{T} = \emptyset$). It follows that if all ciphertexts $s_0, \ldots, s_h$ are submitted in sequence the pirate decoder will start by returning the color-label that corresponds to C^0 (since $C^0 = \{1, \ldots, n\}$) and for some i_0 and on it will be returning color-labels that do not correspond to $C^{i_0}, C^{i_0+1}, \ldots, C^h$ (i.e. $C^{i_0+v} \cap \mathcal{T} = \emptyset$ for $v = 0, \ldots, h - i_0$). Now it is easy to see that if j is not a traitor the behavior of the pirate-decoder when given ciphertexts that induce the coloring $\{C_1^{j-1}, C_2^{j-1}, \ldots, C_{j-1}^{j-1}, C^{j-1}\}$ and ciphertexts that induce the coloring $\{C_1^j, C_2^j, \ldots, C_j^j, C^j\}$ is identical. As a result if i_1 is the smallest color index so that when given s_{i_1} the pirate decoder stops returning the color-label that corresponds to C^{i_1} it follows that $C_{i_1}^{i_1}$ contains at least one traitor with very high probability.   □

Tracing Decoders of Type-2 with Sublinear Ciphertext Size. Using proposition 2 it is easy to construct traitor tracing schemes of type-2 black-box list-traceability with sublinear ciphertext size that produce not very large lists of suspects. It is interesting to note here that proposition 2 suggests a trade-off between ciphertext size and uncertainty: the smaller the ciphertext size the bigger the uncertainty becomes. A possible choice for $h(n), m(n)$ is $h(n) := n^{1-c}$, for some constant $0 < c < 1$, and $m(n) := (1 - c)^{-1}$; then by proposition 2 we obtain a $\langle n, n^c, (1 - c)^{-1} n^{1-c} \rangle$-BBTTS of type-2 list-traceability. Depending on the application a suitable c can be chosen. The value of c that yields the smallest value for uncertainty and ciphertext size at the same time is $c = 1/2$ that results in a $\langle n, \sqrt{n}, 2\sqrt{n} \rangle$-BBTTS.

6   Tracing Abrupt/History-Recording Pirate Decoders in Multimedia Multicast

One of the basic assumptions in the TTSs studied in this work so far is that all users decrypt in the same way in normal operation. In this section we show that if we give up this condition it is possible to design BBTTSs successful against abrupt history-recording pirate decoders in the context of multimedia transmission.

Consider the following modification of the underlying MES: in the normal operation of the multicast scheme the material is distributed in slightly varied copies to the subscribers constantly. Watermarking techniques as those of [12,6] aid the tracing process. Because of the fact that not all users are going to decrypt in the same way, the MES cannot be used anymore for distribution of keys or similar data. It can only be used for distributing digital content that is presented by some device Dev (like a TV-set or a monitor screen) — and can be allowed to be different from user to user (users are not affected by a slight modification of a pixel in a figure or slight changes in spaces between words in text display). The presentation of the content M through such a device will be denoted by Dev(M). Formally, we restrict to devices and multimedia plaintext spaces for which the following watermarking assumption is true:

Watermarking Assumption 1 *There is a probabilistic algorithm $\mathcal{W}$ s.t. for some h, given any $M \in \mathcal{M}$ it produces h "versions" of M, $M_1, M_2, \ldots, M_h$, such that the following are true: (i) the Dev(M_i) are "adequate" presentations of M (ii) there is an algorithm $\mathcal{W}'$ that for any algorithm $\mathcal{A}$ that generates an M' given $M_{j_1}, \ldots, M_{j_k}$, $\mathcal{W}'$ given M' traces back to one of the M_{j_ℓ}, provided that Dev(M') is an adequate presentation of M, and that k is below a certain threshold t.*

We note that this assumption has also been used in [9], and can be achieved in most audio or video streams. The normal operation of the new scheme, which combines watermarking with the MES of [5], is described in figure 3 (where h, m are as in section 5).

Repeat the following steps forever:

    For $i = 1, \ldots, m$

    Get next M, and using $\mathcal{W}$ obtain $M_1, M_2, \ldots, M_h$.

    The encryption of M is: $C := \{\langle E_{K_{j,1}}(s_{j,1}), \ldots, E_{K_{j,h}}(s_{j,h})\rangle\}_{j=1}^{m}$

        where for $j = 1, \ldots, m$, $j \neq i$, $l = 1, \ldots, h$ $s_{j,l} = r_j$,

        and for $l = 1, \ldots, h$ $s_{i,l} = M_l - \sum_{j \neq i} r_j$.

    Decryption is done by retrieving some s_{j,l_j} for $j = 1, \ldots, m$

    and summing them up so that one version of M is recovered.

Fig. 3. Operation of the Type-3 Traceability Scheme

Tracing Type-3 Decoders. The tracer sets i to 1 (see figure 3), and records the outputs $M^{(1)}, \ldots, M^{(m)}$ of the pirate box; using $\mathcal{W}'$ it obtains one of the original watermarked versions for each $M^{(i)}$. If the original version that corresponds to $M^{(i)}$ is $M_l^{(i)}$ then the tracer deduces that the key $K_{i,l}$ was used for the decryption of the ciphertext. As a result the tracer collects a set of keys $K_{1,l_1}, \ldots, K_{m,l_m}$ that are used by the pirate decoder. If $h = 2t^2$, $m > 4t^2 \log n$ (see [ ]) and the keys $K_{j,l}$ were assigned to users as in [ ] then the tracer can safely accuse the user that holds most of the recovered keys as a traitor, provided that at most t traitors colluded (cf. [ ]).

Theorem 2. *Given $h, m \in \mathcal{F}$ s.t. $n \leq h(n)^{m(n)}$, $h(n) = 2t^2(n)$ and $m(n) > 2h(n) \log n$, and provided that the watermarking assumption holds for $h(n)$ with threshold $t(n)$, the MES described above is a $\langle t(n), (1 - \sigma(n))^{-1}, m(n)h(n)e \rangle$- BBTTS of type-3 traceability, where e denotes the expansion factor induced by the watermarking assumption, and $\sigma(n)$ is negligible.*

Proof. First observe that the reaction capabilities of the decoder do not apply in this setting since the tracing mode and normal operation coincide. Suppose now that the tracing algorithm does not return a traitor with overwhelming probability. Since the setting of parameters and the assignment of keys are as in [ ] this means that the set of keys collected from each row does not intersect maximally with one of the traitors' sets of keys but with some other innocent user. Provided that the watermarking tracing algorithm fails with negligible probability it follows that the reply of the pirate-decoder for some rows was generated using versions of the plaintext that do not correspond to the traitors' keys. But with overwhelming probability and independently of the history-recording capability of the decoder these versions are not accessible by the pirate-decoder. This is because *every* key in a row encrypts a different watermarked version of the transmitted plaintext and all keys are distinct.   □

Note that the type-0 black-box tracing method of [ ] cannot be used here because of the history-recording features of type-1,3 decoders: a history-recording decoder can easily defeat the black-box tracing method of [ ] by a standard delaying technique (such as the one described in section 4). In the BBTTS we present above, we substitute the step-by-step "walking" black-box tracing technique of [ ] by using the watermarking assumption and generating h different versions of the message which are transmitted in parallel. Reaction capabilities of type-3 decoders are rendered useless since the tracing operation is identical to normal operation.

Remark. Our approach of tracing type-3 decoders that combines tracing and normal operation bears similarities to (and may also be used in) the dynamic traitor tracing setting.

References

1. Ross Anderson and Markus Kuhn, *Low Cost Attacks on Tamper Resistant Devices*, Security Protocols, Springer LNCS 1361, 1997. 23
2. Boaz Barak, Oded Goldreich, Russell Impagliazzo, Steven Rudich, Amit Sahai, Salil Vadhan and Ke Yang, *On the (Im)Possibility of Obfuscating Programs*, CRYPTO 2001. 23
3. Omer Berkman, Michael Parnas, and Jiri Sgall *Efficient Dynamic Traitor Tracing*, 11th SODA, 2000. 24
4. Dan Boneh and Matthew Franklin, *An Efficient Public Key Traitor Tracing Scheme*, CRYPTO 1999. 23, 27
5. Dan Boneh and Matthew Franklin, *An Efficient Public Key Traitor Tracing Scheme*, manuscript, 2001. 27, 28, 35
6. Dan Boneh and James Shaw, *Collusion-Secure Fingerprinting for Digital Data*, CRYPTO 1995. 37
7. Benny Chor, Amos Fiat, and Moni Naor, *Tracing Traitors*, CRYPTO 1994. 23, 27, 28, 39
8. Benny Chor, Amos Fiat, Moni Naor, and Benny Pinkas, *Tracing Traitors*, IEEE Transactions on Information Theory, Vol. 46, no. 3, pp. 893-910, 2000. (originally appeared as [7, 8]). 23, 27, 28, 35, 36, 37, 38
9. Amos Fiat and T. Tassa, *Dynamic Traitor Tracing*, CRYPTO 1999. 24, 28, 37
10. Eli Gafni, Jessica Staddon and Yiqun Lisa Yin, *Efficient Methods for Integrating Traceability and Broadcast Encryption*, CRYPTO 1999. 24
11. Aggelos Kiayias and Moti Yung, *Self Protecting Pirates and Black-Box Traitor Tracing*, to appear in the Proceedings of CRYPTO 2001. 23, 27, 28, 29, 30, 31
12. J. Kilian, F. T. Leighton, L. R. Matheson, T. G. Shamoon, R. E. Tarjan, and F. Zane *Resistance of Digital Watermarks to Collusive Attacks*, Proceedings of the 1998 IEEE International Symposium on Information Theory pp.271, 1998. 28, 37
13. K. Kurosawa and Y. Desmedt, *Optimum Traitor Tracing and Asymmetric Schemes*, Eurocrypt 1998. 23, 27
14. Dalit Naor, Moni Naor, and Jeffrey B. Lotspiech *Revocation and Tracing Schemes for Stateless Receivers*, CRYPTO 2001. 24
15. Moni Naor and Benny Pinkas, *Threshold Traitor Tracing*, CRYPTO 1998. 23, 39
16. Moni Naor and Benny Pinkas, *Efficient Trace and Revoke Schemes* , In the Proceedings of Financial Crypto '2000, Anguilla, February 2000. 23
17. Birgit Pfitzmann, *Trials of Traced Traitors*, Information Hiding Workshop, Spring LNCS 1174, pp. 49-63, 1996. 24, 27
18. Birgit Pfitzmann and Matthias Schunter, *Asymmetric Fingerprinting*, Eurocrypt 1996. 24
19. Brigitt Pfitzmann and M. Waidner, *Asymmetric fingerprinting for larger collusions*, in proc. ACM Conference on Computer and Communication Security, pp. 151–160, 1997. 24
20. Reihaneh Safavi-Naini and Yejing Wang, *Sequential Traitor Tracing*, CRYPTO 2000. 24
21. Douglas R. Stinson and R. Wei, *Combinatorial Properties and Constructions of Traceability Schemes and Frameproof Codes*, SIAM J. on Discrete Math, Vol. 11, no. 1, 1998. 23

Efficient State Updates for Key Management

Benny Pinkas

STAR Lab, Intertrust Technologies
Princeton, NJ, USA
bpinkas@intertrust.com

Abstract. Encryption is widely used to enforce usage rules for digital content. In many scenarios content is encrypted using a group key which is known to a group of users that are allowed to use the content. When users leave or join the group the group key must be changed. The LKH (Logical Key Hierarchy) algorithm is a very common method of managing these key changes. In this algorithm every user keeps a personal key composed of $\log n$ keys (for a group of n users). A key update message consists of $O(\log n)$ keys.

A major drawback of the LKH algorithm is that users must update their state whenever users join or leave the group. When such an event happens a key update message is sent to all users. A user who is offline during t key updates, and which needs to learn the keys sent in these updates as well as update its personal key, should receive and process the t key update messages, of total length $O(t \log n)$ keys. In this paper we show how to reduce this overhead to a message of $O(\log t)$ keys. We also note that one of the methods that are used in this work to reduce the size of the update message can be used is other scenarios as well. It enables to generate n pseudo-random keys of length k bits each, such that any *successive* set of t keys can be represented by a string $\log(t) \cdot k$ bits, without disclosing any information about the other keys.

1 Introduction and Motivation

Digital Rights Management (DRM) systems provide content which is accompanied by rules or controls that define the ways in which the content can be used. The rules are enforced by a governance mechanism that ensures that only legitimate operations can be applied to the content. The most simple governance mechanism is encryption: The content is encrypted and the decryption key is only given to users which are allowed to use the content[1].

To model this setting we consider the following simplified scenario. A group U of n parties is receiving encrypted content from servers (or alternatively the parties are exchanging encrypted communication between themselves). All parties

---

[1] If the usage rules are of the type "User A can get the content and do anything he wants with it" then encryption can be the only governance mechanism that is used. If the rules are more complex. e.g. "User B can use the content at most three times" then more complex mechanisms should be used (e.g. based on tamper resistance), but typically encryption is used as a first line of defense.

T. Sander (Ed.): DRM 2001, LNCS 2320, pp. 40–56, 2002.

share a group key which is managed by a group controller (GC). We assume that the GC can communicate with each of the other parties using secure one-to-one channels, which are realized using standard encryption and authentication techniques. In order to do so the GC typically shares a different key with each of the users.

The content servers deliver the content encrypted with the group key, to ensure that only group members can use it. The system therefore enforces the rule "Group members are allowed to use content sent by content servers", since knowledge of the group key enables to decrypt the content. This system can model a content subscription group, namely where members of the group U are subscribers which are allowed to use the content.

In order to enforce the usage rules the group key must be changed when users join or leave the group. This is essential in order to

- Prevent leaving members from decrypting content that will be sent to the group in the future.
- Prevent joining members from decrypting content that was previously sent to the group (namely, provide *backward secrecy*).

Joins are usually trivial to handle. When a user u' wants to join U the GC should pick a new group key, send a message to the group containing the new key encrypted with the old group key, and also inform u' of the value of the new key. (There are many ways in which these messages can be sent, but they are mostly irrelevant for the discussion of this paper.) All further content sent to the group should be encrypted with the new key, until other members join or leave the group. This procedure supports backward secrecy and prevents u' from decrypting old content that was sent to the group. (We note that in the LKH key management scheme, which is the focus of this paper, the join operation is more complicated. We discuss this issue below.)

The main design challenge is to efficiently handle events in which users leave the group, or are forced by the GC to leave the group (say, because they violated usage rules). When a user u leaves the group a new group key should be generated by the GC and become known to every user remaining in the group. The keys known to u should be revoked in a way which prevents u from learning any information about messages encrypted with the new group key.

There is a trivial method for rekeying the group in the case of a leave: The GC chooses a new group key k, and sends it independently and privately to each of the users, except for the leaving member. For example, the GC can share a different key with each user, and encrypt k using this key. The problem with this approach is that the GC has to send a total of $n - 1$ encryptions (the length of each is of the same order as the length of the new key). The total length of the messages it has to send is therefore $O(n)$ keys (or $O(n|k|)$ bits) and might be too high if the number of group members n is large (say, a few millions).

1.1   The LKH Scheme

A very appealing user revocation method was suggested in [13,14]. In this method, commonly denoted as LKH (Logical Key Hierarchy), the GC associates a binary tree with the group, and associates each user with a different *leaf* of this tree. Therefore for a group of n users the tree is of depth $d = \log(n)$. The tree is used for key management and is not used as part of the mechanism in which messages are sent to users (in particular, it has no relation with distribution trees used in multicast communication).

The GC associates a random key with each node of the tree, and therefore knows the keys of all the nodes in the tree. The GC also provides each user with all the keys in the path from the user's leaf to the root. Since all these paths converge at the root of the tree, every user knows the root key and therefore this key can serve as the group key. In the example depicted in Figure 1, user U_0 is associated with the leftmost leaf and knows keys K, K_0, K_{00} and K_{000}. The root key K is the group key.

When a user is removed from the group the GC must change all the keys in the path from this user's leaf to the root. All the users that remain in the group must update their keys, namely change the keys in the intersection between the path from their leaf to the root and the path from the removed user's leaf and the root. In particular, this means that every remaining user learns the new root key. The new root key is then used as the new group key. The update of the users' keys can be done by the GC sending a single message that contains an encryption of $2\log(n) - 1$ keys. (The details of this message appear in Appendix A and are not important for understanding the rest of this manuscript.) Improved schemes

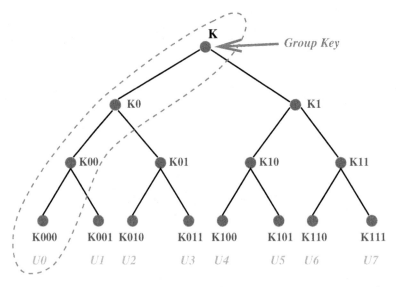

Fig. 1. The LKH key data structure (the keys of U_0 are encircled)

in [8, 10] reduce this overhead to a single message with $\log(n)$ encryptions of keys, i.e. with total length of $\log(n)|k|$ bits.

If backward secrecy is required then a join operation is similar to a remove operation in the sense that the keys that the joining user receives must be different than the keys previously used in the system. This is required in order to prevent the joining user from learning previous messages that were sent to group encrypted with the group key (it is not sufficient to change only the root key because other keys in the path might have been used in previous revocation messages to encrypt the root key itself or information that reveals it). The joining user is assigned a leaf, and all the keys in the path from this leaf to the root must be updated, using the same method and the same overhead as in user deletion.

1.2 The State Update Problem

The LKH method is quite efficient: each user has to keep a personal key with $\log n$ keys, i.e. of length $\log(n)|k|$ bits, and the length of a key update message is also $\log(n)|k|$ bits. The main drawback of the basic LKH method and its variants is the requirement that group users update their state whenever users join or leave the group. Suppose that t users join or leave the group and that a user was offline when these updates took place. This user must now update the keys in the path from its leaf to the root, in order to be able to process future update messages. If the user also desires to decrypt content that was sent during the period it was offline, it must also learn the t group keys that were in effect during that period. The straightforward way for the user to learn this information is for it to receive and process all t key update messages. The total length of these messages is $t \log(n)|k|$ bits. Typical values for these parameters are, say, $n = 1,000,000$, $t = 1000$, and $|k| = 128$. In this case the total overhead is about $2,500,000$ bits. The computation overhead is almost always negligible, since it only involves efficient "private key" cryptographic operations.

The LKH method was suggested in the context of secure multicast, that builds secure communication on top on the Internet's multicast layer. In that context the state update problem must be addressed since multicast communication is lossy and therefore the key update messages might not be received by all users. Note though that in many scenarios the security is applied to live broadcasting and then users who were offline are not interested in obtaining group keys that were in effect during their offline period. This means that an update message to a user can contain only the current keys in the path from its leaf to the root.

The state update problem might be even more relevant in a digital rights management setting. There might not be continuous communication between the GC and the users, which can be offline most of the time. Content can be delivered to users in separation from the rules and the cryptographic keys that enable the use of the content. The content itself can be delivered in different channels such as a webcast, web servers, a peer-to-peer network, or in static devices such as CDs, DVDs, or other similar types of media. The rules are typically delivered to users when they connect directly with servers, such as the GC.

In this setting it is natural that users do not have continuous communication with the GC, but rather contact it from time to time. Users might acquire content while being disconnected from the GC (e.g. by users "beaming" music from one device to the other), and when they connect with the GC they should obtain keys that enable access to that content[2]. Since key updates might occur frequently, it is reasonable to assume that during the period in which a user is offline there are several updates to the group key. Once the user is online again it should get the group keys that were used since the last time it was connected.

A recent approach taken by Naor, Naor and Lotspiech [ ] is to design a system in which users can be completely *stateless*. That is to say that users do not have to change their personal data when revocations or joins take place. Instead of requiring users to change their state, the GC attaches to each message a header which depends on the list of active users, and enables only these users to decrypt the message (the header information is similar to the list of key update messages that must be available to all users at all times if the LKH scheme is used). They suggest two new key update algorithms, which require each user to store a personal key of $\log n$ and $\frac{1}{2}\log^2 n$ keys, respectively. After t key updates the length of the header information is $t \log n$ and t keys, respectively. The second scheme is very efficient in terms of the length of the header information, which does not even depend on n, at the cost of increasing the length of the personal key. (Note however that the overhead analysis of this scheme requires n to be an upper bound on the number of users *throughout* the lifetime of the system.)

Our approach: We take a different approach, of using the original LKH scheme (and its immediate variants, such as [ ]), and reducing the overhead of users who were offline and need to update their state. Namely, the overhead of learning the group keys that were sent in key update messages which were not received, and also updating the personal keys.

This task can be accomplished by a "universal" solution that applies to all users. For example by making all the key update messages of the LKH scheme available on a web site or constantly retransmitted, or by using one of the stateless methods of [ ] and attaching a header to every message (or posting the header on a web site).

We are able to make the update information much shorter by using a different update message per user, depending on the period during which the user was offline and the content which it is allowed to receive. In particular, the personal key of every user contains only $\log n$ keys as in the LKH scheme, and the update message is of length $O(\log t)$ keys.

---

[2] "Beamed" content might have a rule that enables it to be used a few times for free, but require that a user should get a key from the GC in order to use the content more times.

1.3   Contributions

We address the problem of making state updates as efficient as possible, mostly from the perspective of the communication between the GC and the user. Consider a group U in which there are n users, that uses the LKH scheme for key management. Consider now a user u who was offline during a period in which t users were removed from the group. The length of a key is $|k|$. The trivial state update message contains all the key update messages that were sent during the t key updates, and its length is $t \log(n)$ keys or $t \log(n)|k|$ bits. A naive analysis of the run time reveals also that given this message the user should perform $O(t \log(n))$ decryptions in order to update its state.

The first trivial improvement is to note that after being offline there is no need for the user to learn the actual key update messages. The information that it should learn consists of the group keys that were used while it was offline, which are needed in order to decrypt messages that were sent when these keys were in effect, and the current keys of the nodes in the path from the user's leaf to the root, which are required in order to process future key update messages. The total is t group keys, and $\log(n)$ node keys, which can be sent in a message of length $t + \log(n)$ keys (this message is directed to a specific user, rather than being a universal message that can be used by all users).

In the rest of the paper we present additional improvements:

- Group keys can be generated in a method that enables a concise representation of a sequence of consecutive keys. This enables a list of t consecutive keys to be sent using a shorter message. Namely,
  - t consecutive keys can be sent using a message of length $O(1)$ keys ($2|k|$ bits). This method is not secure against collusions between users.
  - t consecutive keys can be sent using a message of length $O(\log t)$ keys ($2 \log t |k|$ bits). This method is secure against collusions between any number of users.
- We observe that not all the keys in the path from the user's leaf to the root are changed by the update messages, but rather only keys that intersect with the paths from the leaves of deleted or joining users. A probabilistic analysis shows that in most cases only $O(\log t)$ of the $\log n$ keys in the path should be updated. The expected number of keys that have to be changed is $\log(t) + \log \log(n/t)$.

To sum up, the communication overhead of updating the state of a user which was offline during t key updates is reduced for most users from $O(t \log(n)|k|)$ bits to $O(\log t |k|)$ bits. If we do not care about security against collusions of users then this overhead is composed of $O(\log t |k|)$ bits for updating the path, and $O(|k|)$ for sending old group keys. If security against user collusions is required, the overhead is $O(\log t |k|)$ bits for each of these tasks.

1.4   Related Work

User revocation schemes can be traced back to the *broadcast encryption* scheme of Fiat and Naor [ ]. This system enables the removal of any number of users as long as a limited number of them collude (the number of colluding users must be smaller than a system parameter which affects the overhead).

The Logical Key Hierarchy scheme (LKH), which was suggested independently by Wallner et. al [ ] and Wong and Lam [ ], enables to revoke any number of users with security against any number of colluding users. The motivation for this scheme was providing security for multicast groups. Since the scheme requires users to change their keys (state) whenever other users leave or join the group, the users must be connected most of the time. The communication overhead of the LKH scheme was improved in [,] by a factor of 2 (see discussion in Appendix A).

In the information theoretic scenario, Luby and Staddon [ ] provide lower bounds for any revocation algorithm. Kumar et. al [ ] design a *one-time* revocation system for removing s users in which the message length is $O(s \log n)$ and the length of the personal key is $O(s^2)$ and does not depend on n. Since this system is good for a single revocation the question of updating the user's state does not exist. Other, more efficient systems for one-time revocation, based on polynomial interpolation, were by suggested Anzai et. al [ ] and Naor and Pinkas [ ]. In these schemes the length of the revocation message is s keys and the personal key contains only a single key. The scheme of [ ] can be generalized for many revocations, and provides traitor tracing capabilities.

The MARKS system [ ] is a key assignment method that addresses multicast scenarios in which premature removal of users is rare and it is known in advance what content each user is allowed to obtain. It is assumed that in these scenarios there is no need for revocation messages. It is further assumed that users subscribe in advance for a sequence of consecutive "content" events, e.g. for a pay-TV movie (which is composed of consecutive minutes). Fine granularity is achieved by dividing time into short "application data units", ADUs, (e.g. an ADU being a minute of a video) and providing a different key for every ADU. A user should receive the keys of the ADUs which it is entitled to use. The key assignment to ADUs is done using the same method we suggest in Section 2.2 (however, no proof of security or rigorous complexity analysis is given in [ ]).

2   A Concise Representation of Keys

Let us denote the group key that is used between the ith and $(i + 1)$th key updates as k_i. A user which did not receive the t key update messages numbered $i, i + 1, \ldots, j$, where $j - i = t - 1$, must learn keys $k_i, \ldots, k_j$ in order to decrypt content that was sent during these periods. This can be trivially achieved using a message containing these t keys. We show below two methods of reducing this overhead to two keys and $O(\log t)$ keys, respectively.

The methods described in this section can be used in more general scenarios. They enable to generate n pseudo-random keys in a way that enables short representations of any subset of *successive* keys, while preserving the pseudo-randomness of the other keys.

2.1   A Method with no Security Against Collusions

Let N be a predefined constant (say, $N = 10,000$), and let F be a pseudo-random generator with input length of $|k|$ bits and output length of $2|k|$ bits. The system uses a seed of length $2|k|$ bits that can be used to send update messages for N key updates. Afterwards new seeds should be generated.

The system operates in the following way. The GC chooses in advance two seeds, L_1 and R_N, each of length k. Denote by $F_0(x)$ and $F_1(x)$ the left and right halves of the output of F. The GC defines the following values

$$L_i = F_0(L_{i-1}) \quad i = 2, \ldots, N \tag{1}$$
$$R_i = F_0(R_{i+1}) \quad i = N - 1, \ldots, 1 \tag{2}$$
$$k_i = F_1(L_i) \oplus F_1(R_i) \quad i = 1, \ldots, N \tag{3}$$

The key k_i is used as the group key after the ith key update[3]. Note that given L_i and R_j, with $i < j$, one can compute all the keys $k_i, \ldots, k_j$. The update message to a user that did not receive key update messages i through j consists therefore of L_i and R_j alone, is of length $2|k|$ bits, and enables the user to compute $k_i, \ldots, k_j$.

The following theorem shows that a user that receives the pair of keys $\langle L_i, R_j \rangle$ (and no other L or R values) cannot use them to learn keys k_ℓ for which $\ell \notin [i, j]$.

Theorem 1. *Given only L_i and R_j, with $i < j$, the sequence of keys k_ℓ, $\ell \notin [i, j]$ is pseudo-random.*

Proof: (Sketch) The proof uses a standard hybrid argument. Suppose that it is possible to distinguish between the keys $\{k_\ell \mid \ell \notin [i, j]\}$ and a random sequence. Namely there is a non-negligible difference (denoted by δ) between the probability that the user outputs 1 in each of these cases. We can then construct a distinguisher between the output of F and random values. Our distinguisher is given a pair (x_0, x_1) which is either $F(y)$ for a randomly chosen y, or a random $2|k|$ bit string.

Suppose first that $j = N$. We construct $N - t$ hybrids. Hybrid H_ℓ (for $1 \leq \ell \leq i$) is defined in the following way:

- Set $k_1, \ldots, k_{\ell-1}$ to random values.
- Set L_ℓ to a random value.
- Set R_N to a random value, and define all other keys using L_ℓ and R_N.

The distribution of keys $(k_1, \ldots, k_{i-1})$ in H_1 is identical to that generated by the construction, whereas the distribution of these keys in H_i is random. The difference therefore between the probability that the user outputs 1 given H_1 and given H_i is δ. This means that there is an $1 \leq \ell < i$ for which the difference

---

[3] In the improvement of LKH described in [,] the root key is defined by a different method and cannot be set to an arbitrary value. Therefore, the root key should be used to encrypt k_i, which should be used as the group key.

between the probabilities associated with H_ℓ and $H_{\ell+1}$ is at least $\delta/(N-t)$ and is non-negligible. Our distinguisher algorithm for F picks a random location $1 \le \ell' < i$, and performs the following operations:

- Sets $k_1, \ldots, k_{\ell'-1}$ to random values.
- Sets $L_{\ell'+1}$ to x_0, and defines L_s for $s > \ell' + 1$.
- Sets R_N to a random value, and defines R_s for $\ell' \le s < N$.
- Sets $k_{\ell'}$ to $x_1 \oplus R_{\ell'}$.
- For $\ell' + 1 \le s \le N$ defines $k_s = L_s \oplus R_s$.

With probability at least $1/(N-t)$, $\ell' = \ell$ for which the difference in probabilities is $\delta/(N-t)$. Therefore our distinguisher succeeds with probability at least $\delta/(N-t)^2$.

Assume now that $j < N$ and $i > 1$. The argument used above can be used with hybrids ranging over all the locations $\ell \notin [i, j]$ and yield the same result. $\square$

The method suggested here is not immune to collusions between two corrupt users receiving update messages. For example consider user A which paid for content during times $[1, 100]$ and user B which paid for content during times $[201, 300]$. Suppose now that user A was offline during times $[50, 70]$, and user B was offline during times $[250, 270]$. User A contacts the GC and receives L_{50} and R_{70}, and user B contacts the GC and receives L_{250} and R_{270}. Now the two users can use L_{50} and R_{270} together to compute the keys $k_{50}, \ldots, k_{270}$. In particular, they can compute the keys $k_{101}, \ldots, k_{200}$ which neither of them is entitled to receive. The same attack can also be run by a single user that receives two update messages (e.g. consider the above example with A and B being the same user who did not pay for receiving the content during times $[101, 200]$). For this reason the scheme must not send two or more updates to a single user, if between two periods in which the user was offline there is a period in which it is not entitled to obtain the group keys.

The communication overhead of the method consists of an update message that contains two keys, namely of length $2|k|$ bits, as long as the sequence of keys that the user should learn is within a single "block" of keys (i.e. generated from the same seeds). If the sequence of keys contains keys from c blocks, then the communication overhead is $2c|k|$ bits. (However, if n is sufficiently long then c is typically very small, i.e. $c = 1$ or 2.)

2.2   A Method Secure Against Collusions

The following key generation method supports short update messages which are secure against collusions of any set of corrupt users.

Let N be a predefined constant which is a power of 2 (say, $N = 2^{20}$). The method enables to generate N group keys (of length $|k|$ bits each) while enabling to compute any t *consecutive* keys from at most $O(\log t)$ values of length $|k|$ each. If the GC generates the group using this method then a user which does not receive t key update messages can receive a message of length $O(\log t)$ keys from the GC and use it to reconstruct the t group keys that were sent in the key update messages.

The keys are generated in the following way (similar to the Goldreich-Goldwasser-Micali [ ] or the Naor-Reingold [ ] constructions of pseudo-random functions).

- Let F be a pseudo-random generator with input of length $|k|$ bits and output of length $2|k|$, and denote by $F_0(x), F_1(x)$ the left and right halves of the output of F for the input x.
- Imagine a full binary tree of depth $\log(N)$ which has N leaves.
- The GC chooses a random key of length $|k|$ for the root node, and defines a key for every other node of the tree in the following way, going from the root down: Let v be a node, and let $v0, v1$ be its two sons. Denote by k_v the key of node v. Then $k_{v0} = F_0(k_v)$ and $k_{v1} = F_1(k_v)$.
- The key of the ith leaf is used as the group key after the ith key update.

The construction ensures that a key of a node v enables to compute the keys of all the leaves of the subtree rooted in v, using the same key computation method that was used in the initial generation of the tree. (Generating the keys in the leaves of the subtree requires keeping at most $\log n$ internal key values in memory, and doing an amortized computation of $O(1)$ applications of F per key.)

Security: Theorem 2 shows that knowledge of any number of leaf keys, and of the keys of any internal nodes that are the roots of these leaves (and of no other leaves) reveals no information about the keys of other leaves.

Theorem 2. *Given any set S of leaves, and the values of the keys of a set of nodes R (either internal nodes or leaves) such that S is exactly the union of the leaves of the subtrees rooted by nodes in R, the values of the other nodes of the tree are pseudo-random.*

Proof: (Sketch) The proof is based on the proof of the pseudo-randomness of the GGM construction in [ ]. It assumes that there is a distinguisher that distinguishes between the values of the leaves of the tree and random values, and constructs an adversary that distinguishes between the output of the pseudo-random generator and random values, based on queries that it makes to values of the leaves of the tree. The adversary first constructs a full binary tree, chooses a random value to its root and sets the values of the nodes according to the procedure described above. The values of the nodes in R and their descendants are then fixed and will not be changed. The values of the other nodes are defined during the interaction with the distinguisher, based on a hybrid construction, as in the proof in [ ]. Define the number of leaves of the subtrees rooted by R as t. These subtrees have between t and $2t - 1$ nodes. The total number of nodes is $2N - 1$ and therefore there are at most $2N - t - 1$ hybrids, where in the first one (which is the tree defined by the construction) the probability that the distinguisher outputs 1 is equal to this probability in the case the tree is built according to the construction, and in the last one (in which all the nodes except the descendants of R have random values) the probability is the same as if the tree (except the descendants of R) is random. Therefore if the difference between these two probabilities is δ, there is a hybrid which distinguishes between the output of the generator and a random value with probability at least $\delta/(2N-t)$.

$\square$

The key update method: Consider a user which did not receive the messages of t successive key updates and needs to learn the keys of the t successive leaves which were associated with the group keys sent in these key updates. Denote this set of leaves as S. In order to enable the user to learn these keys it is sufficient to provide it with the keys of a minimal set R of nodes, such that S is *exactly* the union of the leaves of the subtrees rooted by the nodes in R. The GC should therefore send to the user the keys of the nodes in R, and the user can use these keys to compute the group keys.

Theorem 3 proves, using an inductive argument, that for every sequence S of t *successive* leaves there is such a set R of at most $O(\log t)$ nodes. The length of the message sent to the user is therefore $O(\log(t)|k|)$ bits.

In order to analyze the size of R we first prove the following lemma.

Lemma 1. *Let T be a complete binary tree with $N = 2^n$ leaves. Then given any set S of consecutive leaves, there is a set R of at most $2n - 2$ nodes such that S is exactly the union of the leaves of the subtrees rooted by the nodes in R.*

Proof: The proof is by induction. Let T_i be a complete binary tree with 2^i leaves. Define the following two values for T_i:

- R_i is the maximum, taken over all sets S of consecutive leaves, of the size of the minimal set of nodes R such that S is exactly the union of the leaves of the subtrees rooted by the nodes in R.
- E_i is defined in a similar way, but taking the maximum over all sets S that contain either the leftmost or the rightmost leaf of T_i. Namely, E_i is the maximum, taken over all sets S of consecutive leaves that contain the leftmost or the rightmost leaf of T_i, of the size of the set of nodes R such that S is exactly the union of the leaves of the subtrees rooted by the nodes in R.

It holds that

$$R_i = \max(R_{i-1}, 2E_{i-1}) \tag{4}$$
$$E_i = \max(E_{i-1}, E_{i-1} + 1) = E_{i-1} + 1 \tag{5}$$

Equation 4 holds since there are only two options for the sequence S that maximizes R_i: If it is contained in one half of the tree (e.g. in the left half rooted by the left son of the root of T_i) it is actually a sequence of leaves in a tree of depth $i - 1$ and the number of nodes in R is bounded by R_{i-1}. If S is contained in both halves of the tree, it is a union of two sequences in two trees of depth $i - 1$, where each of these sequences contains either the leftmost or the rightmost leaf of its subtree. The size of R is then bounded by $2E_{i-1}$.

Equation 5 holds since the sequence S that maximizes E_i is either contained in one half the tree (in which case the size of R is bounded by E_{i-1}), or contains one half of the tree and in addition a sequence of leaves from the other half. In this case R contains the root of the first half, and at most E_{i-1} additional nodes.

For a tree of depth 1 (namely with two leaves), $R_1 = E_1 = 1$. It therefore holds that

$$R_i = 2E_{i-1} = 2i - 2 \tag{6}$$
$$E_i = i \tag{7}$$

This proves the lemma. (Note that if instead of using a binary tree the tree has more descendants per node, the overhead increases.) □

The lemma provides the same bound for any sequence S regardless of the number of leaves it contains. The following theorem provides a bound which depends on $|S|$.

Theorem 3. *Given any set S of t consecutive leaves in a complete binary tree, there is a set R of at most $2\lfloor \log(t) \rfloor + 1$ nodes such that S is exactly the union of the leaves of the subtrees rooted by the nodes in R.*

Proof: Let $N = 2^n$ be the number of leaves in the tree. Let $r = \lfloor \log(t) \rfloor$, namely the largest power of 2 which is not greater than t. We consider the tree as a collection of $N/2^r$ subtrees of depth r, with 2^r leaves in each subtree.

Since it holds that $t/2 < 2^r \leq t$ the sequence of leaves in S can span at most three consecutive such subtrees. The leaves of the inner subtree are completely contained in S, whereas some or all of the leaves of the outer subtrees are contained in S. Applying lemma 1, the number of nodes that cover the leaves in S is at most $E_r + 1 + E_r = 2r + 1 = 2\lfloor \log(t) \rfloor + 1$. □

3 Updating Keys on the Path from a Leaf to the Root

The fact that a user is offline during t key updates does not necessarily mean that all the keys in the path from the user's leaf to the root were changed by the key updates. In fact, if the locations of the users that are leaving or joining are random, then for each key update there is a $1/2$ chance that only the root key is affected, a $1/4$ chance that two keys on the path to the root are affected, and in general a $1/2^i$ chance that i keys on that path are changed.

The update message from the GC to the user should contain only the keys that need to be updated, rather than all the $\log n$ keys in the path from the user's leaf to the root. In this section we prove the following theorem:

Theorem 4. *For any user, after t key updates of random leaf keys using the LKH protocol,*

– It holds with high probability that $\log t + O(1)$ keys need to be updated, and

– *The expected number of keys that have to be updated is* $\log(t) + \log\log(n/t) + O(1)$.

Proof: Fix a certain leaf (the leaf of the user who was offline), and assume that the key updates are applied to randomly chosen users. The probability that the intersection between the path from the user to the root, and the path from a updated key to the root, contains exactly i nodes is 2^{-i}. This is also the probability that the length of the intersection is strictly greater than i.

Considering t key updates, the probability that the intersection with all the paths from the leaves of the updated keys are of length at most ℓ, is $(1 - 2^{-\ell})^t$. Setting $\ell = \log t + c$, yields that the probability of an intersection of length at most ℓ is $(1 - 2^{-\ell})^t = (1 - \frac{1}{t2^c})^t \approx e^{-2^{-c}} \approx 1 - 2^{-c}$. In particular, $\ell = \log t + 2$ yields a probability of $(1 - \frac{1}{4t})^t = 0.78$. Similarly setting $\ell = \log t + 3$ and $\ell = \log t + 4$ yield probabilities of 0.88 and 0.94, respectively. The length of the intersection is therefore greater than $\log t + 4$ nodes with probability at most 6%.

As for the calculation of the expected length of the intersection, let us again set $\ell = \log t + c$, where c is a parameter whose value we will define below. The probability that all the t intersections are of length ℓ or less is $(1 - 2^{-\ell})^t = (1 - \frac{1}{t2^c})^t = e^{-2^{-c}}$. The expected length of the intersection with all paths is therefore bounded by

$$(\log t + c) \cdot e^{-2^{-c}} + \log n \cdot (1 - e^{-2^{-c}}).$$

Assuming that 2^c is large, we can use the following approximation

$$\approx (\log t + c) \cdot (1 - 2^{-c}) + \log n \cdot 2^{-c}$$
$$= \log t + c + 2^{-c}\log(n/t) - 2^{-c}c$$

Setting $c = \log\log(n/t)$ cancels out the third element and reveals that the expectation is $\log t + \log\log(n/t) + O(1)$. This is therefore the expected length of the update message. □

Using the Revocation Protocol of Canetti et. al [ ]: Further improvement can be achieved if one employs the revocation method of [ ], described in Appendix A. See details in A.2.

References

1. J. Anzai, N. Matsuzaki and T. Matsumoto, *A Quick Group Key Distribution Scheme with Entity Revocation*. Adv. in Cryptology – Asiacrypt'99, Springer-Verlag LNCS 1716 1999, pp. 333–347.   46
2. B. Briscoe, *MARKS: Zero side effect multicast key management using arbitrarily revealed key sequences*, Proc. First International Workshop on Networked Group Communication (NGC'99), 1999.   46
3. R. Canetti, J. Garay, G. Itkis, D. Micciancio, M. Naor and B. Pinkas, *Multicast Security: A Taxonomy and Some Efficient Constructions*, In Proc. INFOCOM '99, Vol. 2, pp. 708–716, New York, NY, March 1999.   43, 44, 46, 47, 52, 54, 55

4. A. Fiat and M. Naor, *Broadcast Encryption*, Advances in Cryptology – CRYPTO '93, Springer-Verlag LNCS vol. 773, 1994, pp. 480–491, 1994. 45, 53

5. O. Goldreich, S. Goldwasser and S. Micali, *How to construct random functions*, J. of the ACM, Vol. 33, No. 4, 1986, pp. 792-807. 49

6. R. Kumar, S. Rajagopalan and A. Sahai, *Coding constructions for blacklisting problems without computational assumptions*, Adv. in Cryptology – Crypto '99, Springr-Verlag LNCS 1666, pp. 609–623, 1999. 46

7. M. Luby, **Pseudorandomness and Cryptographic Applications**, Princeton Computer Science Notes, 1996. 49

8. M. Luby and J. Staddon, *Combinatorial Bounds for Broadcast Encryption*, Adv. in Cryptology – Eurocrypt '98, Springer-Verlag LNCS 1403, 1998, pp. 512–526. 46

9. D. Naor, M. Naor and J. Lotspiech, *Revocation and tracing schemes for stateless receivers*, Adv. in Cryptology – Crypto '01, Springer-Verlag LNCS 2139, 2001, pp. 41–62. 44

10. D. McGrew, A. T. Sherman, *Key establishment in large groups using one-way function trees*, submitted to IEEE Transactions on Software Engineering (May 20, 1998). 43, 46, 47, 55

11. M. Naor and B. Pinkas, *Efficient Trace and Revoke Schemes*, Proceedings of Financial Crypto '2000, February 2000. 46

12. M. Naor and O. Reingold, *Number-Theoretic constructions of efficient pseudo-random functions*, Proc. 38th IEEE Symp. on Foundations of Computer Science, 1997, pp. 458–467. 49

13. D. M. Wallner, E. G. Harder and R. C. Agee, *Key Management for Multicast: Issues and Architecture*, RFC 2627, June 1999. 42, 46, 53, 54

14. C. K. Wong and S. S. Lam, *Digital Signatures for Flows and Multicasts*, IEEE ICNP '98. Also, University of Texas at Austin, Computer Science Technical report TR 98-15. 42, 46, 53

A   LKH Based Schemes

A.1   The LKH Scheme

Tree based group rekeying schemes were suggested by Wallner et. al [ ] (who used binary trees), and independently by Wong et. al [ ] (who consider the degree of the nodes of the tree as a parameter). We concentrate on the scheme of [ ] since it requires a smaller communication overhead per user revocation. When this scheme is applied to a group of n users it requires each user to store $\log n + 1$ keys. It uses a message with $2 \log n - 1$ key encryptions in order to delete a user and generate a new group key. This process should be repeated for every deleted user. The scheme has better performance than the Fiat-Naor [ ] scheme when the number of deletions is not too big. It is also secure against any number of corrupt users (they can all be deleted from the group, no matter how many they are). A drawback of the scheme is that if a user misses some control packet relative to a user deletion operation (e.g., if it temporarily gets disconnected from the network), it needs to ask for the missed control packets. This also applies for a user who misses join operations if the scheme is set to support backward secrecy.

We now describe the scheme of [ ]. Let $u_0, \ldots, u_{n-1}$ be n members of the group (in order to simplify the exposition we assume that n is a power of 2). They all share a group key k with which group communication is encrypted. There is a single group controller, which might wish at some stage to delete a user from the group and enable the other members to communicate using a new key k', unknown to the deleted user.

The group is initialized as follows. Users are associated with the leaves of a tree of height $\log n$ (see Figure 1). The group controller (GC) associates a key k_v with every node of the tree, and sends to each user (through a secure channel) the keys associated with the nodes along the path connecting the user to the root. For example, in the tree of Figure 1, user u_0 receives keys k_{000}, k_{00}, k_0 and k. Notice that the root key k is known to all users and can be used as the group key and encrypt group communication.

In order to remove a user u from the group the GC performs the following operations. For all nodes v along the path from u to the root, a new key k'_v is generated. New keys are encrypted as follows. Key $k'_{p(u)}$ is encrypted with key $k_{s(u)}$, where $p(u)$ and $s(u)$ denote respectively the parent and sibling of u. For any other node v along the path from u to the root (excluded), key $k'_{p(v)}$ is encrypted with keys k'_v and $k_{s(v)}$. All encryptions are sent to the users. For example, in order to remove user u_0 from the tree of Figure 1 the following set of encryptions is transmitted (see Figure 2): $E_{k_{001}}(k'_{00}), E_{k'_{00}}(k'_0), E_{k_{01}}(k'_0), E_{k'_0}(k'), E_{k_1}(k')$. It is easy to verify that each user can decrypt only the keys it is entitled to receive. If backward secrecy is required then a user join operation is similar to user removal (see Section 1.1). The update of the keys in the path from the leaf of the joining user to the root is performed in a similar manner to the key update in the case of user removal.

A.2   The Scheme of Canetti et. al [ ]

This scheme reduces the communication overhead of [ ] by a factor of two, to only $\log n$ key encryptions.

The initialization of the scheme is as in the scheme of [ ]. Let f be pseudorandom generator which doubles the size of its input. The security of the user deletion scheme can be formally reduced to the security of f. Denote by $f_0(x)$, $f_1(x)$ the left and right halves of the output of f on an input x. To remove a user u the group controller associates a value r_v to every node v along the path from u to the root: It chooses r_u at random and sets $r_{p(v)} = f_1(r_v)$ for all other v. It also defines for each v the new key $k'_{p(v)} = f_0(r_v)$ and encrypts r_v with key $k_{s(v)}$. The encryptions are sent to all users. For example, in order to remove user u_0 from the tree of Figure 1, we send encryptions $E_{k_{001}}(r_{000}), E_{k_{01}}(r_{00}), E_{k_1}(r_0)$. One can easily verify that each user can compute from the encryptions all and only the keys it is entitled to receive.

Advantages: The construction in [ ] halves the communication overhead of the basic scheme to only $\log n$, and its security can be rigorously proven based on the

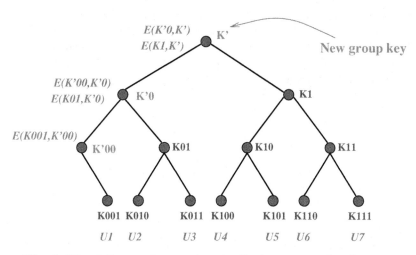

Fig. 2. The delivery of new values to the keys surrendered to u_0

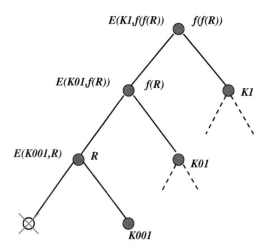

Fig. 3. The delivery of new key values to the keys in the scheme of [ ]

widely used assumption of the existence of pseudo-random generators. Independently, McGrew and Sherman [ ] have presented a tree based rekeying scheme which has the same overhead as [ ]. However, the security of that scheme is based on non-standard cryptographic assumptions and is not rigorously proven.

More Efficient Key Update The scheme of [ ] enables to perform the key update procedure of Section 3 more efficiently. The main idea is that in order to enable a user to update the keys in the path from its leaf to the root a new key should only be sent for nodes v for which

- v is the intersection point between the path from the leaf of the ith revoked user to the root, and the path from the user's leaf to the root; and
- The paths to the root from the leaves of the users which were revoked *after* the ith user do not intersect the path from the user's leaf to the root in a node which is in a lower layer than v.

A probabilistic analysis shows that in this case, too, the expected length of an update message to the user is of length $O(\log(t)|k|)$ bits, although with a smaller constant.

Collusion Secure q-ary Fingerprinting for Perceptual Content

Reihaneh Safavi-Naini and Yejing Wang

School of Information Technology and Computer Science
University of Wollongong
Wollongong 2522, Australia
{rei,yejing}@uow.edu.au

Abstract. We propose a q-ary fingerprinting system for stored digital objects such as images, videos and audio clips. A fingerprint is a q-ary sequence. The object is divided into blocks and each symbol of the fingerprint is embedded into one block. Colluders construct a pirate object by assembling parts from their copies. They can also erase some of the marks or cut out part of the object resulting in a shortened fingerprint with some unreadable marks. We give constructions of codes that can identify one of the colluders once a pirate object is found.

Keywords: Traceability, fingerprinting codes, watermarking schemes.

1 Introduction

Protecting digital media against illegal copying and redistribution is one of the main concerns of the owners and distributors of digital objects. Access control techniques such as encryption ensure that a digital object is only accessible to the person who has a special piece of information, called 'key'. However when the content is decrypted, no mechanism is left to prevent illegal copying and re-distribution of the object.

Fingerprinting is a commonly used technique in which a unique sequence is embedded in each copy of the object so that an illegal copy can be traced to a buyer who has misused his privileges. Collusion secure fingerprinting [1,2,10] ensures that a pirate copy can be traced to one of the colluders if the object is constructed by a collusion of up to c buyers. To embed a fingerprint in an object a *watermarking* system is used. A watermarking system embeds the fingerprint into the object in an imperceptible way such that only an authorised person with access to secure key information can recover the fingerprint.

Boneh and Shaw considered fingerprinting codes and did not concern themselves with the actual embedding process. According to their model the fingerprint is a string of *marks* over an alphabet Σ of size q. Each mark can take one of the q values and is embedded into the content using an embedding system. They assumed the place that a mark is embedded is unknown (otherwise a buyer can remove the mark) and considered a collusion attack in which colluders construct an illegal copy by comparing their copies of the object to detect the mark

T. Sander (Ed.): DRM 2001, LNCS 2320, pp. 57–75, 2002.
© Springer-Verlag Berlin Heidelberg 2002

positions and then use one of the marks, or erase the mark (*unreadable state*) in the detected positions. However an undetected position remains unchanged. Colluders' action is modelled by a *marking assumption*. Boneh and Shaw considered c-secure codes that allow tracing of one of the colluders if a pirate copy is found. They proved that under the above assumption a *totally c-secure code* which can always (deterministically) trace a colluder cannot exist. They also gave constructions of *binary* c-secure code with ε-error in which the chance of erroneous tracing is at most ε.

Guth and Pfitzmann [10] argued that Boneh and Shaw's marking assumption was strong and allowed the undetected positions to be erasable too but assumed that the adversary can only erase a percentage of the marks. With this assumption, called *weak marking assumption*, they modified a binary code proposed in [1,2] to provide protection under the new marking assumption. Again tracing is probabilistic and there is a small chance of falsely accusing an innocent user or not identifying a colluder.

We consider q-ary fingerprinting for objects with perceptual content. Matheson et al noted [16] that Boneh and Shaw's marking assumption reflects properties of *representational watermarks* used for text over natural languages or programming languages and not watermarks used for perceptual content such as still images, audio and video signals in which change to the media is continuous. This observation is true if the embedding of the fingerprint is by using a watermarking system. That is if the fingerprinting sequence is used as the key in a watermarking algorithm, then the watermark signal is spread over the whole object and construction of the pirate object cannot be modelled by Boneh and Shaw's model. In other words components of the fingerprinting sequence are not linked to a small area in the object and so the pirate copy cannot be modelled by an object whose embedded fingerprint is the combination of colluders' fingerprints, as proposed in [ ]. This approach to fingerprinting does not offer any protection against a 'cut and paste' attack where colluders cut their objects into *parts* and reassemble a pirate object by pasting parts from different colluders. This is because in the pirate object each part is from a different watermarked copy and so applying the verification method of the watermarking system will not detect a watermark.

In our approach the object is broken into segments and a mark from the fingerprint sequence is embedded in each segment. Collusion security is obtained mainly through the design of the sequence and the underlying watermark. While the marking assumption captures properties of the underlying watermarking systems.

The basic idea of having a two tier system, that is, using watermarking to embed a mark and a fingerprint sequence to provide collusion security, is not new. It has been used by Boneh and Shaw (for non-perceptual content) and others following their model, and also the work reported in [ ]. However this latter, as noted by the authors, has a different approach. Using an embedding method similar to the one proposed in [ ] will allow us to use a q-ary version of Boneh and Shaw's marking assumption for perceptual content. In particular, we consider the following embedding process. The object to be fingerprinted is divided into *segments*, for example blocks of 8 × 8 pixel in an image. Next a subset of these segments are randomly chosen and one component of the fingerprinting sequence is embedded in each chosen segment using a watermarking algorithm. The subset of segments is fixed for all copies and is kept hidden. Watermarking a segment creates one of the q *versions* of that segment. Watermarking algorithms that can embed more than one bit information are studied by numerous authors [4,23]. As noted in [16] the main properties of perceptual contents is that the space of possibilities is continual and "has some relatively simple geometry". This means that two different versions of a segment are dis-similar and so are distinguishable. However two copies of the same version of a segment (belonging to two colluders) are *similar*. (The two copies will not be identical but will be very similar.)

In a collusion attack, colluders compare their copies of an object and construct a pirate copy in which each segment is obtained from a corresponding segment of one of the colluders. That is, when colluders detect a mark position, they can use one of their versions *but cannot construct a version that they do not have* and so the version of that segment in the pirate copy will be one of their versions. They may also be able to make some of the detected marks unreadable: that is modify the segment such that no mark can be extracted from it. This is a reasonable way of modelling watermarking schemes that use a different random sequence for embedding the q marks. A group of colluders have a number of versions of a segment but do not know the actual random sequences used in the embedding process and so cannot construct a version that they do not have. However they can use attacks such as *averaging* (for example pixel values in a segment) versions of a segment to make the embedded mark unreadable. The effectiveness of the averaging attack will depend on the underlying watermarking system and the number of colluders [15].

Using the above scheme for the fingerprinting sequence means that the pirate sequence will be a q-ary sequence with some positions having '?' representing on unreadable mark.

We also allow the sequence recovered from the pirate copy to have *deleted* positions and so have shorter length than the original fingerprint. This can happen because of modifications to the object geometry resulting from operations such as cropping an image, or removing frames from a video clip. Deletions need not be considered if we assume that the tracer always has an original copy of the object and can recover the lost positions by comparing the pirate object with the original one. However this could become very expensive and impractical for large objects such as a video clip when there are a number of distribution centres for the same object. In this case, each centre must either keep an original copy of the object, or be able to securely access such a copy over the Internet, or send the pirated copy to a central location for tracing. All these solutions have drawbacks and weaknesses and so it is desirable to be able to trace without having access to the original copy. We note that watermark recovery could be performed without the original object and so if the original object is not required for recovering the deleted positions in the fingerprint of pirate object, tracing will be completed with accessing the original object.

Our approach to fingerprinting still images (or video data), provides protection against 'cut and paste' attack as long as the number of errors generated through this process is bounded. For example if averaging attack on all parts is used then the quality of the pirate copy will be reduced but also many mark positions will become unreadable in which case our systems will become ineffective.

Our Results

We first define and construct The tracing algorithm is by finding the minimum Hamming distance between the pirate word and all the codewords in the code and ensures that one colluder can be correctly identified.

Increasing protection against erasure is important because colluders can always average their versions of a segment to reduce the strength of the mark [ ]. We show that higher resilience against erasure can be obtained by using repetition and randomisation of the code. This is similar to the approach used by Boneh and Shaw for constructing binary c-secure codes with ε-error and using a different marking assumption. We will construct a c-secure code with ε-error using n copies of a were $n > \log_{p_0}(\varepsilon/L)$ and p_0 is the probability of erasure of a mark in the fingerprint. Guth and Pfitzmann used multiple copies of binary c-secure codes for providing protection against erasure. Although compared to q-ary case, the required number of copies for the same value of ε is higher but the size of the segment to embed a q-ary mark is in general larger and so the total size of the object in the two cases could be the same.

Finally we consider codes that can recover deleted marks, that is, when the pirate sequence is shorter than the embedded fingerprint. We propose two solutions. The first one uses a special mark, called 'buffer mark', used as a position marker in the fingerprint. The second solution is by using Levenshtein distance instead of the Hamming distance for tracing a colluder, and employing deletion correcting codes with high minimum distance for providing protection against deletion of the marks. This latter approach is particularly interesting and is in parallel with using Hamming distance and error-correcting codes for tracing.

Related Work

There are a number of closely related works.

The aim of our work is to construct collusion secure fingerprinting schemes for objects with perceptual content to protect digital content stored on media such as CD and DVD.

In *collusion-resistant watermarks*, each buyer receives a watermarked copy of the object. Ergun et al showed [ ] an averaging attack that can defeat any watermark system when enough watermarked copies (colluders) exists. However for small number of copies the mark cannot be erased.

Frame-proof codes [1,2] ensure that no collusion of up to c buyers can construct a pirate copy that contains the fingerprint of another buyer. A number of constructions for these codes are proposed in [21,20,18,20].

Boneh and Shaw studied *totally c-secure*, and *c-secure codes* with ε-error, under *strong marking assumption*. Guth and Pfitzmann [10] constructed binary c-secure with ε-error under *weak marking assumption*. Although Boneh and Shaw's definitions and existence results are for q-ary codes but all their constructions, including the one modified by Guth and Pfitzmann, are for binary case.

Staddon et al [20] defined q-ary *c-traceability codes*. The allowable operations for colluders is similar to our marking assumption but does not include erasure. They gave a sufficient condition for an error-correcting code that can be used as a traceability code.

Traceability systems are also studied in the context of broadcast encryption schemes [3,21,22,12,9]. *Broadcast encryption* systems [7] allow targeting of an encrypted message to a privileged group of receivers. Traceability schemes in this context are also called *key fingerprinting* and a number of constructions are proposed [3,21,12].

Other related works are *dynamic tracing* scheme proposed by Fiat and Tassa [8] and *sequential tracing* proposed by Safavi-Naini and Wang [17]. Sequential tracing is particularly related because the mark allocation table is in fact a static code similar to the fingerprinting codes considered here. The colluders' attack can be modelled by a marking assumption similar to the one used in this paper but without erasure. However the system operation is different in the two cases and in particular in sequential tracing detected colluder will be *disconnected*.

In the following section we give the model and construction of q-ary c-secure codes that protects against erasure of the marks. In Section 3 we introduce sequence deletion attack and give two constructions that provide protection against this attack. Section 4 concludes the paper.

2 q-ary c-Secure Codes

A *c-robust watermarking system* consists of a set of q marks $\Sigma = \{1, 2, \cdots, q\}$ and a pair of algorithms (I, D). The *insertion algorithm* I takes a digital object O, a symbol i and a key k and produces a *version* O_i of the object, watermarked with i. The *detection algorithm* D takes an object O', the key k and produces an element of $\Sigma' = \Sigma \cup \{?\}$ or produces *False* that indicates no watermark is present. The algorithm will produce '?' if it cannot decide if a watermark is present. The c-robustness refers to the property that collusion of up to c colluders who have access to c versions of O cannot construct a different version of the object, but they may construct an object such that the detection algorithm produces a '?'.

A *q-ary fingerprinting system* consists of a q-ary fingerprinting code and watermarking system. The code is a collection of q-ary sequences. To embed a fingerprint $(i_1, i_2, \cdots, i_L)$, where $i_j \in \Sigma, 1 \leq j \leq L$, in an object O, the object is first broken into basic segments. Next, a sequence of L basic segments $O = (o_1, o_2, \cdots, o_L)$, are chosen and the watermarking insertion algorithm is used to embed i_j in o_j. When a pirate object is found, the watermark detection algorithm is used to find the marks embedded in the basic segments of the sequence. The resulting sequence is the pirate fingerprint and is a sequence over Σ'. We will concentrate on the fingerprinting code and the recovered sequence.

Let $C = \{u_1, u_2, \cdots, u_c\}$ be a set of c colluders, each having a copy of the object O. The basic strategy for constructing a pirate object is to compare the objects segment by segment, detect mark positions and construct a pirate object in which the mark position is one of the colluders' versions, or is unreadable. Undetected position may also be averaged to become unreadable.

Let Our marking assumption is as follows

Marking Assumption: A collusion $C = \{u_1, \cdots, u_b\}, b \leq c$, is only capable of creating an object whose fingerprint lies in the following set

$$\mathcal{P}(C) = \{x = (x_1, \cdots, x_L) : x_j \in \{w_j^{(i)} : 1 \leq i \leq b\} \cup \{?\}, 1 \leq j \leq L\}$$

This is a q-ary version of Guth and Pfitzmann's marking assumption and allows erasure to occur both in the detected and undetected positions.

We note that colluders might use other strategies. For example cutting their objects into parts that are not aligned with the original segments and construct the pirate object by re-assembling parts from colluders' objects. In this strategy as long as a part is bigger than a basic segment, the pirate object will have complete basic segments of colluders. We assume there are enough large parts so that the pirate fingerprint does not have too many basic segments with erased mark.

Definition 1. *Let $\varepsilon > 0$. A code $\Gamma \in \Sigma^L$ is called q-ary c-secure with ε-error if there exists a tracing algorithm A such that for any pirate word x generated by a colluding group C, $|C| \leq c$, then*

$$Pr(A(x) \in C) > 1 - \varepsilon.$$

A q-ary c-secure code with ε-error of length L and with N codewords, is denoted by c-$S_q(L, N; \varepsilon)$.

We call the code q-ary c-secure to emphasise the similarity of the marking assumption with that of [ ] and [ ].

2.1 Constructing c-Secure Codes from Error-Correcting Codes

Collusion attack on q-ary codes *without erasure* is studied in the context of traceability codes. Staddon et al [ ] defined traceability codes and proved the following results.

Definition 2. *Let $\Gamma \subseteq \Sigma^L$ be a code, $C = \{u_1, \cdots, u_b\} \subseteq \Gamma$ be a collusion. Define*

$$desc(C) = \{(x_1, \cdots, x_L) : x_j \in \{w_j^{(i)} : 1 \le i \le b\}, 1 \le j \le L\}$$

Γ is called c-traceability code if the following condition is satisfied: for any $(x_1, \cdots, x_L) \in desc(C)$, there is a $u_i \in C$ such that

$$|\{j : x_j = w_j^{(i)}\}| > |\{j : x_j = w_j\}|$$

for any $(w_1, \cdots, w_L) \in \Gamma \setminus C$.

A c-traceability code with number of codewords N and length L is denoted by c-TA$_q(L, N)$. Let $(L, N, D)_q$-ECC denote an error-correcting code of length L with N codewords and with minimum Hamming distance D over an alphabet of size q.

Theorem 1. *([ ]) Let Γ be an $(L, N, D)_q$-ECC, and c be an integer. If*

$$D > (1 - \frac{1}{c^2})L \tag{1}$$

then Γ is a c-TA$_q(L, N)$.

We can extend Theorem 1 to the case that there are erasures but tracing only succeeds if the number of erasures is bounded. Let $\mathcal{P}(C; e)$ denote the subset of $\mathcal{P}(C)$ with at most e erasures. That is

$$\mathcal{P}(C; e) = \mathcal{P}(C) \cap \{(x_1, \cdots, x_L) : |\{j : x_j = ?, 1 \le j \le L\}| \le e\}$$

Definition 3. *Let $\Gamma \in \Sigma^L$ be a code and $C = \{u_1, \cdots, u_b\} \subseteq \Gamma$, $b \le c$, be a collusion. Γ is called a c-traceability code tolerating e erasures, and denoted by c-TA$_q(L, N; e)$, if the following condition holds: for any $(x_1, \cdots, x_L) \in \mathcal{P}(C; e)$, there is a $u_i \in C$ such that*

$$|\{j : x_j = w_j^{(i)}\}| > |\{j : x_j = w_j\}|$$

for any $(w_1, \cdots, w_L) \in \Gamma \setminus C$.

Theorem 2. *Let Γ be an $(L, N, D)_q$-ECC, and c and e be integers. If D satisfies*

$$D > (1 - \frac{1}{c^2})L + \frac{e}{c^2} \tag{2}$$

then Γ is c-TA$_q(L, N; e)$.

Proof. Let $C = \{u_1, \cdots, u_b\}$ be a collusion, and assume $x \in \mathcal{P}(C)$. If $|C| \le c$ then there exists $u_i \in C$ such that u_i and x have at least $(L - e)/c$ in common, that is $\lambda(u_i, x) \ge (L - e)/c$.

On the other hand, for any $u \in \Gamma \setminus C$

$$\lambda(u, x) \leq \lambda(u, u_1) + \cdots + \lambda(u, u_b) \leq c\lambda_{max}$$

Because of (2) we have $c^2(L - D) < L - e$. Noting that $L - D = \lambda_{max}$, then $c^2\lambda_{max} < L - e$, and hence

$$\lambda(u, x) \leq c\lambda_{max} < \frac{L - e}{c} \leq \lambda(u_i, x)$$

So $\lambda(u_i, x) > \lambda(u, x)$ for any $u \in \Gamma \setminus C$, and u_i is identified correctly.

Theorem 2 shows that pirate words with not too many erasures can be de-terministically traced. In the following we use multiple copies of the above code to increase erasure tolerance, but tracing will be with a small error. A similar approach is used by Boneh and Shaw [1,] but for a different marking assumption.

Increasing Erasure Tolerance

We start with a c-$TA_q(L, N; e)$. The basic idea is to repeat the codeword enough times so that at least one copy of u can be recovered. The chance of tracing for the resulting code is the same as the initial code multiplied by the probability of recovering a codeword.

We assume that *the probability of erasing the mark in a segment is indepen-dent of other segments and is at most equal to p_0.* That is, we do not make any distinction between detected and undetected marks.

Theorem 3. *Let $\varepsilon > 0$ and $p_0 > 0$ be given. Suppose there exists a c-$TA_q(L, N; e)$, and an embedding system with erasure probability p_0 for each sym-bol. Then there exists a c-$S_q(nL, N; \varepsilon)$ where n is an integer satisfying,*

$$n > \log_{p_0}(\varepsilon/L). \tag{3}$$

Proof. Suppose we have a code Γ, c-$TA_q(L, N; e)$. Repeating each mark n times results in a new code consisting of L blocks denoted by $B_1, B_2, \cdots, B_L$, where B_i consists of n copies of the same mark. For a block B_i, the probability that all marks are corrupted is p_0^n, and so the probability that at least one mark is left within B_i is $1 - p_0^n$. We know that a sequence of $L - e$ marks can detect one of the traitors using the code Γ. The probability that there are $L - e$ unerased blocks with at least one correct mark in each is,

$$p = \binom{L}{e}(1 - p_0^n)^{L-e}. \tag{4}$$

So p is the probability of correctly tracing one colluder. Let $x = \log(L/\varepsilon)$. Noting that

$$1 - (1 - 2^{-x})^L \leq L \cdot 2^{-x}, \quad \text{for } x > 0,$$

we have

$$\varepsilon = L \cdot 2^{-x} \geq 1 - (1 - 2^{-x})^L \geq 1 - (1 - 2^{-x})^{L-e} \geq 1 - (1 - 2^{-x})^{L-e} \binom{L}{e}.$$

So

$$1 - \varepsilon \leq (1 - 2^{-x})^{L-e} \binom{L}{e}$$

and

$$1 - (1 - \varepsilon)^{1/(L-e)} \left(\frac{L}{e}\right)^{1/(e-L)} \geq 2^{-x}$$

That is

$$- \log \left(1 - (1 - \varepsilon)^{1/(L-e)} \left(\frac{L}{e}\right)^{1/(e-L)} \right) \leq x.$$

Since $- \log p_0 > 0$, we have

$$\frac{- \log \left(1 - (1 - \varepsilon)^{1/(L-e)} \left(\frac{L}{e}\right)^{1/(e-L)} \right)}{- \log p_0} \leq \frac{x}{- \log p_0}.$$

If n satisfies (3), then $n > x/(- \log p_0)$. So we have

$$1 - (1 - \varepsilon)^{1/(L-e)} \left(\frac{L}{e}\right)^{1/(e-L)} > p_0^n.$$

And finally,

$$1 - \varepsilon < \binom{L}{e} (1 - p_0^n)^{L-e}.$$

The right-hand side is equal to (4), and so the probability of correctly tracing one traitor is $> 1 - \varepsilon$.

2.2 Bound for c-$TA_q(L, N)$ and c-$TA_q(L, N; e)$

One of the efficiency measures of a q-ary code is the size of the alphabet, q. The higher value of q requires larger segments for embedding and so less number of segments in the object. Theorems 5 and 6 can be used to bound q.

Theorem 4. *(Plotkin bound) For an $(L, N, D)_q$-ECC, if $D > (1 - 1/q)L$, then*

$$N \leq \frac{D}{D - (1 - 1/q)L}$$

Theorem 5. *Let c and e be integers, and Γ be an $(L, N, D)_q$-ECC with D satisfying (1). If $N > q > 2$, then $q > c^2$.*

Proof. Assume otherwise, that is $c^2 \geq q$. Then

$$1 - \frac{1}{c^2} \geq 1 - \frac{1}{q}.$$

Condition (1) gives that $D > (1 - 1/c^2)L \geq (1 - 1/q)L$. Applying Theorem 4, we have

$$N \leq \frac{D}{D - \theta \cdot L} = \frac{D}{D - (1 - \frac{1}{q})L}$$

and so

$$D \leq \frac{(1 - \frac{1}{q})NL}{N - 1}.$$

From (1) we have

$$(1 - \frac{1}{c^2})L < \frac{(1 - \frac{1}{q})NL}{N - 1}$$

and so when $N > q > 2$

$$c^2 < \frac{1}{1 - \frac{(1 - \frac{1}{q})N}{N - 1}} < \frac{1}{1 - 2(1 - \frac{1}{q})} = \frac{1}{1 - 2 + 2\frac{1}{q}} = \frac{1}{-1 + 2\frac{1}{q}} < 0$$

This is a contradiction and so $c^2 < q$.

Corollary 1. *In a c-$TA_q(L, N)$ obtained from Theorem 1, $q > c^2$.*

Following a similar argument, Theorem 6 gives a bound on q for a c-$TA_q(L, N; e)$ obtained from Theorem 2.

Theorem 6. *Let c be an integer, Γ be an $(L, N, D)_q$-ECC with D satisfying (2). If $N > q > 2$, then $q > \frac{L}{L-e}c^2$.*

Proof. Assume otherwise, that is $\frac{L}{L-e}c^2 \geq q$. Then $\frac{L-e}{c^2} \leq \frac{L}{q}$. Now from condition (2) we have

$$D > (1 - \frac{1}{c^2})L + \frac{e}{c^2} = L - \frac{L - e}{c^2} \geq (1 - \frac{1}{q})L.$$

The theorem can be proved by using Theorem 4.

Corollary 2. *In a c-$TA_q(L, N; e)$ obtained from Theorem 2, $q > \frac{L}{L-e}c^2$.*

To give examples of $(L, N, D)_q$-ECC with D satisfying (2) we use algebraic-geometry codes (*AG*-codes). Let $[L, k, D]_q$ denote a *linear error-correcting code* of length L, dimension k and minimum distance D over a q-ary alphabet. It is known [ ] that AG codes with parameters $[L, k, L + 1 - k - g]_q$ exists, if there exists an algebraic curve of genus g over $GF(q)$ having n rational points. For $g = 1$, the curves of genus 1 are elliptic curves which are known to exist for any $L \leq N_q(1)$ where $q = p^m$ and $N_q(1)$ is defined as

$$N_q(1) = \begin{cases} q + \lceil 2\sqrt{q} \rceil, & p \mid \lceil 2\sqrt{q} \rceil, \text{ and } m \geq 3 \text{ is odd} \\ q + \lceil 2\sqrt{q} \rceil + 1, & \text{else} \end{cases} \tag{5}$$

So an AG code exists for any k, $1 \le k \le L - 1$. When $g = 2$, the curve of genus 2 exists for any $L \le N_q(2)$, where $q = p^m$ and $N_q(2)$ is given as follows.

If $m \equiv 0 \,(mod\,2)$

$$N_q(2) = \begin{cases} q + 4\sqrt{q} + 1, q \ne 4, 9 \\ 10, \qquad\qquad q = 4 \\ 20, \qquad\qquad q = 9 \end{cases} \tag{6}$$

If $m \equiv 1 \,(mod\,2)$

$$N_q(2) = \begin{cases} q + 2\lceil 2\sqrt{q} \rceil + 1, q \text{ is non-special} \\ q + 2\lceil 2\sqrt{q} \rceil, \qquad q \text{ is special and } 2\sqrt{q} - \lceil 2\sqrt{q} \rceil > (\sqrt{5} - 1)/2 \\ q + 2\lceil 2\sqrt{q} \rceil - 1, q \text{ is special and } 2\sqrt{q} - \lceil 2\sqrt{q} \rceil < (\sqrt{5} - 1)/2 \end{cases} \tag{7}$$

here q is *special* means that either $p \,|\, \lceil 2\sqrt{q} \rceil$ or q is of the forms: $q = \ell^2 + 1$, $q = \ell^2 + \ell + 1$ or $q = \ell^2 + \ell + 2$ for some integer ℓ. The corresponding code exists for any k, $1 \le k \le L - 2$.

In AG codes, the minimum distance is given by $D = L + 1 - k - g$. If D satisfies (2) then we obtain a c-$\text{TA}_q(L, q^k; e)$ with parameters,

$$L \le N_q(1), 1 \le k \le L - 1, 0 \le e \le L - 4L, \qquad c = \lfloor \sqrt{\tfrac{L-e}{k}} \rfloor, \text{ where } g = 1,$$
$$L \le N_q(2), 1 \le k \le L - 2, 0 \le e \le L - 4k - 4, c = \lfloor \sqrt{\tfrac{L-e}{k+1}} \rfloor, \text{ where } g = 2. \tag{8}$$

2.3   Comparison and Trade-Offs

Theorem 3 gives a general method of constructing a c-$S_q(L, N; \varepsilon)$ code from a c-$\text{TA}_q(L, N; e)$ code. Suppose we use an AG code with parameters in row one of (8), as a c-$\text{TA}_q(L, q^k; e)$ code. In this code $c^2 = (L-e)/k$, or equivalently, $L = e + c^2 k$. Moreover, $N = q^k$ which gives $k = \log_q N$. So $L = e + c^2 \log_q N > c^2 \log_q N$, and the length of the c-$S_q(nL, N; \varepsilon)$ obtained from Theorem 3 is

$$n \cdot L > \log_{p_0}(\varepsilon/L) \cdot L > \frac{\log(L/\varepsilon)}{\log(1/p_0)} \cdot c^2 \log_q N > \frac{\log(q/\varepsilon)}{\log(1/p_0)} \cdot c^2 \log_q N$$
$$> c^2 \frac{\log(1/\varepsilon)}{\log(1/p_0) \log q} \log N$$

That is the length of c-$S_q(L, N; \varepsilon)$ is of the form

$$O\left(c^2 \frac{\log(1/\varepsilon)}{\log(1/p_0) \log q} \log N \right) \tag{9}$$

Boneh and Shaw [1, 2] constructed a binary c-secure code for $\varepsilon > 0$, with L of the order

$$O\left(c^4 \cdot \log \frac{N}{\varepsilon} \log \frac{1}{\varepsilon} \right). \tag{10}$$

Guth and Pfitzmann's modification of Boneh and Shaw's code to provide erasure tolerance results in codewords that are slightly longer than (10), and so the length of codes obtained from AG code is smaller than Guth and Pfitzmann's construction. This is not surprising because q-ary marks, rather than binary ones, are used.

3   Removing Segments

A digital object can be shortened. For example the first 50 milliseconds of a video clip may be removed without affecting its content, or an image might be 'cropped'. In this section we consider pirate objects where the recovered fingerprints is shorter than the fingerprint in the colluders' copies. In this case the recovered fingerprint sequence cannot be compared with the codewords in the fingerprinting codes and so the previous tracing system will not work.

Let r be an integer, define

$$\mathcal{P}(C; e, r) = \{y = (y_1, \cdots, y_{L'}) : y \text{ is a subword of some}$$
$$x \in \mathcal{P}(C; e), L' \geq L - r\}$$
$$\Sigma^{L,r} = \{x \in (\Sigma \cup \{?\})^* : L - r \leq |x| \leq L\}$$

Definition 4. *Let e, r, c be integers, $\Gamma \subseteq \Sigma^L$ be a code, and $C = \{u_1, \cdots, u_b\}$, $b \leq c$, be a collusion.*

1. *Γ is c-$TA_q(L, N; e, r)$ if there is a tracing function $A : \Sigma^{L,r} \longrightarrow \Gamma$ such that $A(x) \in C$ for any $x \in \mathcal{P}(C; e, r)$.*
2. *Γ is c-$S_q(L, N; r, \varepsilon)$ if there is a tracing function $A : \Sigma^{L,r} \longrightarrow \Gamma$ such that $Pr(A(x) \in C) > 1 - \varepsilon$ for any $x \in \mathcal{P}(C; e, r)$.*

We give constructions for c-$TA_q(L, N; e, r)$ and c-$S_q(L, N; r, \varepsilon)$, one by protecting symbols of a fingerprinting sequence using buffer blocks, the other by using a deletion/insertion correcting code.

3.1   Constructing c-$TA_q(L, N; e, r)$ Using Buffer Blocks

We construct a code, c-$TA_{q+1}(\bar{L}, N; e, r)$, using a c-$TA_q(L, N; e)$ by employing a 'buffer' mark. In the construction below we assume that the deleted segments are consecutive. This assumption is removed in the construction given in section 3.2. Assume the watermarking system has $q + 1$ marks, *buffer mark* 0. Let $\Gamma^{(b)}$ be a $(q + 1)$-ary code, which is obtained from c-$TA_q(L, N; e)$ by inserting b buffer marks between any two normal marks. Tracing will have three steps: (i) recover synchronisation, (ii) find a collection of at least $L - e$ normal marks, and (iii) identify a traitor using the tracing algorithm of the code c-$TA_q(L, N; e)$.

In the recovered sequence, existence of i buffer marks between two normal marks implies that $b - i + m(b+1)$ segments are deleted (m is a positive integer). Since the length of the recovered sequence is not shorter than $L - r$, so as long as $b + 1$ is bigger than r, consecutive segments will retain their correct positions.

The following theorem shows that with appropriate choice of parameters it is always possible to find the correct positions of all marks.

Theorem 7. *Let Γ be a c-$TA_q(L, N; e)$. Then $\Gamma^{(b)}$ is c-$TA_{q+1}(L + (L-1)b, N; e, b)$. Furthermore, $\Gamma^{(b)}$ can trace $x \in \mathcal{P}(C; e, b)$ to $u \in C$ provided that x satisfies the following:*

- *there are at most e erasures among the normal mark positions, or at most b erasures among the buffer mark positions;*
- *there are at most b deletions around two successive normal marks in every non-cross intervals.*

The proof can be found in a long version.

3.2 Using Deletion/Insertion-Correcting Codes

The construction in section 3.1 requires the deleted part of the object to be contiguous. In the following we give a different approach that allows random deletion, and reduce the problem of tracing to the construction of a special class of codes.

Preliminaries Let Γ be a collection of codewords over an alphabet Σ. Denote by Σ^* the set of strings of finite length over Σ. A *word* x is a sequence

$$x = x_1 x_2 \cdots x_L, \quad x_i \in \Sigma$$

and its length L is denoted by $|x|$. A *subword* w of x is a string where

$$w = x_{i_1} x_{i_2} \cdots x_{i_{|w|}}, \quad 1 \le i_1 < i_2 < \cdots < i_{|w|} \le L.$$

A word w is said to be a *common subword* of $x, y \in \Sigma^*$ if w is a subword of both x and y. For $x, y \in \Sigma^*$ define

$$\rho(x, y) = \max\{|w| : w \text{ is a common subword of } x \text{ and } y\}$$

and denote by $\rho(\Gamma) = \max_{x, y \in \Gamma, x \ne y} \rho(x, y)$. Suppose we have the words:

$$
\begin{array}{lll}
x = x_1 \cdots x_{i-1}\, x_i & x_{i+1}\, x_{i+2} \cdots x_{L-1} x_L, & |x| = L \\
y = x_1 \cdots x_{i-1}\, x_{i+1}\, x_{i+2}\, x_{i+3} \cdots x_L, & & |y| = L - 1 \\
z = x_1 \cdots x_{i-1}\, x_i' & x_i \quad x_{i+1} \cdots x_{L-2} x_{L-1} x_L, & |z| = L + 1
\end{array}
$$

We use the following terms: *a deletion* is an operation that gives y from x; and *an insertion* is an operation that gives z from x. We write $x \xrightarrow{(d,i)} y$ if there exists a common subword w of x and y such that

$$d = |x| - |w|, \quad i = |y| - |w|.$$

The *Levenshtein distance* between two words $x, y \in \Sigma^*$ is defined as

$$D_l(x, y) = \min_{(d,i)} (d + i).$$

It has been shown [ ] that

$$D_l(x, y) = |x| + |y| - 2\rho(x, y). \tag{11}$$

The *minimum Levenshtein distance* of a code Γ is denoted by $D_l(\Gamma)$, and is defined as follows

$$D_l(\Gamma) = \min_{x,y \in \Gamma, x \neq y} D_l(x, y).$$

Tracing with Shortened Fingerprint To prove the main theorem of this section (Theorem 8), we need the following lemma.

Lemma 1. *Let $e, r, c > 0$ be integers, and $\Gamma \subseteq \Sigma^L$ be a code. If*

$$\rho(\Gamma) < \frac{L - e - r}{c^2} \tag{12}$$

then the following property is satisfied: for any $C \subseteq \Gamma$, $|C| \leq c$, and any $x \in P(C; e, r)$, there exists a u_i such that $\rho(x, u) < \rho(x, u_i)$.

Proof. Suppose a group $\{u_1, \cdots, u_b\}$ of colluders produces a pirate word x,

where $|x| = a_1 + a_2 + \cdots + a_b + a = L' = L - t$, $t \leq r$ and $a \leq e$. Let $a_i = \max_{1 \leq i \leq b}(a_j)$. Then

$$a_i \geq \frac{L - a - t}{c} \geq \frac{L - e - r}{c}.$$

Since $w = w_{i1} \cdots w_{ia_i}$ is a common subword of u_i and x, so $\rho(x, u_i) \geq a_i$. Let u be another codeword, $u \in \Gamma \setminus C$, given by

then

$$\rho(x, u) = a'_1 + a'_2 + \cdots + a'_b \leq \rho(u, u_1) + \rho(u, u_2) + \cdots + \rho(u, u_b) \leq c\rho(\Gamma)$$

If $\rho(\Gamma)$ satisfies condition (12), then

$$\rho(x, u_i) < \rho(x, u) \quad \text{for } \forall u \in \Gamma \setminus \{u_1, \cdots, u_b\}.$$

Theorem 8. *Let $e, r, c > 0$ be integers, and $\Gamma \subseteq \Sigma^L$ be a code with N codewords. If*

$$D_l(\Gamma) > 2\left(1 - \frac{1}{c^2}\right)L + \frac{2}{c^2}(e + r) \tag{13}$$

then Γ is a c-$TA_q(L, N; e, r)$.

Proof. Follows from Lemma 1 and (11).

Existence of Deletion/Insertion Correcting Codes

Consider a code Γ in which all codewords have the same length L. Let $x, y \in \Sigma^*$. We write

$$x \xrightarrow{(d,i)} y$$

if there exists a common subword w of x and y such that

$$d = |x| - |w|, \quad i = |y| - |w|.$$

A code Γ is said to be *t-deletion/insertion correcting code* if, for each word $y \in \Sigma^*$, there exists at most one codeword $x_0 \in \Gamma$ such that

$$x_0 \xrightarrow{(d,i)} y, \quad d + i \leq t.$$

The following theorem is given in [ ].

Theorem 9. *(Theorem 4.1, [ ]) A code $\Gamma \subseteq \Sigma^*$ is t-deletion/insertion correcting code if and only if $2t < D_l(\Gamma)$.*

For more about deletion/insertion correcting codes, see [,] and references therein. It is not difficult to prove the following Lemma.

Lemma 2. *Let $\Gamma \subseteq \Sigma^L$. For any $x, y \in \Gamma$, $D_l(x, y) \leq 2t$ if and only if y can be obtained from x by t deletions and t insertions, that is*

$$D_l(x, y) \leq 2t \iff x \xrightarrow{(t,t)} y. \tag{14}$$

To construct a q-ary t-deletion/insertion correcting code we follow an approach proposed in [ ]. The following algorithm gives a t-deletion/insertion-correcting code for any $t > 1$. Suppose the size of Σ is q. Choose $x_0 \in \Sigma^L$ and let $X_0 = \{x \in \Sigma^L : D_l(x_0, x) \leq 2t\}$. (14) shows that each word in X_0 can be obtained from x_0 by t deletions followed by t insertions. For t deletions, we can choose arbitrary t positions from L positions, and delete the symbols at chosen positions. For the remaining $L - t$ symbols, we choose $L - t$ positions from L positions. Then we choose t symbols from Σ, and finally insert the chosen symbols into the chosen positions. This means that X_0 contains

$$\binom{L}{t} \cdot \binom{L}{L-t} q^t = \binom{L}{t}^2 q^t$$

words. Using Stirling formula it is not difficult to see that when

$$\frac{q^L}{L^2} > q^t \tag{15}$$

we have

$$\binom{L}{t}^2 q^t < q^L$$

Let $B(x_0; 2t) = \{x \in \Sigma^L : D_l(x_0, x) > 2t\}$. Then $B(x_0; 2t) \neq \emptyset$, and there is a word $x_1 \in \Sigma^L$ such that $D_l(x_0, x_1) > 2t$. We follow the same process. After i steps, the word $\{x_0, \cdots, x_{i-1}\}$ are chosen. Let

$$B(x_0, \cdots, x_{i-1}; 2t) = \{x \in \Sigma^L : D_l(x_0, x) > 2t, \cdots, D_l(x_{i-1}, x) > 2t\}.$$

If $B(x_0, \cdots, x_{i-1}; 2t) \neq \emptyset$, then $x_i \in B(x_0, \cdots, x_{i-1}; 2t)$ is chosen such that the Levenshtein distance between any two of them is bigger than $2t$. This step is repeated N times where

$$B(x_0, \cdots, x_{N-1}; 2t) = \emptyset.$$

This is essentially a brute force method. Constructions for t-deletion codes are found in [14,24,19,27].

A c-$S_q(L, N; r, \varepsilon)$ can be constructed using a method similar to section 2.1 using a c-$TA_q(L, N; e, r)$. We state the following theorem whose proof is similar to Theorem 3.

Theorem 10. *Let $\varepsilon > 0$, $p_0 > 0$, $r > 0$ be given. Suppose there exists a c-$TA_q(L, N; e, r)$, and an embedding system which ensures an erasure probability p_0 for symbol. Then there exists a c-$S_q(nL, N; r, \varepsilon)$, where n be an integer satisfying (3).*

4 Concluding Remarks

In this paper we considered fingerprinting schemes for digital objects with perceptual content, such as video clips and still images. Rather than embedding a single watermark in the whole object we proposed a two tier system consisting of a q-ary fingerprinting sequence, and a watermarking system that embeds the marks of the fingerprinting sequence into the segments of the object. This results in a fingerprinting model similar to Boneh and Shaw's, but this time for objects with perceptual content. We extended their marking assumption to capture properties of watermarking systems for perceptual contents and allowed the marks to be erased in both detected and undetected segments. Using this model, we defined q-ary c-secure codes and proved that a q-ary error-correcting code with high enough minimum distance gives a c-secure code that can detect one of the colluders. To increase resilience against erasure, we proposed a repetition construction similar to Boneh and Shaw's, but using a weaker q-ary weak marking assumption and showed that the length of the code for the same number of colluders is smaller than that of a binary code constructed by Guth and Pfitzmann for the binary version of the same marking assumption.

We also allowed the mark positions in the pirate fingerprint to be completely deleted. We proposed two constructions, one using a special buffer mark, and the second one using a deletion/insertion code. An interesting open question is the trade-off between efficiency parameters of a code, that is the number of codewords, the length of the code, the number of colluders and the size of the alphabets. Also efficient construction of deletion/insertion correcting codes will be of high interest.

Acknowledgements

Authors would like to thank Takeyuki Uehara for interesting discussions.

This research is in part supported by Australian Research Council Grant Number 227 26 1008.

References

1. D. Boneh and J. Shaw. Collusion-secure fingerprinting for digital data. In *Advances in Cryptology – CRYPTO'95, Lecture Notes in Computer Science,* volume 963, pages 453-465. Springer-Verlag, Berlin, Heidelberg, New York, 1995. 57, 58, 61, 62, 64, 67

2. D. Boneh and J. Shaw. Collusion-secure fingerprinting for digital data. *IEEE Transactions on Information Theory, Vol.* 44, No. 5:1897-1905, 1998. 57, 58, 61, 64, 67

3. B. Chor, A. Fiat, and M. Naor. Tracing traitors. In *Advances in Cryptology – CRYPTO'94, Lecture Notes in Computer Science,* volume 839, pages 257-270. Springer-Verlag, Berlin, Heidelberg, New York, 1994. 61

4. I. Cox, J. Killian, T. Leighton, and T. Shamoon. Secure spread spectrum watermarking for multimedia. *IEEE Transaction on Image Processing, Vol.* 6, No. 12:1673-1687, 1997. 59

5. J. Dittmann, A. Behr, M. Stabenau, P. Schmitt, J. Schwenk, and J. Ueberberg. Combining digital watermarks and collusion secure fingerprinting for digital images. In *Proceedings of SPIE,* volume 3657, pages 171-182, 1999. 58

6. F. Ergun, J. Kilian, and R. Kumar. A note on the limits of collusion-resistant watermarks. In *Advances in Cryptology – EUROCRYPT'99, Lecture Notes in Computer Science,* volume 1592, pages 140-149. Springer-Verlag, Berlin, Heidelberg, New York, 1999. 60

7. A. Fiat and M. Naor. Broadcast encryption. In *Advances in Cryptology – CRYPTO'93, Lecture Notes in Computer Science,* volume 773, pages 480-491. Springer-Verlag, Berlin, Heidelberg, New York, 1994. 61
8. A. Fiat and T. Tassa. Dynamic traitor tracing. In *Advances in Cryptology – CRYPTO'99, Lecture Notes in Computer Science,* volume 1666, pages 354-371. Springer-Verlag, Berlin, Heidelberg, New York, 1999. 61
9. E. Gafni, J. Staddon, and Y. L. Yin. Efficient methods for integrating traceability and broadcast encryption. In *Advances in Cryptology – CRYPTO'99, Lecture Notes in Computer Science,* volume 1666, pages 372-387. Springer-Verlag, Berlin, Heidelberg, New York, 1999. 61
10. H. Guth and B. Pfitzmann. Error- and collusion-secure fingerprinting for digital data. In *Information Hiding'99, Lecture Notes in Computer Science,* volume 1768, pages 134-145. Springer-Verlag, Berlin, Heidelberg, New York, 2000. 58, 61, 62
11. H. D. L. Hollmann. A relation between Levenshtein-type distances and insertion-and-deletion correcting capabilities of codes. *IEEE Transactions on Information Theory, Vol.* 39, No. 4:1424-1427, 1993. 70, 71
12. K. Kurosawa and Y. Desmedt. Optimum traitor tracing and asymmetric schemes. In *Advances in Cryptology – EUROCRYPT'98, Lecture Notes in Computer Science,* volume 1462, pages 502-517. Springer-Verlag, Berlin, Heidelberg, New York, 1998. 61
13. G. Langelaar, I. Setyawan, and R. Lagendijk. Watermarking digital and video data. *IEEE Signal Processing Magazine,* Sept.:20-46, 2000. 58
14. V. I. Levenshtein. Binary codes capable of correcting deletions, insertions and reversals. *Soviet physics – doklady, Vol.* 10, No. 8:707-710, 1966. 72
15. L. R. Matheson, S. G. Mitchell, T. G. Shamoon, R. E. Tarjan, and F. Zane. Robustness and security of digital watermarks. In *Financial Cryptography – FC'98, Lecture Notes in Computer Science,* volume 1465, pages 227-240. Springer-Verlag, Berlin, Heidelberg, New York, 1998. 58, 59, 60
16. B. Pfitzmann and M. Waidner. Asymmetric fingerprinting for large collusions. In *Proceedings of* 4th *ACM conference on computer and communications security,* pages 151-160, 1997. 57
17. R. Safavi-Naini and Y. Wang. Sequential traitor tracing. In *Advances in Cryptology – CRYPTO 2000, Lecture Notes in Computer Science,* volume 1880, pages 316-332. Springer-Verlag, Berlin, Heidelberg, New York, 2000. 61
18. R. Safavi-Naini and Y. Wang. New results on frameproof codes and traceability schemes. *IEEE Transactions on Information Theory, Vol.* 47, No. 7:3029-3033, 2001. 61
19. L. J. Schulman and D. Zuckerman. Asymptotically good codes correcting insertions, deletions, and transpositions. *IEEE transactions on information theory, Vol.* 45, No. 7:2552-2557, 1999. 71, 72
20. J. N. Staddon, D. R. Stinson, and R. Wei. Combinatorial properties of frameproof and traceability codes. *IEEE transactions on information theory, Vol.* 47, No. 3:1042-1049, 2001. 61, 62, 63
21. D. Stinson and R. Wei. Combinatorial properties and constructions of traceability schemes and frameproof codes. *SIAM Journal on Discrete Mathematics,* 11:41-53, 1998. 61
22. D. R. Stinson and R. Wei. Key preassigned traceability schemes for broadcast encryption. In *Proceedings of SAC'98, Lecture Notes in Computer Science,* volume 1556, pages 144-156. Springer-Verlag, Berlin, Heidelberg, New York, 1999. 61
23. M. Swanson, M. Kobayashi, and A. Tewfik. Multimedia data-embedding and watermarking technologies. *Proceedings of IEEE, Vol.* 86, No. 6:1064-1087, 1998. 59

24. G. Tenengolts. Nonbinary codes, correcting single deletion or insertion. *IEEE Transactions on Information Theory,* IT-30, No. 5:766-769, 1984. 72
25. M. A. Tsfasman and S. G. Vladut. *Algebraic-geometric codes.* Kluwer Academic Publishers, 1991. 66
26. Y. Wang. Contributions to traceability schemes. Ph.D Thesis, School of Information Technology and Computer Science, University of Wollongong, Australia, 2001. 61
27. J. Yin. A combinatorial construction for perfect deletion-correcting codes. *Designs, Codes and Cryptography,* 23:99-110, 2001. 72

Privacy Engineering
for Digital Rights Management Systems

Joan Feigenbaum[1][*], Michael J. Freedman[2][**],
Tomas Sander[3], and Adam Shostack[4]

[1] Computer Science Dept., Yale University
PO Box 208285, New Haven, CT 06520 USA
joan.feigenbaum@yale.edu
[2] MIT Lab for Computer Science
200 Technology Square, Cambridge, MA 02139 USA
mfreed@lcs.mit.edu
[3] InterTrust STAR Lab
4750 Patrick Henry Drive, Santa Clara, CA 95054 USA
sander@intertrust.com
[4] Zero-Knowledge Labs
888 Maisonneuve East, Montreal, Quebec H2L 4S8 Canada
adam@zeroknowledge.com

1 Introduction

Internet-based distribution of mass-market content provides great opportunities
for producers, distributors, and consumers, but it may seriously threaten users'
privacy. Some of the paths to loss of privacy are quite familiar (*e.g.*, mining of
credit-card data), but some are new or much more serious than they were in
earlier distribution regimes. We examine the contributions that digital-rights-
management (DRM) technology can make to both compromising and protecting
users' privacy. We argue that the privacy-enhancing technology (*e.g.*, encryption,
anonymity, and pseudonymity) that absorbs most of the attention of the security
R&D community cannot by itself solve the privacy problems raised by DRM,
although it can play a role in various solutions. Finally, we provide a list of
"privacy engineering" principles for DRM systems, some of which are easy to
implement and potentially quite effective.

The goal of DRM technology is distribution of digital content in a manner
that protects the rights of all parties involved, including (but not necessarily
limited to) copyright owners, distributors, and users. Appendix A below contains
a detailed description of a generic DRM system and its technical components.
Here, we give a high-level description that suffices for our purpose, which is
exploration of the interplay among DRM systems, user privacy, and business
and legal issues.

[*] Supported in part by ONR grants N00014-01-1-0795 and N00014-01-1-0447 and
NSF grant CCR-0105337.
[**] This work was largely done while the author was visiting InterTrust STAR Lab.

T. Sander (Ed.): DRM 2001, LNCS 2320, pp. 76–105, 2002.

The following is a list, adapted from Chapter 5 of [27], of some of the security technologies that often play a role in DRM:

- *Security and integrity features of computer operating systems* include, for example, the traditional file-access privileges enforced by the system.
- *Rights-management languages* express in machine-readable form the rights and responsibilities of owners, distributors, and users, enabling application programs to determine whether requested uses should be allowed.
- *Encryption* scrambles digital content so that it can be transmitted or stored in an unusable form (and later decrypted and used, presumably by an application that is authorized to do so and has legitimate possession of the decryption key).
- *Digital signatures* provide assured provenance of digital content and nonrepudiation of transactions.
- *Fingerprinting and other "marking" technology* embeds (usually imperceptible) ownership or rights information in digital content so as to facilitate tracking of copying, distribution, or usage.

DRM-system development consists of putting these pieces together into an end-to-end system that serves the needs of owners, distributors, users, and all other major stakeholders. For high-quality, popular content, this is a daunting development task, and we are not claiming that it is a solved (or even solvable) problem. Nor are we claiming that DRM technology alone can protect everyone's interests perfectly; laws, social norms, and (most importantly) business models will play major roles in making mass-market distribution work, and it will probably never work perfectly. Our claim is simply that the use of these techniques can affect user privacy and that this fact should be taken into account at every stage of DRM-system design, development, and deployment.

At the risk of stating the obvious, we note that there can be inherent tension between the copyright-enforcement goals of owners and distributors who deploy DRM systems and the privacy goals of users. Rights enforcement may be facilitated by user tracking or by network control of users' computers, but both of these are potentially destructive of user privacy. One of the major ways in which privacy can be compromised is through data collection by distributors and network operators. We discuss typical DRM loci of collection in more detail in Section 2 below.

Privacy engineering for DRM is made significantly more complicated by the fact that there are legitimate reasons for distributors and network operators to collect data about users and their activities. These include traffic modeling for infrastructure planning and QoS enhancement; risk management; backup and archiving; targeted marketing and recommendations; mining of aggregated, depersonalized datasets for trend-spotting and (untargeted) marketing and advertising; and counting or statistical sampling (*e.g.*, by clearinghouses like AS-CAP/BMI for payments to artists). However, data collected for legitimate reasons can also be used in illegitimate (or perhaps just distasteful or annoying) ways. Furthermore, in today's dynamic business environment, mergers, acquisitions, bankruptcies, and other changes over the life-cycle of a corporation can radically change who has access to what information and how that information may be used and cross-referenced. The merger of DoubleClick and Abacus Direct exemplified how changing access to data can have radical privacy implications [ ].

It is our thesis that sound privacy engineering of content-distribution and DRM systems can help defuse at least some of this inherent tension. If properly designed, implemented, and used, DRM can provide reasonable user-privacy protection[1] and simultaneously supply businesses with information necessary for their basic functionality at a fair cost. We give a list of privacy-engineering principles in Section 4 below; perhaps the most important overarching theme of these principles is that data-collection procedures should be tailored very precisely for the business purposes they serve and that personally identifying information (e.g., names and addresses) should be omitted from all data collections whose purposes don't require it.

We focus our discussion on mass-market content. For niche-market content, we believe that privacy issues are less pressing or at least are more easily solved by technology, legal contracts, or some combination of the two.

The rest of this paper is organized as follows. In Section 2, we review the ways in which DRM can impact user privacy. In Section 3, we explain why this problem cannot be solved straightforwardly by the considerable number of tools that have already been explored at length in the security and privacy literature. In Section 4, we suggest a practical approach to privacy engineering using the Fair Information Principles and privacy audits. We provide several *simple, yet effective* principles that engineers should observe for privacy-friendly system design. We conclude in Section 5.

2   How Digital Distribution and DRM Affect User Privacy

In this section, we review how Internet content distribution and DRM can lead to privacy loss. We also point out which of these paths to privacy loss are common to all Internet-based commerce or to all forms of mass-market content distribution and which are specifically created or exacerbated by DRM. In order to do this, we must examine some of the ways in which commercial distributors might use DRM to build profitable businesses.

First, consider a straightforward distribution model that does not involve DRM. The user downloads a digital work from the distributor's website; this transaction may or may not involve payment, and, if it does, the user will provide a credit-card number or some other information that allows the payment to work its way through the financial system. Once the user has the digital content on his computer, he is subsequently technologically untethered to the distributor and may use the content in any way that he chooses (albeit at his legal risk if he

---

[1] In this paper, we use the term "privacy" to mean end-user privacy, *i.e.*, privacy of the individual consumer. We acknowledge that other constituencies, *e.g.*, content owners and technology providers, have privacy concerns, but those concerns are the subject of another paper.

violates copyright or other laws). There are two main ways in which this type of transaction can pose a threat to the user's privacy. His Web activity can be monitored (*e.g.*, through client-side cookies, server-side logs, or a variety of other means), and his credit-card or other payment data can be mined. The first threat is common to all Web-based commerce (and to non-commercial Web activity, for that matter) and has nothing to do with content distribution specifically. The second is a long-standing concomitant of non-cash (or, more precisely, non-anonymous) payment systems, and it has nothing to do with content distribution or with Web-based transactions, except insofar as the migration of commerce to the Web could greatly increase the extent to which payment data are mined. Many more parties can collect and access payment data online than can do so offline.

Our concern in this paper is the effect on privacy of introducing DRM to this straightforward model. Before going on, it is worth asking why DRM is needed. The standard answers are that owners and distributors need some post-download control over their content (*i.e.*, that the user in the basic DRM-free transaction described above would copy, distribute, or modify the content in ways that violate copyright), that users need a way to verify provenance and authenticity of content, and that, in general, business models that are used for physically embodied works such as books and CDs will break if the works are embodied in digital files and sold through the type of straightforward purchase described above. This hypothesis may be correct, but it has not been adequately tested. Mass-market distributors have not yet put much high-quality content online and tested the proposition that, if they offer it at a reasonable price through an easy-to-use channel, their users will buy it rather than steal it. Some niche-market distributors are doing so, and the results of these experiments will be interesting. In the meantime, because DRM systems are under development and will apparently be used by big distributors, their potential effects on user privacy are important.

There are several different DRM strategies, and their potential effects on privacy differ as well. We consider them in turn. Note that we are not claiming that the DRM technology needed to implement these strategies would "work," in the sense that it could not be circumvented; we're asking what its effect on privacy would be if it did work.

One strategy is to distribute persistent, complete DRM metadata with digital content. In the basic transaction described above, each digital work available on the distributor's website would be formatted for use only by approved application programs, and each of these applications would be able to interpret the distributor's DRM metadata as well as the content. Each file downloaded by a user would include both the content and the metadata that describes the "rights" that the user has acquired. Content and rights need not be downloaded from the same website; the point is that, in this general DRM strategy, they are each transferred once to the user's computer (after payment if this is a commercial transaction) and thereafter unmonitored by the distributor. Using an approved application, the user could only access the content as specified by the rights metadata. Approved actions for text, for example, might include viewing and printing but not editing or redistributing via email. Promotional music or video might be distributed free but restricted via DRM metadata to a fixed, small number of plays. Under this strategy, rights metadata is added to the collectible, minable information about a user. Otherwise, the strategy has no effect on user privacy; in particular, *actual* use of the digital content, as opposed to approved but not necessarily executed use, can take place in private, offline.

Another strategy is to tie downloaded content to a particular device or set of devices. Before downloading a digital work, the user would have to provide serial numbers (or other IDs) of the devices on which he intends to use it. The DRM metadata distributed with the work would then have to include this set of devices, and the set would thus become yet another type of user-specific information that can be collected and mined. In addition, this strategy requires ongoing, periodic contact between user and distributor. Users who have purchased content will insist on being able to continue to use it when they replace old devices with new ones, *e.g.*, because the old ones malfunctioned or because the users bought more powerful devices or received them as gifts. Thus, the rights server, which may or may not be the distributor, will have to save and periodically update a record of the user and the device set. Users can thus be "tracked" to some extent under this DRM strategy. This is a departure from the previous scenarios in which a user downloaded some content and possibly some metadata, paid for it if necessary, and from then on did not need to have any further contact with the content distributor or rights server. Such tracking for the purpose of tying content to a set of devices obviously puts at risk some previously private information about the user.

A third DRM strategy involves tying the downloaded content to the user. After downloading a digital work from a legitimate distributor (and paying for it if necessary), the user would have the right to use the work on any device at any time, *after* proving that he's a legitimate user. Here, the amount of user-tracking can be much greater than it is in other strategies. Potentially collectible and minable information about a user includes his complete listening, reading, and viewing history. This is a qualitatively more serious threat than those previously described. Many people would be willing to risk others' knowing that they downloaded a pornographic video; fewer would want others to know that they watched this video 1,000 times.[2]

Finally, a radical and interesting strategy consists of dispensing altogether with content downloads. Some conventional wisdom has it that sale of digital content can never be profitable (in part because users will expect to pay much less for it than they have traditionally paid for physically embodied content, while distributors' costs will not be much lower than they are in the physical world) but that subscriptions to content services may be. In the "content becomes a service" scenario, paid-up subscribers to Internet content-delivery services can get any of the content in their subscription package streamed to their devices

---

[2] In a more realistic example, a friend of ours who is not a technology professional said "All of the Barry Manilow fans out there would be blackmail victims."

whenever they want it, but they don't actually acquire copies of the content. Such subscriptions might be attractive to users if they are reasonably priced, but they create the potential for massive collection of usage data and the resulting loss of privacy.

These are not the only possible DRM strategies, but they illustrate the basic, important point that some potential threats to user privacy derive from monitoring of content and rights acquisition, some from the need to update rights, and some from the collection of usage data.

As we explained earlier, some of the potential threats to privacy are caused by Web-based distribution and not by DRM *per se*. It is worth noting that there are also ways in which Web-based distribution is potentially *more* conducive to user privacy than older distribution channels. For example, because delivery is done via a data network, there is no intrinsic need to supply identity-exposing real-life information, such as a delivery or billing address, in order to complete a transaction. Furthermore, certain digital distribution channels, such as decentralized peer-to-peer systems, naturally make user-tracking harder than it is in other channels and could thus lead naturally to more privacy. When DRM systems are introduced in order to have fine-grained control over the usage of content, they can also dispense fine-grained anonymous payment tokens, thus allowing *usage* tracking (*e.g.*, for the purposes of efficiently provisioning networks or accurately compensating artists) without *user* tracking. More generally, DRM systems can segregate personally identifying information (PII) such as names, addresses, and phone and credit-card numbers into precisely the databases and operations systems of the distributor that actually need to make use of it, keeping it out of digital credentials, tokens, and other objects that are used by content-rendering applications and other system components that do not need PII.

3   Why Cryptography Is Insufficient

Twenty-five years of cryptographic research has yielded a vast array of privacy-enabling technologies that support many types of two-party and multi-party interactions. Thus, cryptographic researchers might wish to believe that user privacy in content distribution and DRM is a solved problem. You pay for content with anonymous electronic cash. You connect to content providers and rights lockers via an anonymizing mixnet. You authenticate yourself with anonymous credential schemes or zero-knowledge identification protocols. You download content via private information retrieval or oblivious transfer. You use secure function evaluation when interacting with services that require some information.

Despite the apparent profusion of such technologies, few are in widespread use. Furthermore, even if they were in widespread use, they would not necessarily eliminate the user-privacy problems that we have described. In this section, we seek to understand why this is so. We first examine this issue from a technical perspective, then consider relevant economic and business aspects.

3.1   Technological Failures of Privacy Solutions

Privacy-enhancing technologies developed in the research community are not stand-alone, adequate solutions to privacy threats. We claim that these technologies are insufficient: They solve only part of the problem and are open to technical attacks, they are often difficult to integrate with the rest of the mass-market content-distribution infrastructure, and they sometimes have unacceptably high costs.

Our Abstractions Don't Model Our Reality   The cryptographic research community models interactions and protocols in terms of very distinct entities and information. For instance, the traditional communication confidentiality model is that Alice wants to communicate with her friend Bob without adversaries Eve and Lucifer being able to read her message. We may abstract general privacy-enhancing protocols by saying that users try to hide information by performing computations in some trusted private environment (the trusted computing base, or *TCB*) and then using the results of these computations to communicate with the outside world. We suggest that this model is inadequate for commercial content distribution, where the clean dichotomies of good guy vs. bad guy, trusted vs. untrusted, and private vs. public do not exist.

DRM comes into the picture because users want to obtain mass-market content online and commercial distributors want to sell it to them. Many users are unconcerned about the commercial distributors knowing the details of the purchases in which they participate directly and using this knowledge for straightforward business purposes (such as order fulfillment and billing), but many are concerned about how such knowledge could be misused or shared. This problem is further complicated by the fact that "misuse" is ill-defined; pairs of parties that have some interests in common also have some conflicting interests. Alliances, partnerships, and commercial relationships are constantly in flux and will remain so. Not only are users battling from the low ground, but it is difficult for them even to identity the enemy from whom they should hide all of their private data. In a network where businesses bundle valuable content and personalization services, and users want anytime anywhere access from any number of devices, who is Alice, who is Bob, who is the enemy, and what is the TCB? Cryptographic research cannot answer these questions. Cryptographic protocol specifications assume that one knows exactly what is "legitimate use" of data and what is "misuse," and they assume that there is a single, well-defined relationship between Alice and Bob.

Technical Limitations: Security Breaches and Usability   Even if cryptographic research could answer these questions, attackers are likely to find technical exploits and information leakage in a purely technical solution to user-privacy problems. The research community is relatively good at designing secure protocols, but secure implementation is much harder, much more complex, and not something over which the research community has complete control. Brady *et al.* argue in [ ] that very moderate attackers will always find vulnerabilities in large and complex systems: Statistics favor the attacker as such software systems evolve.

One critical technical concern with privacy-enhancing technology is the apparent tradeoff between ease-of-use and security. Even "simple" technology like encrypted email, for which toolkits such as PGP were offered in the early 1990s, is still confusing and difficult for the average consumer to use [ ]. In DRM systems, managing separate pseudonyms for accessing content or interacting with separate entities for content versus rights management may prove to be similarly confusing.

Many ease-of-use issues relate to the problem of consumer authentication. Most client authentication techniques, *e.g.*, passwords and Web cookies, are relatively weak and prone to attacks [,]. Furthermore, recovery techniques for forgotten passwords are arguably weaker: They are often based on something a user has (such as an physical or email address) or something he knows (such as answers to Web-form questions). These techniques generally require a large amount of PII and offer marginal security. In fact, privacy may turn out to be infeasible in some information-theoretic sense if we also want to provide recovery.[3]

These security weaknesses have privacy implications. Even ignoring business misuse (accidental or otherwise), if PII is collected and an attacker compromises a server, he may learn embarrassing or destructive information. For instance, cracking a DRM rights locker and exposing that a CEO recently purchased "How to survive after bankruptcy" will certainly not help the company's stock price. The distinction between "system security" and "user privacy" may be increasingly hard to make.

Legacy System Integration Privacy considerations should be part of system design from the beginning, as should security considerations. Privacy decisions should be made when one maps out data flows and the format of data exchanges; they are hard to change after standardization or wide acceptance. Unfortunately, if businesses choose to engineer privacy at all, they will probably have to integrate privacy solutions into legacy systems, because of switching costs. System integration poses several difficulties:

– **Dual operation:** Legacy software may have to support dual modes for backwards compatibility, one that supplies information, one that doesn't. There have been classic attacks (*e.g.*, SSL version rollback [ ]) against such designs. What good are advanced privacy options if a vendor does not update his software, and a user's DRM client happily supplies full information? One natural response to dual operation problems is forced updates for client software, which has its own drawbacks with respect to security, privacy, and consumer acceptance.

---

[3] That is, the user can have no private input to the recovery procedure.

- **Information:** Legacy systems may expect more information than new privacy-friendly exchanges provide. It has been the experience of the authors
  that businesses often do not fully recognize the purpose or effect of such
  information. For instance, businesses may decide to replace social security
  numbers (SSNs) with random numeric ids in a database, without realizing
  until later that SSNs were used for risk management to reduce collection
  costs. As usual, system documentation is often incomplete.
- **Performance:** Legacy systems may expect grossly different performance
  from that offered by new privacy-enabling protocols. Fiddling with timers
  may not be sufficient for complex, adaptive protocols, especially for multi-
  party situations, multiple network layers, and many-node systems.
- **Load:** The increased computational and communication load of cryptographic protocols may cause a congestive collapse of networking and routing
  protocols, as well as client/server operations.

Excessive Technical Costs? There are two sets of costs in respecting customer
privacy. They are the cost of deploying and operating the privacy technology and
the opportunity cost of the activities rendered impossible by respect for privacy.
The latter business incentives are described in Section 3.2.

The direct costs of privacy solutions include development, operation, policy-
management, and performance problems caused by increased communication
and computationally more expensive protocols. We show how the costs of several
cryptographic technologies would apply to privacy solutions for DRM.

- **Public-key crypto is slow:** Most privacy-enabling protocols, *e.g.*, blinding or oblivious transfer, heavily use modular multiplications and exponen-
  tiations for public-key operations. This creates a significant computational
  load in comparison to basic symmetric primitives. Aging DES can process
  13 MB per second, and the AES standard Rijndael can process 30 MB per
  second. With 1024-bit RSA, we can perform only 98 decryption operations
  per second [ ].[4] We recognize that cryptographic accelerators are becoming
  inexpensive, with a $700 card from Cryptographic Appliances able to per-
  form 1000 RSA operations per second. Still, users should certainly not be
  expected to purchase additional hardware, and large server farms may still
  find this cumulatively pricy.
- **SSL is slow:** Consider the cost of public-key operations in SSL. Network-
  shop found that a typical Pentium server (running Linux and Apache) can
  handle about 322 HTTP connections per second at full capacity but only 24
  SSL connections per second. A Sun 450 (running Solaris and Apache) fell
  from 500 to 3 connections per second [ ].
  Crypto often plays a large role in DRM system for content protection but
  mostly through symmetric-key operations. If privacy technologies require

---

[4] As reported in the Crypto++ 4.0 benchmarks, run on Win2000 on a Celeron 850
MHz chip.

extensive use of public key primitives, *i.e.*, do not use them only for initialization, they might not only throttle the rate of new connections but also greatly reduce the maximum number of simultaneous connections.

- **Small devices are slow:** Although one trend of computers is to faster and cheaper, they also trend towards smaller and more mobile. Even if cryptography is inexpensive (computationally and otherwise) on the server side, it may add an unacceptable burden on devices in which grams of mass and minutes of battery life are important engineering goals.
- **Public-key infrastructures (PKIs) are a false panacea:** The Gartner Group reported that average in-house PKI development and installation costs around $1 million, and 80% of PKIs today are in test pilot stages and may never get off the ground [ ]. These numbers refer mainly to business-to-business applications. There are very few serious PKI pilots that are trying to get certificates into the hands of consumers.

  While DRM systems will likely require a PKI for vendors and distributors, users themselves do not seem to need public keys. Privacy-enhancing technologies such as attribute certificates or private credentials [ ] change all this. One technical reason that SET failed was that it required a PKI for all customers, not merely for vendors.
- **Traffic analysis may vitiate anonymous cash and credentials:** One might wish to replace credit-card payments with anonymous tokens that serve as proof of purchase. This may not work very well with practical ecash schemes, because consumers will often buy a token and then immediately redeem it for the rights or the content to which it entitles them. The computational expense of using blinding or some other cryptographic technique to create the token will buy us nothing, because observers can link these two actions by the consumer and learn exactly what they would have learned from a credit-card transaction. Forcing the consumer to delay redemption of the token would probably be a poor business decision. Convenience and ease-of-use trump security for most consumers; there is little reason to expect that the same won't be the case for privacy. The traffic-analysis problem would be mitigated if ecash were widely used and accepted.
- **Mixnets absorb bandwidth:** Ignoring vulnerabilities to complex traffic-analysis attacks or simple JavaScript and cookie exploits, mixnets are ill-suited for mass-market content distribution for another reason: At best, bandwidth use scales linearly with the number of hops. Even worse, widely deployed mixnets may greatly randomize traffic patterns, as messages are thrown across North America, Europe, Asia, and Africa in order to cross jurisdictional lines. This randomization works counter to network-load balancing and current infrastructure deployment (*e.g.*, the pipes to Africa are much smaller). Protocol redesign is prohibitively expensive.

These are merely a few examples of the technical costs of privacy-enhancing technologies. In describing them, we do not mean to suggest that these technologies can never be made efficient and cost-effective; on the contrary, we encourage R&D efforts to make them so (and we participate in such efforts ourselves!). Rather, our goal is to point out the harsh reality of current gaps between real-world efficiency requirements and real-world performance of techniques that satisfy the definitions of "efficiency" given in the research literature.

3.2   Economic Aspects of Privacy Engineering

The major constituencies involved in a privacy-enabling protocol or system must be willing to sacrifice the information that may normally be collected about the other parties or their inputs. However, in e-commerce transactions, these constituencies have conflicting interests and asymmetric power. Why should a powerful content provider wanting to learn information about his users agree to run a protocol that deprives him of this very information? The industry is likely to the follow the "Know your customer" mantra.

Many of the problems facing privacy-technology adoption can be framed in microeconomic terms: network externalities, asymmetric information, moral hazard, and adverse selection. Shapiro and Varian expose the role of incentives in the information economy in [ ]. Ross Anderson poses a similar argument in [ ], relating the lack of information *security* to perverse economic incentives.

Network Externalities   The utility of privacy technologies on the Internet may be related to *Metcalfe's law*, which states that the usefulness of a network is proportional to the square of the number of nodes. The result is that networks can grow very slowly at first but then rapidly expand once a certain size is reached. This growth pattern is not limited to communication systems, such as the telephone network or the Internet, but is applicable in many situations in which a number of parties need to coordinate investments for a new system to take off. Television, credit cards, and recently DVDs have faced such startup difficulties.

It is easy to see that many privacy technologies obey Metcalfe's law and therefore exhibit network externalities – their marginal value to a user increases with their expected number of users. Anonymous file-sharing systems will become truly beneficial to users only when a large array of content can be readily, easily accessed. Anonymous email is unidirectional (and therefore less useful) unless both parties use the anonymizing network [ ]. The anonymity offered by such a network is bounded by the number of users. Similarly, electronic cash will only become useful if many merchants will accept it. We may infer from this that DRM systems are unlikely to push the acceptance of cryptographic ecash but rather will continue with existing technologies, *e.g.*, credit cards. As we design DRM systems for practical use in the near term, we should therefore expect that vendors will learn who is paying how much.

Several other features of network economics are of particular importance. Technology often has high fixed cost and low marginal costs, and switching costs for infrastructural technologies are also quite large, leading to lock-in. Assuming that corporate entities using DRM systems make decisions motivated primarily by profit (and that a good reputation for respecting customers' privacy has a measurable positive impact on profitability), these entities should only switch infrastructural technologies if the expected net present value of the benefits of switching is greater than its costs. Experience shows that this makes infrastructural switching rare, slow, and painful. Consider, for example, the nonexistent migration from IPv4 to IPv6.

Often, part of what makes a business an "Internet business" is that it can use pre-existing Internet infrastructure to get a cost advantage over its competitors. If privacy technologies require widespread infrastructure redesign, they vitiate this principle of Internet business success, and content providers probably won't adopt them. If ubiquitous onion routing requires changing network protocols and routers, and the only benefit is consumer privacy, we had better not have to wait for onion routing to be in place in order to be able to buy and read e-books in private!

Once again, we are not suggesting that Internet infrastructure will never evolve to a state in which it seamlessly and efficiently incorporates privacy-enabling protocols. Our point is that such a state is quite far from the state we're in now, that evolution will be slow, and that the desire for user privacy in DRM may not be sufficient motivation to force infrastructural change. Interim steps are needed to ensure reasonable privacy options in today's infrastructure.

Asymmetries, Moral Hazard, and Demand An asymmetry of information between entities in a DRM system makes privacy more difficult to achieve. Moral hazard arises from the principal-agent problem, in which the principal (*i.e.*, consumer) cannot observe the effort of the agent (*i.e.*, content/service provider) and thus has to incentivize the agent using something other than a payment per unit of effort. The hazard arises when the results of the agent's effort (*i.e.*, the "amount" of privacy) cannot be measured accurately, and thus the agent is tempted to slack off.

The obvious conclusion of this economic argument is that content providers will be tempted not to provide privacy if providing it costs money (and we have just argued that it does), and consumers cannot really measure their "units of privacy" and make educated demands.

Consumers are largely unable to differentiate between privacy options, and there are not even good methods for evaluating privacy. "Best practices" for privacy engineering have not yet been standardized. It is noticeable that Earthlink launched a new $50 to $60 million ad campaign, focusing strongly on offering "the totally anonymous Internet" [ ]. In reality, this means they promise to abide by their privacy policy and will not share individual-subscriber information. What is the technical difference from many other ISPs? Likely none. How does the average consumer differentiate this "trust me" approach from technological ones such as the Zero-Knowledge Freedom network [ ], which provides pseudonymity based on cryptographic onion-routing [ ]? Likely poorly, notwithstanding greater latencies. Even if businesses decide to offer privacy, this consumer inability to differentiate motivates companies not to invest in expensive technological options.

Business Incentives Two main issues face businesses that are considering privacy practices: why they *should* collect information and why they *should not* offer privacy.

There are legitimate reasons for businesses to collect data, such as customer retention, statistics, risk management, customization, and billing. For instance, network operations can (and perhaps should) collect usage data for traffic-modeling and provisioning purposes. Lack of good Internet traffic models is a big problem, and Internet-traffic modeling is a very active area of research; it requires the collection of usage data. In the content-distribution and DRM space, network operators would want to know which content is accessed from where, especially in rich media formats, in order to distributively cache replicas for bandwidth-saving, latency-reducing, and load-balancing purposes (an approach taken by Akamai for dynamic content routing [20]). In a subscription-service model, content providers would still need to know how often a song is accessed in order to determine artist compensation. For risk-management purposes in DRM systems, businesses want to be able to blacklist compromised devices or revoke compromised public keys. Similarly, most payment mechanisms require additional information to mitigate fraud, *e.g.*, asking for billing address information for online credit-card payments.

Businesses also have incentives not to offer privacy, in addition to the value of the information itself. Information security is difficult and expensive. Businesses still spend large amounts of money and many person-hours trying to achieve it, because it protects their own interests. Information privacy seems to be comparably difficult, similarly requiring secure design, implementation, and operation. However, businesses do not have the same incentives for privacy, and this results in little spending for technological innovation and development.

However, there are also motivations for minimizing the information collected. One of the strongest reasons, regulation, is concerned with both compliance and avoidance. Companies must comply with regulations such as the E.U. Data Protection Directive, and a large number of laws have been proposed in the U.S. Congress and state legislatures, as Americans grow increasingly concerned about their privacy. Businesses are starting to see that collecting and correlating data can present a public-relations risk. Lastly, extensive data collection and distribution can substantially increase the cost and effort that a business must undergo in order to be audited. We return to these issues in Section 4.3.

To summarize, it is likely that, in content distribution and DRM, as in many other realms, businesses will fight tooth and nail for the right to collect information they deem necessary. Depending on the nature of the information, consumers probably will not fight as hard to prevent them from collecting it. One major consideration for practical privacy engineering is that information *collected* for legitimate purposes may also be *used* in illegitimate ways, including sharing it with third parties who do not have a need to know. In Section 4, we recommend several steps that businesses and DRM-technology developers can take to limit the extent of this sharing and the damage it can cause.

4   Approaches to Practical Privacy Engineering

Our recommendations fall into two general categories: (1) Fair Information Principles and ways to implement them and (2) the need for privacy audits and privacy-policy enforcement.

4.1   The Fair Information Principles Approach

We have argued that definitions of "privacy" found in the cryptographic research literature are inadequate for most real-world privacy-enhancing solutions. If one accepts this claim, what should be the goals for practical privacy engineering? The best general answer we can give today is the Fair Information Principles (FIPs) [33], an early and commonly used framework for examining information-collection practices in privacy-sensitive areas such as health care. The FIPs have been widely accepted as describing desirable privacy goals. Variants of these principles underlie most privacy-protection laws and principles, *e.g.*, European privacy legislation [12,13,31].

The OECD version [12] of the FIPs is the following:

- Collection Limitation
- Data Accuracy
- Purpose Disclosure
- Use Limits
- Security
- Openness
- Participation
- Organizational Accountability

These are useful guidelines, in part because they do not specify any technological approach but rather set general goals. This differs significantly from the cryptographic approach, in which defining the terms of information-theoretic privacy or computational indistinguishability almost automatically suggests a technological approach, leading us to use expensive cryptographic tools such as public-key encryption, blinding, zero-knowledge protocols, *etc.* The FIPs allow us to consider low-cost solutions for privacy-enhanced electronic-commerce technologies.

This is important in light of many of the reasons that *businesses* have not widely adopted privacy-enhancing technologies (as described in Section 3.2). Even if the R&D community makes great strides on some of the problems pointed out in Section 3.1, it is unclear how quickly this technology would be developed and adopted; privacy may remain a low enough priority for the major constituencies to make serious investment unlikely.

On the *consumer* side, privacy studies continually report that consumers are very concerned about privacy. Yet today, we do not have evidence that consumers have broadly adopted software to enhance their privacy, *e.g.*, cookie blockers. Asking consumers to install and learn new, privacy-respecting software has been largely unsuccessful: The average user apparently does not want to pay for this stuff, in the broad sense of the word "pay." Rapid adoption of new technologies on the Internet is driven by the next "killer app," *e.g.*, Napster has done a lot to introduce consumers to digital music. Privacy does not fall into such an exalted category.[5]

Therefore, we suggest an alternative approach to privacy engineering that avoids some of these pitfalls:

1. The Fair Information Principles are an adequate notion of privacy.
2. Privacy enhancement should be built directly into the DRM technology that powers consumer applications. Consumers should not be burdened with needing to take additional steps to protect their privacy.
3. The business costs of introducing privacy enhancement into DRM should be low.
4. The consumer costs of using privacy-enhanced DRM should also be low. These costs include both the monetary cost of the service and the ease-of-use, latency, and other "user-experience" issues.

Why the FIPs apply to DRM One may view DRM technology as security middleware. It is typically targeted towards international markets, *e.g.*, towards European and Asian, as well as American, jurisdictions. One of the most compelling arguments for the FIPs is that they already underlie most privacy-friendly legislation and best-practice standards. Businesses that operate in (or plan to expand into) these jurisdictions will minimize their compliance costs if DRM technology can be easily configured to comply with these regulations. Furthermore, because the FIPs are emerging as the *de facto* measure for good privacy practices, business PR needs may largely be satisfied by complying with them.

The Fair Information Principles clearly stress the notion of the purpose for which information is collected and used. This is particularly well suited for relatively complex systems like DRM, in which there are a number of legitimate purposes for collecting and using information, as pointed out in Section 3.2.

4.2   Simple Principles for Privacy Engineering

Although the FIPs are well understood, the technological literature has said relatively little on how to translate them into engineering principles. In this section, we describe some system-architectural, system-engineering, low-tech, and no-tech principles that begin to allow one to meet these goals for content distribution and DRM.

Customizable Privacy Many businesses may deploy DRM middleware, with possibly different preferred information-collection and privacy policies. This makes DRM systems different from specific, unilaterally deployed e-commerce

---

[5] An analogous phenomenon has been observed in the security field.

solutions. A DRM system should therefore offer *customizable privacy*, within which system participants can easily configure the system to accommodate their preferred information-collection and handling procedures.

This customization principle has several simple consequences. A system should work with *minimal data exchanges*, and personally identifying information should not be included by default. Creating additional channels for information flow is significantly easier than trying to remove existing information flows. A first step in privacy-aware system design is to analyze the need for information, to graph flows among the various system participants, to analyze how the information flow can be minimized, and to design the message formats accordingly. This point further demonstrates the following, of no surprise to security engineers:

> Privacy considerations should be part of the initial system design phase. They should not be considered a property that can be added on later.

As the only widely available payment mechanism on the Internet is currently credit cards purchasing of electronic goods, and for that matter any type of goods, on the Internet is effectively non-anonymous. Purchases happen at web retailers, which use the currently available non-anonymous ecommerce infrastructure. However on the DRM layer no PII needs to be collected. Simple pseudonyms appear to be sufficient to allow for most DRM functionalities including user account management and risk management tasks, such as, individualization of client software or devices and revocation. This is an interesting observation as it shows that a lot of the privacy intrusive behavior that has been attributed to DRM does in fact happen on the ecommerce layer and not on the DRM layer itself. It comes from the fact digital goods are sold online and is quite independent of the copyright protection measures that are taken. Clearly from an privacy engineering viewpoint system designers can and should disassociate the non-anonymous ecommerce and payment layer from the DRM layer by not passing PII from the Web retailer to the DRM servers that manage rights and keys and the rest of the DRM infrastructure.

Collection Limitation A business needs to determine which information is necessary for business practices and legacy-system integration, as well as the purpose for this information. For example, credit-card security requires the transfer of billing address information. However, many applications may not require PII. In DRM systems, one should give special consideration to collection-limitation issues for the activation and individualization of DRM clients, during which these clients are endowed with public/secret key pairs. (One main purpose of individualization is to ensure that compromised devices can be identified and revoked; this does not necessarily mean that individual users must be identified.) Statistical purposes, *e.g.*, user profiling, recommendation services, and customization, similarly do not require full disclosure of PII. A unique identifier or pseudonym can be used to link the appropriate information together.

A business should only collect information that it really needs and should disclose how this information will be used.

A business can avoid a "vacuum cleaner" approach to information collection by analyzing its real importance. Certainly this analysis is difficult, especially within the realm of a new technology such as DRM. But, as *The Economist* points out in [11], "Firms are more likely to collect information sensibly and thoughtfully if they know why they want it."

Database Architecture and Management Database design offers a prime opportunity to provide a layer of data-privacy technology. In fact, database design will affect the set of privacy choices businesses can offer their customers. Data may be segmented according to the different groups that are interested in it – a principle of *split databases* and *separation of duty*. For example, accounting needs customer names and billing addresses, and customer service may need some proof of purchase to verify warranty validity. Marketing and risk-management departments, which may require usage data, can function with only a pseudonym. This weak *pseudonymization* is likely to be a simple pointer into another database, but this separation may aid privacy audits, simplify sharing arrangements, and provide an easy means for access control within an organization.

A DRM system should provide easy pseudonymization that can be used to key databases.

According to good collection-limitation practices, some DRM systems may not require a user's name.[6] In those systems that do not require full PII disclosure, splitting usage data from billing data is even simpler; there may be no need to manage a secure mapping between separate databases.

Indeed there are already laws that explicitly prescribe that user profiles should only be collected in pseudonymized profiles, like the German Teleservices Data Protection Act [21] and the "Gesetz zu dem Staatsvertrag uber Mediendienste"[22]. These laws likely apply to DRM systems (among other online services). One noticeable fact is here that these laws also make requirements about the *internal* technical workings of a system, such as, that pseudonymization techniques should be used. These laws have been enacted already in 1997. So why have the technical provisions not been widely implemented in Germany since then for a variety of Internet services? Firstly their need to be parties who actively work on their enforcement. Secondly and more importantly the law requires the implementation of certain privacy protecting measures, *if they are "feasible and reasonable"*. Thus we believe that a big contribution the R&D community could make would be to demonstrate that the deployment of some basic

---

[6] In fact, given that experienced or professional troublemakers are likely to engage in identity theft before buying their devices or services, not requiring a name prevents anyone from laboring under the false expectation that they can track down and punish troublemakers.

privacy protecting measures are both technologically and economically feasible and reasonable in real world commercial contexts. This may create the foundation for data protection agencies and others to effectively demand that these measures will actually be implemented.

The practice of *data erasure* should also be performed as a privacy-friendly data-management technique. Data fields that contain PII should be erased after their immediate need has been fulfilled. The removal of PII from usage records before those records are inserted into a long-lived data warehouse can definitely be done efficiently on a massive scale; in fact, it is *already* done efficiently on a massive scale.[7]

Purpose Disclosure (Notice) Several considerations must be taken into account for purpose disclosure: a means to express the relevant practices in an *understandable* way, a channel to transport these various choices to the user at the *proper* time, and a channel to transport the user's decision to *other* system participants that need to observe these choices. For example, banks have complied with the letter of the Gramm-Leach-Bliley Financial Services Modernization Act, but not its spirit, by sending out notices that are densely worded and incomprehensible [ ].

Notices should be easily understandable and thoroughly disseminated.

In the DRM world, a consumer should be notified about privacy practices that accompany a certain content offer before any actual purchase. In the current DRM world, content acquisition typically occurs through a Web retailer. This provides an easy channel for notification, either by linking to a privacy policy in HTML or by automating tools for notice such as P3P [ ][8]. A DRM system may want to enable several different information-collection practices, with some requiring usage-data collection and others not requiring it. For server-side data collection, a user's decision should be transferred to the rights-fulfillment server and/or content provider. For client-side data collection, we should prevent any reporting (through simple access control) to usage-clearinghouse servers unless the user has been notified – and has agreed – to such practices.

After this paper was accepted, a lawsuit was filed against Fahrenheit Entertainment and Music City Records for distributing a CD whose content was not amenable to standard "ripping" techniques. Among the major claims of the suit are that listening to the music was no longer anonymous and that this was improperly disclosed [ ].

Choice One of the most difficult challenges for FIPs compliance is giving users reasonable choices for information collection. One of the reasons for this is that

---

[7] We have personal experience with the responsible use of depersonalized telephone calling records for traffic modeling and other information-sciences research purposes.

[8] We consider P3P in greater depth in Section 4.4.

businesses may not *wish* to give consumers real choices; they may want to collect more information than what is actually needed to complete transactions.

Businesses should attempt to minimize bias when presenting consumer privacy choices. In public policy, there is a known and studied phenomenon whereby a planning organization presents a set of options that are all roughly similar, thus allowing the appearance of debate (respecting choice) while knowing what the outcome will be. The consequences of various choices should be made readily apparent. We note that businesses already seem to think that simplicity is an effective differentiator in the service industry: Advertisements for "$0.05 anytime, anywhere" long-distance phone service arose from consumer frustration with hidden and exploding phone rates.

Another wrong way to approach privacy is to offer no reasonable choice at all, such as offers for "(1) free subscription service with usage-data collection, (2) gold-star privacy service for $20 per month," or worse, "(1) no privacy, (2) no service." The majority of consumers will seek the cheapest type of service, leading to no real privacy enhancements, and businesses will still incur the capital costs of implementing and deploying privacy-protected service for the small minority. On the Internet, there have been few situations in which consumers have been willing to pay for privacy.

Client-Side Data Aggregation Client-side data aggregation can provide low-tech privacy enhancement for statistics-based services, as in profiling or recommendation services. The granularity of reported usage data will automatically affect the amount of privacy that a user enjoys. If profiling can be based on categorization and "binning" techniques[9], then users can aggregate data according to simple categorization criteria: "Last week, accessed 30 blues albums, 16 classical; played 14 hours rock, 16 hours hip-hop ...".

Transferring Processed Data Many of the data flows in a DRM system will not need to be "complete." For example, an organization such as ASCAP does not need to know who listened to a given song in order to distribute royalties, only that an aggregator will properly pay. There may be audit requirements to ensure that all payments flow through, but those can be accomplished in a number of ways that do not require the sharing of personal information. This is similar to the client-side aggregation suggestion, but the disclosure of data from the consumer to a counterparty makes it qualitatively weaker and requires greater trust.

Competition of Services Competition in the content-provider and distribution market generally motivates service providers to offer better services to consumers, the traditional argument for a free market economy. Thus privacy could become a distinguishing feature among the offers of various service providers.

---

[9] For example, a Beatles, Gerry and the Pacemakers, or Kinks album can all be placed in one "British Rock" bin, which similarly protects our Barry Manilow-loving friends.

Unfortunately, content ownership is largely restricted to a few organizations: 80% of music is controlled by five parties, and a few huge Hollywood studios control most of U.S. (and world) video. We believe that a liberal licensing model to competing content distributors would best suit consumer needs.

Keeping Business Interests in Mind DRM demonstrates another important phenomenon for privacy engineering. There are many components in the system – Web retailers, content servers, rights-fulfillment servers, lockers, usage clearinghouses, *etc.* – that may be operated by different entities. A user interacting with various participants will disclose different types of information and PII. The *overall* privacy that such a system provides is upper-bounded by the privacy that any one entity provides: The overall privacy is as strong as the privacy offered by the "weakest" link. To make privacy-engineering efforts effective, it is essential to understand the business interests of the various system participants. Misguided privacy efforts may simply *not* improve the level of overall privacy. If a party's business model is based largely on datamining, that party will reject restrictions on its data-collection practices.

This phenomenon demonstrates that system privacy is as much a policy issue as a technological one. Certainly, a DRM technology provider can make privacy standards mandatory for parties involved, but their effectiveness will depend upon the leverage that this technology provider can exercise. It is much more likely that overall privacy features of a DRM system will be determined by the powerful interest groups, *e.g.*, the content providers and large distributors on the one side, and consumers (or, more precisely, consumer-interest groups and privacy-activist groups that have effective media leverage) on the other side.

This leads to our key argument about how DRM may become a key enabler of privacy in the content-distribution space. DRM is conceived to support "real" content business: the exchange of money for access to and usage of content. This provides payment for content creators and other parties in the value chain, *without* their having to resort to "free" business models that are typically supported by targeted advertising and datamining revenues that most likely involve privacy intrusions.

4.3   Enforcement and Auditability of Privacy Solutions

One may argue that the FIPs approach is "weaker" than cryptographic privacy. This is certainly true in a purely theoretical sense; it is not "provably strong." Adherence to the FIPs indeed requires honest behavior by the party obtaining the information, as well as the initial goodwill decision to offer a strong privacy policy, although this is certainly coupled with a concern for reputation and legal compliance. However, we note that running cryptographic protocols also requires the goodwill of the parties involved. Cryptography only enforces practice *after* this goodwill decision to run the relevant cryptographic protocol has been made. Thus, the (only) essential parts we are missing in a relatively "cryptography free" implementation of the FIPs are effective mechanisms to enforce information-collection practices that have been agreed upon.

The combination of notice and auditability is strong. Arguably the worst thing U.S. companies can do with regards to handling customer information is to be exposed violating their advertised privacy policies. In some cases, this has triggered class-action law suits and Federal Trade Commission investigations [10]. Along these lines, we believe that the FIPs do actually provide consumers with relatively strong privacy assurances. Requiring or incentivizing companies to make their privacy policies public – already mandatory under European privacy law – is an important step towards providing users with strong privacy. Some companies are already taking such a privacy-friendly approach: All websites on which IBM advertises are required to post a privacy policy, as are all sites that use Microsoft Passport authentication services.[10] The integration of P3P into Internet Explorer 6.0 may turn out to be another driver for websites to post privacy policies.

The combination of notice and auditing would certainly be stronger if tools were available to more effectively ensure that companies actually follow their privacy claims. For this purpose, we describe some useful principles for the enforcement and auditing of privacy practices. At the low end of the auditing solutions (actual costs to businesses that are below $10,000 [2,30]), we have trust seals such as BBBOnLine and TRUSTe for privacy policies themselves. These services rate privacy policies and ensure that they simply and understandably state which PII is gathered, how this information will be used, with whom it is shared, which choices are available to users, *etc.* At the high end, major auditing firms audit the privacy practices of corporations. These auditing costs have reportedly been in the $2M to $5M range for large corporations [25].

We note that virtually all of these large corporations fail these rigorous audits [17]. Many of the problems result from "process" issues. The collected information is used by many separate parts of the company; tracking where and how information moves around is difficult. Enterprise privacy auditing would be facilitated by keeping comprehensive access logs for databases containing PII. Logging itself must be carefully designed, however, to not reveal PII, and it should be similarly secure. These failures support our points that PII flow should be simple and minimized. Cryptographic approaches alone are unlikely to solve these process issues.

In fact, facilitating and standardizing qualified audit methods could lead to cost savings for businesses. This is another example of how businesses currently lack (and need) a good understanding of how PII should be handled, both internally and externally.

We expect that privacy-auditing technologies will fit into any satisfying and practical solution for user-privacy concerns. The purpose for which data is used is at least as important as whether it is collected. Auditing practices have proven successful and adequate in other sensitive business areas, such as financial controls. And selling privacy audits and supporting technologies may be much easier

---

[10] We do not try to address here the privacy problems posed by a service like Microsoft Passport itself.

than selling cryptographic protocols, because upper management in large corporations is much more familiar with audits than with cryptography.

4.4   Adding Higher Tech Solutions

Although we devoted Section 3.1 to pointing out the limitations of cryptographic technologies, we revisit some simple higher-tech approaches that may make FIPs compliance easier.

Proxies Straightforward third-party data proxying can be used to regulate and enforce data-collection practices. We can already note such "trust me" solutions, with Anonymizer.com and SafeWeb for anonymized Web surfing. The important property is a clear separation of duty and enforcement procedure. The proxy can verify that the user received notice and agreed to provide such information before passing the data (or some subset of it permitted by the privacy-policy agreement) on to the requester. Similarly, we can help ensure that relevant data are disclosed only to an appropriate party through the use of proxied serial connections, *e.g.*, via HTTP posts and redirects. This collection-limitation approach (through a trusted third party that provides some seal of approval) may be preferable and more justifiable than audits that happen *after* data collection.

P3P While notice and choice principles sound simple and straightforward, they are relatively difficult to engineer in an easy-to-use, transparent fashion. In a general sense, we wish to create an abstract framework that allows one to map the plethora of privacy practices into some standard framework that can be handled in an automated, integrated fashion. The Platform for Privacy Preferences (P3P) is attempting to achieve this very goal. We should consider such an approach from two different viewpoints: system capability and language expressibility.

A tool's capabilities affect the complexity and type of system that one can handle with it. The P3P specification indeed appears to be sufficiently capable to handle privacy notice within even complex DRM systems: Privacy-policy references can be dynamically generated, including references to external partner sites. Consider the desired property that users be given notice *at a proper time* of all policies that may apply for the lifecycle of a transaction. One (advanced) implementation of the P3P spec is the following: A user downloads the list of relevant policies (included in the Web retailer's HTML page), his browser automatically contacts the relevant rights-fulfillment and content servers for their policies, then his P3P-enabled browser performs some logical inferences to determine whether the policies comply with his expressed privacy preferences. One large downside of this P3P model is that the complexity devolves onto the client. One alternative is for the Web retailer to prefetch all the relevant privacy policies, compute their privacy impact itself, and present only one unified policy to the user. While this level of indirection would simplify P3P client requirements, it would add complexity and policy-synchronization requirements to the system backend.

Language expressibility impacts how deeply or granularly specific privacy practices can be represented in some standard form. Relevant to this paper: Can P3P adequately express DRM data collection and usage? Indeed, many of the possible uses of DRM data (as listed in Appendix A.2) map well into P3P purpose classifications. One major difference, however, is that P3P is precisely built for Web-based activity, not hybrid systems such as DRM. Usage data and other information generated on the client-side, as opposed to on-site, do not have any obvious coverage under the P3P statement and purpose disclosures. Furthermore, we can only classify third-party recipients of data into rough groups according to the equivalence of their data practices. We cannot easily identify recipients in a machine-readable format, even though we may wish to express very specific relationships between business entities in a DRM system. In short, P3P's expressive capabilities are somewhat inadequate for our needs.

Microsoft's adoption of the platform in IE 6 is a step in the right direction, as consumers do not have to take substantial steps to protect their own privacy, especially given default settings that block third-party cookies that use PII without explicit consent. However, Microsoft's implementation only considers compact policies, which in P3Pv1 only contain policy information related to cookies. Not supporting full privacy policies with rich user preferences, this deployment might mislead users into believing that their privacy is already being adequately protected.

P3P seeks to automate and integrate privacy-preference notice into normal Web activity. While P3P may be sufficient for DRM from a systems-engineering perspective, various sources have challenged its ability to provide real privacy protections. For instance, EPIC and Junkbusters have criticized P3P for not complying with fair information practices, for providing only a "take it or leave it" flavor of choice, and for not establishing privacy standards [ ]. We remain hesitant to believe that P3P in its current incarnation will lead to actual improvements in privacy, either for DRM systems or for Web privacy in general. We fully admit general-purpose standardization is a hard problem; perhaps one may conclude that DRM languages should themselves include privacy expressibility.

Monitoring Tools Note that the Fair Information Principles put a high emphasis on monitoring and restricting how collected information is actually used. Recently, companies such as IBM, Zero-Knowledge, and Watchfire have begun to build tools that help automate portions of the FIPs. For example, IBM's Tivoli SecureWay Privacy Manager is designed to monitor and enforce security and privacy policies, Zero-Knowledge's PRM Console discovers and analyzes databases containing personal information, and Watchfire analyzes websites, where much data collection takes place. We believe such tools will play an important role in privacy-policy enforcement and auditing in the future.

5   Outlook

The technical community widely accepts that building secure systems is difficult. However, there has been an enormous amount of practical and theoretical work done in the last 25 years to improve this situation. An organization that wishes to build a secure system has a large pool of resources and a number of options at its command: educating its engineers through books and professional courses, hiring experienced consultants and contractors, buying and integrating existing security products, or using standard security solutions.

Privacy engineering does not enjoy this wealth of available resources. There is great interest in privacy, but most work to date has focused on theoretical research; most actual solutions exist only in a lab context and have not been tested in large-scale deployments. A system designer building a privacy-enhanced system is very much on his own. There is no good and practical book to use; most privacy consultants focus on policy issues rather than technology; and standard software solutions or tools for development and system integration are not available.

We believe that the R&D community could make its largest contribution through the development of a *practical methodology for privacy engineering*, involving procedures for the analysis of privacy-relevant aspects of a system. This paper shows that developing such a methodology even for the subproblem of DRM systems is quite challenging. This methodology should involve a list of dos and don'ts for privacy engineering, guiding principles for white-board design, standard suggestions about how naming and pseudonymization can be handled, and the tradeoffs among various design decisions.

However, such a methodology may be a long way away. There are complex technical and social questions that are implied by the phrase "*practical methodology for privacy engineering.*" The social issues revolve around the need to define privacy so that the engineering issue can be judged. However, there are multiple definitions, many of which are mutually incompatible (*i.e.*, information self determination vs fair information practices). Privacy is a highly emotional and important topic for many people, and what information is considered private may differ substantially from person to person. Designing a practical engineering methodology that addresses all of these issues is challenging indeed. Because privacy means different things to different people in different situations, designing a *single* technical set of recommendations for handling all of them may be an unachievable goal.

The difficulty of defining requirements aside, we claim in section 3 that not all of the issues that prevent the deployment of privacy are technical. However, many engineers and technologists are deeply concerned about privacy issues. As such, the first and perhaps most achievable value of such a methodology could be in helping those concerned address the real issues preventing us from building systems with privacy.

This paper takes a step in this direction, in the context of DRM technology and system engineering.

References

1. Ross Anderson. Why information security is hard - an economic perspective, January 2001. http://www.cl.cam.ac.uk/~rja14/. 86
2. BBBOnLine. Privacy seal. http://www.bbbonline.com/privacy/. 96
3. R.M Brady, R.J. Anderson, and R.C. Ball. Murphy's law, the fitness of evolving species, and the limits of software reliability. Technical Report 476, Cambridge University Computer Labority, 1999. 83
4. Stefan Brands. *Rethinking Public Key Infrastructures and Digital Certificates; Building in Privacy.* The MIT Press, Cambridge, MA, August 2000. 85
5. Jason Catlett, Marc Rotenberg, David Banisar, Ed Mierzwinski, Jeff Chester, and Beth Givens. Open letter to Kevin Ryan, June 2001.
   http://www.junkbusters.com/doubleclick.html. 78
6. Electronic Privacy Information Center and Junkbusters. Pretty poor privacy: An assessment of p3p and internet privacy, June 2000.
   http://www.epic.org/reports/prettypoorprivacy.html. 98
7. Lorrie Cranor, Marc Langheinrich, Massimo Marchiori, Martin Presler-Marshall, and Joseph Reagle. The Platform for Privacy Preferences 1.0 (P3P1.0) Specification, W3C Candidate Recommendation, December 2000.
   http://www.w3.org/TR/P3P/. 93
8. Wei Dai. Crypto++ 4.0 benchmarks.
   http://www.eskimo.com/~weidai/benchmarks.html. 84
9. Complaint, DeLise vs. Fahrenheit Entertainment, No CV-014297, Sup. Ct. Cal. Marin County, September 2001. http://www.techfirm.com/mccomp.pdf. 93
10. John D. Dingell, Edolphus Towns, and Edward J. Markey. Letter by House Democrats asking FTC to investigate TiVo, March 2001.
    http://www.house.gov/commerce_democrats/press/107ltr30.htm. 96
11. Economist. Keeping the customer satisfied, July 2001. 92
12. Organisation for Economic Co-operation and Development. Guidelines on the protection of privacy and transborder flows of personal data, September 1980.
    http://www.oecd.org/dsti/sti/it/secur/prod/PRIV-EN.HTM. 89
13. FTC advisory committee on online access and security: Final report, May 2000.
    http://www.ftc.gov/acoas/. 89
14. Kevin Fu, Emil Sit, Kendra Smith, and Nick Feamster. Dos and don'ts of client authentication on the web. In *Proceedings of the 10th USENIX Security Symposium*, Washington, D.C., August 2001. 83
15. Ian Goldberg and Adam Shostack. Freedom network 1.0 architecture, November 1999. http://www.freedom.net/. 87
16. Carl Gunter, Stephen Weeks, and Andrew Wright. Models and languages for digital rights. Technical Report STAR-TR-01-04, InterTrust STAR Lab, March 2001. http://www.star-lab.com/tr/. 102
17. Dana Hawkins. Gospel of privacy guru: Be wary; assume the worst. USNews.com, June 2001. 96
18. Kelly Jackson Higgins. PKI: DIY or outsource? InternetWeek.com, November 2000. 85
19. Mark Hochhauser. Lost in the fine print: Readability of financial privacy notices, July 2001. http://www.privacyrights.org/ar/GLB-Reading.htm. 93
20. David Karger, Eric Lehman, Tom Leighton, Rina Panigrahy, Matt Levine, and Danny Lewin. Consistent hashing and random trees: Distributed caching protocols for relieving hot spots on the world wide web. In *Symposium on Theory of Computing*, 1997. 88

21. German Legislator. German Teleservices Data Protection Act. 92
22. German Legislator. Gesetz zu dem Staatsvertrag über Mediendienste. 92
23. David Mazieres and M. Frans Kaashoek. The design, implementation and operation of an email pseudonym server. In *5th ACM Conference on Computer and Communications Security*, 1998. 86
24. R. Morris and K. Thompson. Password security: A case history. *Comm. of the ACM*, 22(11), November 1979. 83
25. Stefanie Olsen. Accounting companies tackle online privacy concerns. CNET News.com, September 2000. 96
26. Stefanie Olsen. Earthlink promises 'anonymous' web surfing. CNET News.com, March 2001. 87
27. National Research Council Panel on Intellectual Property (R. Davis chair). *The Digital Dilemma: Intellectual Property in the Information Age*. National Academy Press, Washington, D.C., 2000. 77
28. Carl Shapiro and Hal R. Varian. *Information Rules: A Strategic Guide to the Network Economy*. Harvard Business School Press, Boston, 1999. 86
29. P.F. Syverson, D.M. Goldschlag, and M.G. Reed. Anonymous connections and onion routing. In *Proceedings of the 1997 IEEE Symposium on Security and Privacy*, May 1997. 87
30. TRUSTe. Seal programs. http://www.truste.org/programs/. 96
31. The European Union. Directive 95/46/ec on the protection of individuals with regard to the processing of personal data and on the free movement of such data, July 1995. 89
32. David Wagner and Bruce Schneier. Analysis of the ssl 3.0 protocol. In *2nd USENIX Workshop on Electronic Commerce*, 1996. 83
33. Willis W. Ware. Records, computers, and the rights of citizens. Advisory Committee on Automated Personal Data Systems, July 1973. 89
34. Alma Whitten and J.D. Tygar. Why johnny can't encrypt. In *USENIX Security*, 1999. 83
35. Tim Wilson. E-biz bucks lost under ssl strain. InternetWeek.com, May 1999. 84

A   A Generic Architecture for a DRM Content-Distribution System

In this section, we describe a generic DRM ecommerce architecture, shown in figure 1. We focus on giving an overview of properties and operations that are relevant for DRM operation and are important for our privacy considerations, but we do not optimize this generic architecture for privacy. Instead, we simply describe some of the key components of a DRM system and how they interact, in order to provide readers with some intuition for the terms and notions used throughout the paper.

A.1   Basic Architecture and Extensions

Before content is actually distributed to a user, content is prepared by a *Packager*. This process involves encoding the content in a certain media format and encrypting it under a (symmetric) *content key*. The Packager also adds a content

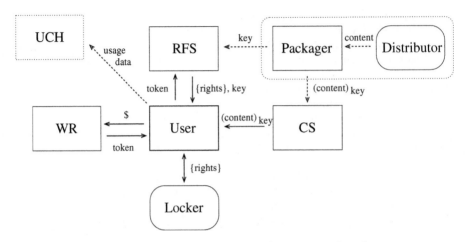

Fig. 1. Generic DRM architecture for content distribution

header to the file that contains metadata that specify the content (*e.g.*, specify
the name and the artist of a song) and also hold additional information such as
a URL from which the content key can be retrieved (or where the rights to play
the content can be obtained). The Packager sends the content key to the *Rights-
Fulfillment Server (RFS)* and the packaged content to a content distribution
server.

A fundamental concept underlying DRM systems is the separation of the
(encrypted) content file from the *rights*. Rights express what a user is allowed
to do with a content file and may be specified in a Rights Management Language (for examples, see [ ]). Business models that are currently commercially
relevant and that a DRM system should therefore support include the download
and purchase of individual content, subscription models (*e.g.*, to a whole music
catalog), pay per play (or pay per view), and a limited number of plays for preview purposes. A simple rights language could specify timeouts, the number of
times that a song is allowed to be played, *etc.*

A user needs to install DRM client software on his machine. This client
decrypts content and manages access to and usage of the content as specified in
the rights it has received.

More precisely, this process could work as follows. A consumer retrieves packaged content from a *Content Server (CS)*. To access the content, a user will
need to retrieve the rights and the content key. In a Web-based system, a user
purchases a certain offer and receives a token from a *Web retailer (WR)*, *e.g.*,
Amazon.com. At the RFS, a user can redeem this token (that proves his purchase) against "digital rights" and the cryptographic content key. After having
received the (encrypted) content, the rights, and the keys, the DRM client will
unlock and render the content as specified in the rights.

Optionally, there may be a *Usage Clearing House (UCH)*. The UCH may collect usage data from certain clients; this may include the time and the frequency with which content was accessed or other data that relate to actual content consumption. Many of our privacy considerations focus on such usage-data collection.

There are various extensions of this basic DRM model that enhance its functionality and value to users:

- **Portable Devices:** Users may have various portable devices to which they wish to transfer the content from a PC. These may include portable music players, wireless phones, or PDAs. The number of portable devices to which content can be transferred may or may not be limited.
- **Rights Locker:** A rights locker is a storage system that contains the digital rights purchased by a user. The rights locker could simply be local to devices, but could also be implemented in some centralized way for anytime, anywhere access. Many devices may wish to interact with these central rights repositories, such as wireless phones, PDAs, *etc.*
- **Peer-to-Peer systems:** The basic architecture described above is client-server. Clearly content could be searched for and retrieved also in a P2P fashion, *i.e.*, the CS would be replaced by a P2P content-distribution service. Additionally, one may also wish to distribute rights and content keys (or implement a distributed rights locker) in a P2P fashion. Distributed rights and key management has inherent security risks from a content-protection viewpoint in a P2P architecture, likely requiring high tamper resistance on the end-points and other difficult security-engineering requirements. We do not study this architecture further in this paper.

A.2   Basic Protocols and Operations to Support

Installation and Initialization of the DRM Client A user needs to install a DRM client on a device, such as a PC. The activation process may involve an individualization step for generating a unique public/secret key pair for this device, which may also involve taking hardware fingerprints to tie the client to a particular device. A user may also open an account with a rights locker, and he may register using his real-world identity or some digital pseudonym.

Searching for Content and Content Delivery The operation of searching for DRM-protected media is not much different from a privacy perspective from using a typical search engine to find other content. When a user downloads content from a Content Server, the CS could certainly log user IP addresses. Users who may wish to protect their privacy from the CS may connect to the CS via an anonymizing network. Packaged content is typically freely superdistributable so that an anonymizing step should not violate the security of a DRM system.

Content Acquisition A users needs to purchase "subscription" or "pay-per-use" tokens from some vendor, typically a Web retailer. Credit cards dominate Internet ecommerce payments, and thus the Web vendor will usually learn the real-world identity of the user. The token is transferred from the Web retailer to the RFS via the user. Note that the token is supposed to be a secure proof of purchase, and so it may specify the terms of the purchase and contain a unique serial number to prevent "double spending" of the token. However, the token does not need to involve the identity of the user.

Rights Delivery The user redeems his token at the RFS to receive the corresponding rights and the cryptographic key to unlock the content. For security reasons, the rights should not be easily transferable to another user. To prevent this, the DRM client should send its public key to the RFS, under which the RFS digital signs the (rights, UID) pair and returns the signed pair to the client. This UID could be specific per user or per device, thereby targeting rights to a particular user or device. The content-decryption key is similarly delivered to the client encrypted under its public key. The RFS does not necessarily learn the user's identity during rights delivery, because a user may only pseudonymously identify himself via the public key. However, the RFS could link or log these transactions and thereby obtain pseudonymous profiling.

For simplicity, we view a rights locker as a central database that stores the digital rights of users, to which a user has to authenticate himself to access his rights. Note that authentication mechanisms to a locker should be *non-transferable*, so that a user cannot publish his user name and password (or public/secret key pair) and thereby enable thousands of people to access the subscription rights that a single user has purchased. A good deterrence mechanism is to ensure that some high-value secret is also accessible through the rights locker, *e.g.*, the authentication mechanism also allows access to a user's credit card information, name, or other information that users may be unwilling to share.

Accessing and Playing Content When a user attempts to access content, the DRM client determines whether the necessary keys and rights are present and, if so, renders the content. Because this process occurs on the user's local device, it does not present any privacy risks.

Risk Management One main goal of a DRM system is to keep unauthorized access to content, or "privacy," under a tolerable threshold. Charged with this goal, a risk management (RM) system participant, most likely connected to the RFS, would be useful to monitor activities in a DRM system to detect misuse or anomalous activities. In particular, there should be a mechanism to revoke compromised devices, *e.g.*, by having the RFS maintain a blacklist of the public keys of compromised devices. Furthermore, the RM should have a method for renewing user software, in order to update security features on the DRM client.

The RM should be able to identify suspicious patterns in the download behavior of users, especially with massive overuse, or crawl popular websites for compromised keys. Clearly, the former approach of log analysis has some privacy implications. However, we note that revocation does not require user PII, but only the public key to be revoked or blacklisted. Still, for legal remedy or simply fraud deterrence, the RM may wish to have the ability to resolve a pseudonym to a real-world identity.

Data Collection in DRM Systems We give some examples as to what information can be collected in a DRM system and for what purposes it may be used. Collected information may include data about content retrieval, rights retrieval, content accessing, frequency, times, access locations, *etc.* This information can be obtained by logging server-side information, or by having client-side DRM software store relevant usage data that may be later sent to a central Usage Clearing House server.

The purposes for collecting data may include the following:

- personalized use for direct marketing
- quality of service enhancement (by network operator)
- backup and archives
- aggregate (depersonalized) usage of info for marketing, *e.g.*, to discover trends in the data set, to perform datamining
- profiling (de)personalized records, *e.g.*, the RIAA (ASCAP) may wish to collect data from a subscription service, such as how often a song is listened to, in order to properly compensate artists.
- customer service and retention
- recommendation services

Secure Open Systems for Protecting Privacy and Digital Services

David Kravitz, Kim-Ee Yeoh, and Nicol So

Wave Systems Corp.

Abstract. This paper describes and analyzes a system architecture that enables consumers to access services and content from multiple providers without jeopardizing the privacy interests of consumers or the intellectual property rights of providers. In order to satisfy these highly desirable objectives, we argue for the necessity of a Trust Server that mediates the conferral and revocation of trust relationships between consumers and providers. The system also calls for the deployment of programmable security coprocessors at vulnerable sites requiring protection, namely at the Trust Server and at each consumer. We define the specific requirements of consumer-side Coprocessors, and their server-side counterparts denoted as Hardware Security Modules (HSMs). A single Coprocessor serves multiple providers by allocating to each of them a virtualized trusted computing environment for software execution and data manipulation. Bearing in mind that the tamper-resistance offered by Coprocessors is subject to more stringent economic pressures than that offered by HSMs, we include in our architecture containment capabilities that prevent compromised Coprocessors from causing damage disproportionate to their numbers. We explain the specific challenges faced with providing containment capabilities while protecting consumer privacy, given that a single Coprocessor must serve the needs of multiple providers. The simultaneous attainment of these goals is one of the highlights of our architecture.

1   Introduction

> ... [The] strongest intellectual property protection requires embedding protection mechanisms throughout the computer hardware and software at all levels ...
>
> *The Digital Dilemma: Intellectual Property in the Information Age*

> The biggest battleground is not the personal computer, where many DRM solutions can run side by side, but consumer electronics, where only one DRM solution will be implemented per device.
>
> *Bill Bernat, Cover Your Assets, Streaming Media, July/August 2001*

Recognition is growing that protection of digital intellectual property must involve the use of consumer-situated hardware [7,9,11,13,15,18]. At the same time, recent work has also pointed to the potentially enormous role that such

T. Sander (Ed.): DRM 2001, LNCS 2320, pp. 106–125, 2002.

hardware may play in protecting the end-user [1,19], where such hardware is already being deployed in the form of smart cards and other personal tokens to achieve safer access-authentication. In the case of providers, dongles may be pointed to as examples of simple consumer-situated hardware that has achieved some success within its circumscribed objective of software copy protection.

Such hardware, however, has almost no impact whatsoever on the Internet economy, where the lack is especially acute in the area of networked digital media. The Napster case, a study in how the costly, traditional recourse of litigation was forced to fill a vacuum of non-existent technological solutions, albeit not before millions of MP3 files had been swapped, spotlights the golden opportunity in harnessing the Internet as a ground-breaking distribution channel if only it could be tamed. The currently unsurmounted challenges have been well articulated as follows:

> It is expensive to design, manufacture, and mass market such a special-purpose device, and an entire content-distribution business based on such a device would necessitate cooperation of at least the consumer-electronics and content-distribution industries, and possibly the banking and Internet-service industries as well. A particular business plan could thus be infeasible because it failed to motivate all of the necessary parties to cooperate or because consumers failed to buy the special-purpose device in sufficient numbers. ([5], p.168)

One possibility for reducing the cost and increasing the appeal of such a consumer-situated security device is by opening up access to more than one provider. In fact, if such hardware rather than serving multiple providers in a preprogrammed and narrowly defined manner instead does so flexibly by incorporating open programmability at its core, barriers preventing widespread consumer deployment could well be substantially reduced. Open hardware would loosen the difficult close-coupling among disparate business entities otherwise necessary in order to actualize a fixed-purpose product. Successful accommodation of rival economic interests motivates the desirability of provider-independent manufacturers specializing in the comprehensive facilitation of security devices (see [19] for related arguments).

But multi-use, provider-independent security hardware brings a fresh set of system-design challenges to the fore, especially when consumer privacy enters the picture. The literature on anonymous service access mainly focuses on the use of tokening systems [1,3,8,10,12], but anonymity on a multi-application trusted execution environment remains very much an open research topic [10]. An important concern that has not been addressed is the fact that a particular system's infrastructure information may be shared among providers to form comprehensive profiles of each consumer. For example, in [19], the certified public key of a consumer's security module is distributed to all providers with whom the consumer wishes to transact. The certified public key may be then shared among an unscrupulous subset of providers to create a revealing profile of the consumer's purchasing habits. Such a weakness in privacy protection could be judged unacceptable. We describe in this paper how privacy may be protected. Note that such features of the system design, while necessary, cannot be sufficient to meet this stringent privacy requirement if the underlying communication transport does not support anonymity features.

Another issue that deserves greater attention is the fact that a coprocessor may be compromised by an adversary with sufficient resources. The trust infrastructure supporting all the goals of the above should feature resilience in such a scenario. A simple example is the prevention of an arbitrary number of clones of a compromised coprocessor from infiltrating the system. However, the context of a shared-usage, high-privacy system described above makes the problem of architecting containment- and damage-limitation- capabilities much harder. Sections 2.3 and 2.4 below explain what can be deployed to achieve these goals.

2   Architectural Components

Each of the sections below explains a core component in Fig. 1, which gives an overview of the entire application and trust framework.

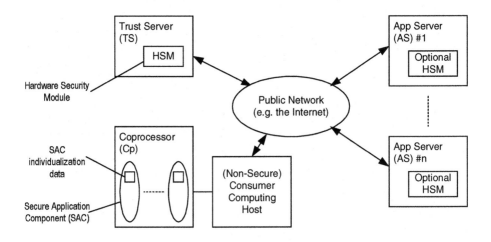

Fig. 1. Application framework

2.1   The Coprocessor

We restrict the use of the term coprocessor here to its use at the level of consumers. We denote its server-class counterpart by the term Hardware Security Module (HSM). While previous work [17] categorizes secure coprocessors into several types, the coprocessor we envision to support the secure open system proposed in this paper overlaps several of these categories. An open programming environment is clearly mandatory, which appears to place such a coprocessor in the same category as that of an HSM, namely, high-end secure coprocessors. On the other hand, the coprocessor may well have to serve within resource-constrained consumer appliances, reminiscent of the category of cryptographic accelerators. In summary, a coprocessor, as used here, is a low-cost microprocessor that enables trusted execution in resource-constrained, possibly embedded, environments that support open programming.

2.2   The SAC

A typical service or application delivered by a provider in this model would involve three entities, namely, (i) an application server (AS), (ii) the conventional, non-secured consumer-situated host device, and (iii) a coprocessor's trusted execution environment. With respect to (iii), we call the component running within this client-side trusted execution environment a Secure Application Component (SAC).

2.3   The Trust Server

We motivate this component by studying the two degenerate cases corresponding to relaxation of either the privacy or the containment objective.

Privacy without Containment. Where containment is not necessary, ensuring that coprocessors are formally indistinguishable coprocessors coupled with any of a number of anonymous access schemes [,], is sufficient to ensure privacy. Note that this result is independent of the feature set of the trusted execution environment; code can be transported confidentially and with both origin authentication and integrity checks to any particular coprocessor. The only requirement is that coprocessors, if indeed cryptographic key material has to be preloaded into them, all obtain the same such data.

Containment without Privacy. Conversely, if only containment is desired, then the problem is easy and has already been solved. For example, the work of [ ] uses unique certified public keys for each coprocessor to allow the provider to track billing and revoke trust in detectably compromised hardware.

Trust Server Rationale. When both containment and privacy are required, a trusted intermediary is necessary to broker the conferral and revocation of trust relationships between consumers and providers. It is this intermediary which we call the Trust Server. Knowledge of the association between a coprocessor and an instance of a SAC must be confined to the Trust Server in order to maximally protect the privacy of the consumer using the coprocessor.

2.4   Individualization

The necessity of coprocessor individualization is obvious from the preceding discussion. The requirement for individualization of a SAC follows from the necessity of a provider to keep track of its separate instances across coprocessors. Two methods for individualizing a SAC are given: Sect. 6 below describes SAC individualization by a provider's Application Server, whereas Sect. 7 describes the process conducted by the Trust Server instead.

A subtle question occurs on the issue of uninstallation and reinstallation of a SAC. After such a cycle, should it be provided with fresh individualization data? On the one hand, by issuing the same data, the provider could unilaterally revoke an instance of a SAC that is behaving suspiciously, possibly indicating the coprocessor on which it runs has been compromised. However, honest consumers should be allowed to break the linkage of individualization if they so desire in the interests of privacy. Fresh individualization for every installation, whether it is new or a repeat, is therefore necessary. This changes the process of revocation of a SAC on a particular coprocessor by the provider responsible for that SAC. The Trust Server, to whom the provider submits the request, must now arbitrate the revocation process. The dual and complementary responsibilities of protecting consumer privacy and of serving provider needs rests on the Trust Server.

3   Notation

Table 1 summarizes the notation used in the rest of the paper.

4   Assumptions Regarding the Trust Server

The HSM within the Trust Server is assumed to act as a slave to its master host, but runs its own secured code and can securely retain static values, such as its private key and a secret for local authentication of data retrieved from the Trust Server databases. The HSM is not assumed to possess dynamic state memory, although to the extent such memory is available (and effectively utilized [ ]), it can be used to help secure the Trust Server against containment attacks which involve large-scale cloning of successfully compromised coprocessors. There are several advantages of exploring which aspects of processing and communications can be secured without being dependent on such memory. Effective backup of a dynamically changing HSM, and determination of the appropriate responses to hardware failure versus sabotage can be thorny issues to resolve. Although we present the Trust Server here as a monolithic host/HSM combination, there can be convincing justification to split up such a server into separate components according to functionality. As an example, there could be a single server that interacts with Application Servers in order to handle SAC publishing and bulk individualization. Such a server could act as an interface between Application Servers and multiple device-servers which each relate to a distinct population of client-side coprocessor users. Examples will be given to show that seemingly

Table 1. Notation used in this paper

Symbol	Meaning
$\langle\rangle$	Delimiters for an n-tuple or a finite sequence
AS	Application Server pertaining to a provider
AS.ID	Identifier for an Application Server. It may be assumed that there is a one-to-one correspondence between (application) providers and Application Servers
AS.key	Symmetric key generated by an Application Server and associated with a SAC-series
AS.privKey	The private key of an Application Server. The corresponding public key is either well-known or authenticated with a public key certificate, with identifier AS.ID
AS.track	Secret information generated by an Application Server. Used to prove continuity of identity to the TS
blob	Individualization data for an instance of a SAC. Generally secret
blobTag	Non-secret information associated with a blob. Contains identifying information for a blob
certID	Identifier for an anonymous public key certificate (or coupon)
Cp	Coprocessor (to consumer computing device)
Cp.ID	Identifier for a coprocessor (to a consumer computing device)
CTblob	SAC individualization data in encrypted form
Enc(pt,pubKey)	Public key encryption of plaintext pt using public key pubKey
H(m)	One-way hash function
HSM	Hardware Security Module
msgKey	Message key
privKey	Private key (of a key pair)
pubKey	Public key (of a key pair)
SAC	Secure Application Component. A software component that executes on the (secure) coprocessor to a consumer computing device. A SAC is protected by physical security
SAC.assign	A cryptographically protected data structure maintained by the TS that binds together different pieces of information associated with a SAC-series
SAC.exe	The representation of the executable for a particular SAC
SAC.ID	Identifier for a particular version of a SAC
SAC.key	Symmetric key generated by an Application Server to encrypt a particular version of a SAC for public distribution, or generated by the TS for a SAC-series
SAC.number	Identifier for a series of versions of a SAC
SAC.src	Representation of the source of a SAC. The executable of a SAC can be derived from SAC.src
SAC.version	Version identifier for a particular version of a SAC
SAC-series	A series of versions of a SAC sharing the same SAC.number
seqAS	A sequence of SAC individualization data blobs together with their associated blobTags
Sign(m,k)	Digital signature operation with message m and signature key k
SymEnc(pt,k)	Symmetric encryption operation with plaintext pt and key k
TS	Trust Server
TS.local	A secret value used by the HSM of the TS to secure local storage
TS.privKey	The private key of the Trust Server.
TS.pubKey	Public key of the Trust Server. Either well-known or authenticated with a public key certificate

small modifications of protocol design can greatly impact the security profile of the overall system. Securing a subsystem under reduced hardware expenditure and maintenance requirements can be particularly important if that subsystem is run remotely from others that already have access to more significant resources.

5   Minimal Assumptions on Secure Communications between Coprocessors and the Trust Server

Any data passing between coprocessors and the Trust Server must be protected by authentication and encryption. Care must also be taken to hide evidence of identity of the coprocessors involved. For example, a known structure of ciphertext with an appended signature over the ciphertext would violate this requirement because armed with an exhaustive list of coprocessor public keys, one could attempt signature verifications. The methods presented here, under the rubric of "Secure Communications" will specifically require that any data encrypted by a coprocessor for the HSM cannot be decrypted by an insider at the Trust Server; any data encrypted for a coprocessor by the HSM cannot be decrypted by a Trust Server insider; a message cannot successfully be spoofed to a coprocessor as coming from the HSM without accessing data currently held in the Trust Server; a message cannot successfully be spoofed to the HSM as coming from a coprocessor without accessing data currently held in the Trust Server. We do not assume that a Trust Server insider cannot successfully spoof data to the HSM as if it came from a coprocessor. Similarly, we do not assume that a Trust Server insider cannot successfully spoof data to a coprocessor as if it came from the HSM.

6   Method 1: SAC Individualization by Application Server

The private key (privKey) corresponding to pubKey is intended to be a coprocessor-level secret that does not leak out of coprocessors that have not been successfully tampered with. Consequently, Application Servers must incorporate the prescribed interactions with coprocessors into their communications code, rather than be given the flexibility to determine the methodology by which alleged coprocessors prove their legitimacy as a condition of successful acquisition of services or content. An unscrupulous application provider might otherwise configure its Application Server to attempt to take advantage of oracles such as those based on the equivalence of Rabin decryption (i.e., the computation of modular square roots) to factoring of the modulus [ ], or on small-subgroup attacks against Diffie-Hellman related protocols [ ]. Such remote acquisition of private keys corresponding to anonymous certificates could potentially be used on a wide scale if such a protocol flaw were to go undetected.

Note that the SAC will not be able to be installed on a compliant coprocessor unless (in Fig. 3, step 11) the AS signature verifies properly and the decrypted

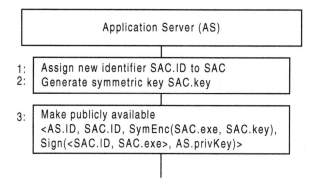

Fig. 2. SAC self-publishing

message yields the key (`SAC.key`) that was originally used by the Application Server to encrypt the SAC prior to public distribution (in Fig. 2, step 3). The `AS.ID` is acquired by the coprocessor from the Application Server's public key certificate. Even if the AS chooses to ignore the validity test of the receipt that the coprocessor obtains in exchange for redeeming the coupon with the Trust Server (in steps 12–16 of Fig. 3), the `AS.ID` has been noted by the TS, so that this information can be logged for tracking (as well as potentially for billing) purposes.

If fresh evidence of a coupon redemption receipt were not made available to Application Servers, coupons corresponding to successfully tampered coprocessors could be "multiply spent." While compliant coprocessors can be tethered to the Trust Server by having them programmed to lose critical functionality if they have not called home after some specified limit on time (or other metric) has been exceeded, successfully tampered coprocessors may avoid such report-back. If they need to report back in order to obtain new keying material, say, they may be able to successfully lie about past activity logs. Note that dependence on the "blob" in the receipt issued by the Trust Server, makes it infeasible for even a tampered device to stockpile usable receipts, where a blob is acquired by a coprocessor from an Application Server during the exchange depicted in steps 7–10 of Fig. 3.

The assumptions on Secure Communications (in Sect. 5) between coprocessors and the Trust Server together with the atomicity of operations performed by the HSM make it infeasible for a Trust Server insider acting without collusion of tampered coprocessors to acquire coupons for which it knows the corresponding private keys.

The SAC individualization process enacted through coupon collection and redemption effectively extends coprocessor individualization into the SAC layer. However, the method intentionally does not specify how the (SAC-level) "blobs" (of SAC individualization data) shared between a compliant coprocessor and an Application Server should be used in SAC-level communications between the

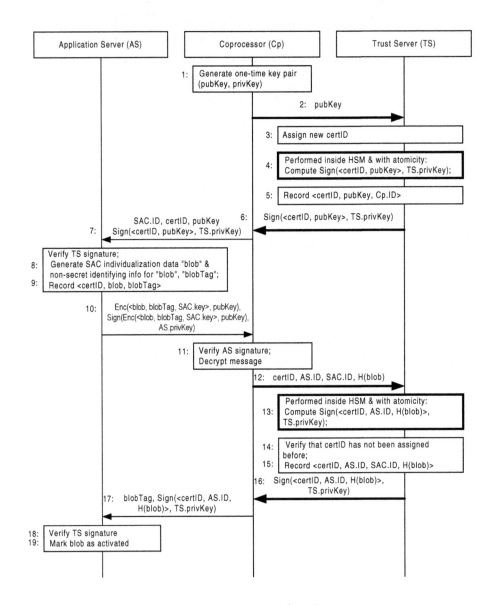

Fig. 3. Coupon collection & redemption

coprocessor and the Application Server. Potential "misuse" of this data does not affect the security of any independently administered SAC.

From a consumer-privacy perspective, a tampered coprocessor alone should not be able to undermine users' confidence that they are communicating with an Application Server in possession of knowledge of the AS private key corresponding to the certified AS public key.

The following attack could be mounted if the signed encryption of step 10 of Fig. 3 as computed by the Application Server were replaced by a separate signature and encryption on the data $\langle$blob,blobTag,SAC.key$\rangle$: A tampered coprocessor could collect coupons and use them at Application Servers without completing the transaction (in order to prevent the coupons from being marked as redeemed at the TS). The tampered coprocessor would presumably be able to extract knowledge of each $\langle$blob,blobTag,SAC.key$\rangle$ based on knowledge of the corresponding Enc($\langle$blob,blobTag,SAC.key$\rangle$,pubKey) and its associated privKey. Since Sign($\langle$blob,blobTag,SAC.key$\rangle$,AS.privKey) has no dependence on coprocessor-related input, the tampered coprocessor would be able to reuse the $\langle$blob,blobTag,SAC.key$\rangle$ encrypted under the target's pubKey value, in order to masquerade as the legitimate Application Server to an unsuspecting target coprocessor user. While the adversary in possession of the tampered coprocessor would have access to the plaintext executable through acquisition of SAC.key, he could, however, be foiled by code within the SAC which expects, say signatures on data randomly generated by the target coprocessor's instance of the SAC. If the adversary had not aborted its use of the coupons before executing step 12, namely coupon redemption with the Trust Server, the target coprocessor would not unwittingly attempt to communicate any potentially confidential information to the adversary following completion of the process in Fig. 3. This is because the reuse of the coupon would be detected at the Trust Server in step 14 thus canceling the transmission of the message in step 16 to the target coprocessor. In any case, this type of attack is thwarted in the actual protocol design, because the signature is over the encryption, which varies based on the particular coprocessor through use of pubKey.

Stepping back from the specific details of the process with respect to a general design criterion relative to privacy, the consumer as user of the client-side coprocessor should be involved in the determination of whether the particular transaction warrants the disclosure of information to the Application Server regarding certificate status, where the authenticity of such information is assured by the Trust Server acting as an anonymizing server. Since this assurance procedure can be designed to be (computationally) unforgeable, such assurances can be requested of the Trust Server by the coprocessor user, and the responses from the Trust Server can be delivered to the Application Server by the coprocessor user as well. If the Application Server does not receive a satisfactory indication of assurance by some self-specified juncture (which may be a function of time, accumulated access to services, or other metric(s)), the Application Server may elect to sever its relationship with the particular coprocessor user. The Application Server can determine the freshness of any assurances it receives, by including appropriate information in the Application Server-specific data that it associates with the coprocessor public key, which it expects to see reflected in the assurances produced by the Trust Server. This procedure has the additional advantage, if so constructed, of exhibiting proof of possession of the private key corresponding to the coprocessor public key, as well as assurance of certificate trustworthiness.

In the particular protocol presented here, server-specific data (namely, `blob`, `blobTag`, and `SAC.key`) is recovered (in step 11 of Fig. 3) by the coprocessor using the private key to decrypt, where some function of the recovered data (namely, `H(blob)`) is forwarded to the Trust Server with the ID of the Application Server (`AS.ID`, along with `SAC.ID`). By having the coprocessor user, rather than the Application Server, handle the request for assurance, this enables increased versatility in billing models. If the Application Server is to be charged for use of a client-side certificate, it could otherwise opt out of requesting assurance in order to hide from the Trust Server its use of the certificate.

By restricting the relationship of a coprocessor to only a single Trust Server at any point in time, this allows for more meaningful tracking of certificate usage. While it is common practice to incorporate expiration dates into certificates, this does not indicate to what extent a certificate has been relied upon and whether it should be considered trustworthy. The use of certificate revocation lists (CRLs) does not satisfactorily address the potential concerns of an Application Server: In addition to the usual problems associated with CRLs, such as guaranteed delivery of latest versions, and scalability, the incorporation of coprocessor user privacy may undermine the effectiveness of CRLs.

The method presented here allows for a different approach to revocations, namely one that uses a Trust Server as arbiter: At the advance request of an Application Server which specifies a list of certificate IDs, a future coprocessor user-request for assurance which is associated with Application Server-specific data relative to the Application Server in question, may be denied if the particular coprocessor is marked at the Trust Server as having been associated with one of the suspect certificate IDs. If these Application Server-initiated requests are properly authenticated, an Application Server will not influence the assurance process relative to other Application Servers.

The suitability of the arbitrated revocation technique is predicated on the fact that there are instances of electronic commerce where an Application Server may be in a better position to catch seemingly fraudulent activity on the part of a coprocessor user than would be a Trust Server, because the Trust Server may not witness the actual electronic commerce transactions such as logging and billing for access to content or services. Furthermore, such transactions may be blinded from the Trust Servers because they may be secured based on secret data shared between the coprocessor and the Application Server as enabled by the present method. One element that may be tracked by an Application Server is the amount of incoming transaction traffic apparently originating from a particular coprocessor, where a suspiciously high volume may indicate possible cloning. The Application Server cannot itself recognize whether two certificate

IDs correspond to the same coprocessor if user privacy is enforced. Unlike a Trust Server, an Application Server may not be able to directly influence coprocessor behavior, even if it can influence the behavior of applications running on the coprocessor that are under control of the particular Application Server.

7   Method 2: SAC Individualization by Trust Server

An important containment goal is achieved for this method on the basis of the minimal assumptions on Secure Communications between coprocessors and the Trust Server, and on the state-invariant HSM: SAC individualization data with respect to an Application Server AS1 legitimately served to an uncompromised coprocessor Cp1, is safe from the combination of an unscrupulous Trust Server insider, a compromised coprocessor Cp2, and a cheating Application Server AS2. Furthermore, if Cp2 can (with the help of a Trust Server insider) get its SAC individualization data instance replayed to unwitting Cp1, the result is a potential attack on the privacy of Cp1's user, but not an attack on containment. Under proper implementation of revocation of Cp2, coprocessor Cp1 should also be revoked, even if it is an unwitting party to abuse the system rather than a direct clone.

In this method, SAC individualization data is delivered in bulk to the Trust Server and stored for the purpose of dispensing to coprocessors during SAC installation and individualization. This procedure is somewhat analogous to the

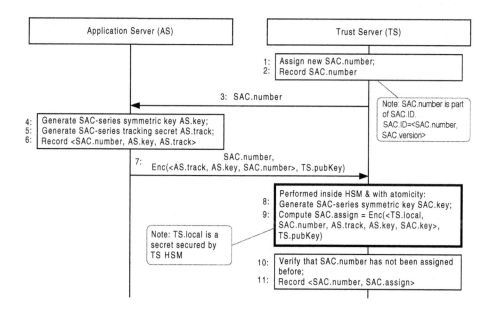

Fig. 4. SAC-series initialization

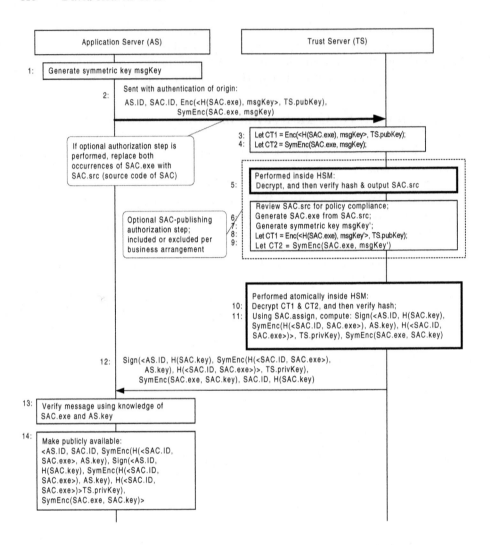

Fig. 5. SAC publishing

filling of a PEZ® candy dispenser followed by the dispensing of one candy tablet at a time, each served up once and consumed. Each individualization-data packet dispensed to a coprocessor may comprise a `blob` of data, as well as a `blobTag` which can be used for tracking purposes by the Trust Server and to identify to the Application Server which `blob` value is purportedly held by any particular coprocessor with which it communicates. Successful delivery of content or services to a client platform may be made contingent upon knowledge of the appropriate blob value as accessed by the SAC within the coprocessor's secure environment. Effective digital rights management (DRM) requires that correct code runs on the client, so that logging of viewed content is not surrepetitiously

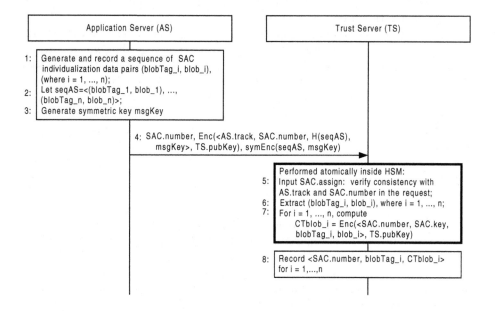

Fig. 6. SAC-series bulk individualization

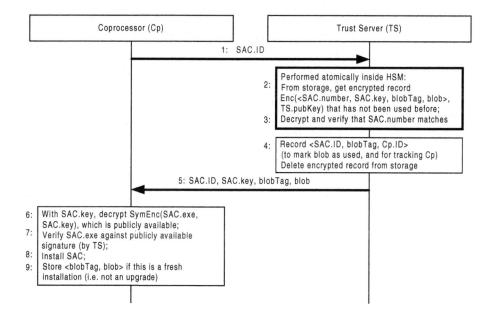

Fig. 7. SAC permissioning (into coprocessors): installation and individualization

removed or altered. In particular, in this model of permissioned-hardware DRM, software emulation are to be rejected.

The bulk transferal of individualization data may be associated with coordination between the Application Server and Trust Server regarding which portions of the data will be deemed to connote which collections of client-side coprocessor attributes, so that the individualization data grouped by coprocessor class may be securely distributed to coprocessors accordingly.

Since all versions or upgrades of a SAC corresponding to a given SAC.number are designed to work off the same (replenishable) pool of bulk individualization data, it is not sufficient (although necessary) to protect this data from attack during bulk delivery from the Application Server, during processing and storage by the Trust Server, and during individualization of a SAC instance being permissioned into a coprocessor. The SAC publishing process must be protected as well, in order to effect the desired level of security. The issue corresponding to this immediate goal is not one of ensuring the authenticity of the Application Server (or provider) requesting that the SAC be published, but rather one of ensuring that once a SAC series is initialized, a strategy has been put into place which denies intruders, whether legitimate Application Servers or not, the ability to get rogue SACs published. A rogue SAC can misappropriate a target Application Server's individualization data by misusing it or exposing it.

Recall that the first method, discussed earlier, handled both the publishing and signing of SACs outside of the Trust Server. Suppose that we handled SAC-series bulk individualization and SAC permissioning as in the current method, but that the Application Server (AS) did its own signing of the SAC and its own publishing, where the AS would generate its own value of SAC.key and send SAC.number, Enc($\langle$AS.track,SAC.key,SAC.number$\rangle$,TS.pubKey) to the Trust Server for SAC-series initialization. A compromise of a single coprocessor would then enable an adversary to publish a rogue SAC using the same value of SAC.number as the target AS and the same (compromised) value of SAC.key. The attack would not require the complicity of a TS insider, since the adversary need not submit a SAC-series initialization vector. His goal is not to submit his own bulk individualization data, but to hijack the target's.

Consider next, if we used all the documented protocols, but allowed an AS to choose its own value of SAC.key rather than having it generated randomly by the TS HSM. Then an attack of a coprocessor yielding the target's value of SAC.key, could be combined with a TS insider attack in which the adversary chooses the same value of SAC.key as did the target, with a forced replay of the same value of SAC.number. The adversary performs the standard SAC-series initialization step with this value of SAC.number, enabling him to have a rogue SAC published which can successfully install and access the target's individualization data, since it shares the same values of SAC.number and SAC.key. Hence, allowing an AS to choose its own value of SAC.key gets around the protection which was offered by including TS.local in SAC.assign (as specified in Fig. 4) in order to prevent insider substitution with an encryption of chosen values.

In order for the actual current method to achieve its resistance against the two-pronged attack of coprocessor compromise and TS insider, a critical aspect of the protocol design is that AS.key is never made available to coprocessors and is thus not subject to compromise in this way. Without knowledge of the target AS.key, an adversary can not provide the missing argument necessary to "finally" publish, i.e., provide a verifiable signature. It is also critical that there is an unspoofable binding between the signature and the presentation of SAC individualization data to the coprocessors. One way to bind a parameter to an existing signature is to input a function of the parameter as an additional argument of the signature. We discuss appropriate choices of parameter below.

The association of AS.track with the bulk individualization data transferal, as indicated in the message of step 4 of Fig. 6, serves to unambiguously designate which encryption-key value of SAC.key should be appended to SAC individualization values ⟨blobTag,blob⟩ as each is delivered to a coprocessor in the message of step 5 of Fig. 7. The association of the SAC.key value to the SAC individualization values is done as part of bulk individualization in steps 5, 6 and 7 of Fig. 6, based on access by the TS HSM to SAC.assign, as originally computed in step 9 of Fig. 4 during initialization of the given SAC-series. Note that maintaining the secrecy of AS.track prevents an adversary from using knowledge of this value in order to resubmit it under the reused SAC.number together with a value of AS.key which he knows, during SAC-series initialization. Such a maneuver, if successful, would allow an adversary to reroute SAC individualization data to a rogue version of the SAC. For the purpose of preventing this rerouting of data for use by a rogue SAC, it would actually suffice to use a non-secret value unambiguously indicative of (but not causing leakage of) the secret value of AS.track (such as H(AS.track)) during bulk individualization, since knowledge of the value of AS.track is necessary in order to submit AS.track together with a known value of AS.key during SAC-series initialization.

Having thus designed a means to securely link individualization data to the correct SAC.key for secure distribution to coprocessors, and having designed a means to thwart the successful usable publishing of rogue SACs under a target's secret value of AS.key, it remains to provide a means of securely binding SAC.key to the signature generated by the Trust Server during SAC publishing. The use of SAC.number or SAC.ID does not suffice for this purpose since a TS HSM without sufficient state memory may not be able to track the fraudulent reuse of these values, and these are not intended to be randomly generated each time. The approach taken in the current design is to input H(SAC.key) as an argument of the signature. Within the secure execution environment of the coprocessor, the value of SAC.key is used to decrypt the ciphertext form of the SAC and as an input to the signature verification process. This design uses the plaintext- (i.e., SAC.key-independent-) version of the SAC within the signature to allow coprocessor-independent verification of the signature by the Application Server making a determination as whether to make publicly available the missing argument of the signature that it computes during signature verification based on its knowledge of AS.key. The explicit (although non-secret) use of H(SAC.key) provides the necessary linkage to effect the binding.

The atomic processing of the signature generation during SAC publishing prevents, in particular, insider substitution of a previously published (legitimate) SAC for which SymEnc(H(⟨SAC.ID,SAC.exe⟩),AS.key) is known, juxtaposed with a different (rogue) SAC for use in computing the unencrypted argument of the signature, H(⟨SAC.ID,SAC.exe⟩).

An alternative means of securing the handling of SAC individualization data, which (unlike the SAC.key-based technique) is independent of encryption of the SAC for the purpose of confidentiality, could proceed as follows: H(SAC.key) as it appears as an argument of the signature in the message transmitted during step 12 of Fig. 5 (SAC publishing), is replaced by H(AS.track). H(AS.track) does not need to be sent along with the signature to the Application Server since, unlike SAC.key (generated by the Trust Server in step 8 of Fig. 4), the appropriate value of AS.track is assumed known by the Application Server that generated it in step 5 of Fig. 4 (SAC-series initialization). While SAC.key in its raw form is transmitted to the coprocessor in step 5 of Fig. 7 (SAC permissioning) for use by the coprocessor, it is important that a non-secret value indicative of AS.track such as H(AS.track), rather than AS.track itself, be communicated to the coprocessor during the step analogous to this one, since the value of AS.track must not be obtainable through coprocessor compromise. Note that SAC.key may be sent along with H(AS.track) to a coprocessor which needs the value of SAC.key in order to decrypt SymEnc(SAC.exe,SAC.key) in the event that this is the form in which it receives the SAC executable, SAC.exe.

Note that during SAC permissioning, an install by a coprocessor of an upgrade versus a fresh install of a SAC (which is characterized by the absence of any currently installed SAC corresponding to that SAC.number), rejects absorption of new individualization data. This attribute makes the system DRM (digital rights management)-friendly in that digital rights data somehow tied to or protected by individualization data, can be maintained across upgrades.

This method addresses legacy provider infrastructure issues, allowing the Application Servers to communicate with multi-application coprocessor users alongside users of already existing client-side devices. No preparatory steps are needed to convert over to a secret shared between the Application Server and the coprocessor, as was necessary in the first method. Furthermore, even if Application Servers never communicate with the coprocessors, instances of a given SAC or mutually trusted SACs can "peer-to-peer" communicate using SAC-level encryption and/or authentication. This can be achieved by having the blobTag include a certificate which corresponds to a private key within blob.

Although not explored further here, there is a potential hybrid approach, which (as in the first method) does not require coordination of SAC individualization data values between the Trust Server and the Application Server, but which handles SAC publishing and installation of SACs through the Trust Server (as in the second method).

The consumer's privacy is protected from an attack in which an impostor outside of the Trust Server gets a SAC published under a targeted Application Server's identity, to the extent that the Trust Server enforces authentication of the origin of the executable/source code. In the case where an optional SAC-publishing authorization procedure is followed, there may be additional review of out-of-band documentation supporting the origin of the SAC source code, as well as examination of the source code itself for compliance. The authentication of the origin can be brought directly into the HSM if there is no need for the SAC publishing authorization process. Of course, even if the HSM verifies digitally signed code against a certified signature key, the registration process that that certificate authority (CA) used to authenticate identity before issuing a certificate is also potentially subject to attack [20].

Undetectably replacing SAC individualization data inside of the Trust Server with known values is potentially an attack against consumer privacy, and not an attack against the provider's goal of containment. Collusion between compromised coprocessors and Trust Server insider attack can result in such substitution by illicitly repeating the dispensing of values of ⟨blobTag,blob⟩ to target coprocessors during SAC permissioning, where such values correspond to those extracted from compromised coprocessors. Because of the assumptions on Secure Communications (as described in Sect. 5) between coprocessors and the Trust Server, and because the input of encrypted bulk individualization data requires authorization (via consistent input of AS.track) by the entity that initialized the SAC series, TS insider attack or compromise of coprocessors alone does not enable such attack.

8   Conclusion

We have introduced two distinct architectures geared toward the same goal of achieving containment of damage to the business of content and service providers while protecting the privacy interests of consumers who participate in the system. These conflicting requirements are best mediated by the introduction of programmable security coprocessors on the consumer end and a Trust Server which can directly access these devices and so offer permissioning of providers' applications into them while still maintaining user privacy. Users have a legitimate right to change their personas with respect to activities conducted over the Internet in order to restrict the amount of valuable information that others can glean, often with no commensurate benefit to the consumer. The Trust Server can deny the permissioning of further services to users who are suspected of noncompliant usage of such services in the analogous way individual providers could handle their relationships with customers who are known to them. We have shown that a considerable degree of defense against both insider attacks and consumer fraud can be achieved by careful protocol design and the measured use of hardware security resources on both the consumer and server end. The first of our two methods is characterized by a strong PKI (public-key infrastructure) flavor which leans toward making minimal use of Trust Server involvement in the process. The second approach is capable of handling legacy infrastructures, although it is adaptable to hybrid approaches which can individualize coprocessors with keying material which is able to support both peer-to-peer PKI and coprocessor-to-Application Server shared-secret based cryptography.

Acknowledgements

We thank Aram Perez and Jon Callas for helpful discussions.

References

1. B. Askwith, M. Merabti, Q. Shi, and K. Whiteley. Achieving user privacy in mobile networks. In Proceedings of the 13th Annual Computer Security Applications Conference, 1997. 107, 109
2. M. Blum, W. Evans, P. Gemmell, S. Kannan, and M. Naor. Checking the correctness of memories. Algorithmica, 12(2/3), pp. 225–244, 1994. 110
3. L. Buttyán and J.-P. Hubaux. Accountable Anonymous Access to Services in Mobile Communication Systems. In Proceedings of SRDS '99, 1999. 107, 109
4. D. Chaum and T. P. Pedersen. Wallet databases with observers. In Advances in Cryptology: Crypto '92, E. F. Brickell, Ed., Lecture Notes in Computer Science 740, pp. 89-105, Springer-Verlag, 1992. 107
5. Committee on Intellectual Property Rights in the Emerging Information Infrastructure. The Digital Dilemma: Intellectual Property in the Information Age. Washington, D. C., National Academy Press, 2000. 107
6. G. Horn and B. Preneel. Authentication and payment in future mobile systems. In Proceedings of ESORICS '98, 1998. 107
7. B. Kaliski. New Challenges in Embedded Security. Consortium for Efficient Embedded Security, Symposium on Embedded Security, Security Ownership and Trust Models, July 10, 2001 (www.ceesstandards.org). 106
8. C. H. Lim and P. J. Lee. A Key Recovery Attack on Discrete Log-based Schemes Using a Prime Order Subgroup. In Advances in Cryptology: Crypto '97, B. S. Kaliski, Jr., Ed., Lecture Notes in Computer Science 1294, pp. 249-263, Springer-Verlag, 1997. 112
9. J. Manferdelli. Digital Rights Management ("DRM"). Consortium for Efficient Embedded Security, Symposium on Embedded Security, Security Ownership and Trust Models, July 10, 2001 (www.ceesstandards.org). 106
10. K. Martin, B. Preneel, C. Mitchell, H. Hitz, A. Poliakova, and P. Howard. Secure billing for mobile information services in UMTS. In Proceedings of IS&N'98, 1998. 107
11. R. Mori and M. Kawahara. Superdistribution: the concept and the architecture. Technical Report 7, Inst. of Inf. Sci. & Electron (Japan), Tsukuba Univ., Japan, July 1990. 106
12. B. Patel and J. Crowcroft. Ticket based service access for the mobile user. In Proceedings of Mobicom' 97, 1997. 107
13. S. Pugh, The Need for Embedded Security. Consortium for Efficient Embedded Security, Symposium on Embedded Security, Security Ownership and Trust Models, July 10, 2001 (www.ceesstandards.org). 106

14. M. O. Rabin. Digitalized Signatures and Public-key Functions as Intractable as Factorization. MIT Laboratory for Computer Science Technical Report 212 (MIT/LCS/TR-212), 1979. 112

15. M. Rotenberg. Consumer Implications of Security Applications. Consortium for Efficient Embedded Security, Symposium on Embedded Security, Security Ownership and Trust Models, July 10, 2001 (www.ceesstandards.org). 106

16. S. Smith. Secure coprocessing applications and research issues. Los Alamos Unclassified Release LA-UR-96-2805, August 1996. 107

17. S. W. Smith, E. R. Palmer, S. H. Weingart. Using a High-Performance, Programmable Secure Coprocessor. In Proceedings, Second International Conference on Financial Cryptography. Springer-Verlag LNCS, 1998. 108

18. M. Stefik. Trusted Systems, Scientific American 276(3), March 1997, pp. 78-81. 106

19. U. Wilhelm, S. Staamann, and L. Buttyán. On the problem of trust in mobile agent systems. In Proceedings of NDSS '98, 1998. 107, 109

20. http://www.verisign.com/developer/notice/authenticode/ 123

MPEG-4 IPMP Extensions

James King and Panos Kudumakis

Multimedia Department, Central Research Laboratories
Dawley Road, Hayes, Middlesex UB3 1HH, England
pkudumakis@crl.co.uk

Abstract. MPEG has further progressed its specification for interoperable Intellectual Property Management and Protection (IPMP) to Committee Draft. This paper describes the MPEG IPMP Extensions as a mapping into an MPEG-4 player. In the future there will also be mappings to both MPEG-7 and MPEG-2. The concepts explained in this paper are to be the basis for content protection throughout the whole of the MPEG family of standards. Detailed within are the reasons for their implementation by MPEG, how these extensions integrate into the current MPEG-4 IM-1 IPMP 'hooks' and the functionality they add to the current standard.

1 Introduction

Today's networks provide the opportunity for media content to be downloaded and distributed with ease. While this has meant that access for legitimate users has increased, it has also lead to a rise in illegal users. Within MPEG it was recognised that content has value to both the user and owner, to ensure that this value is preserved, it must be protected.

MPEG-4 has integrated the concept of the Intellectual Property Management Protection framework into the IM-1 player project to provide this security. The IM-1 player is a collaborative project aimed at creating a reference MPEG-4 compliant player. The framework integrated into the IM-1 player uses the concept of 'hooks' into the content at several stages of the decoding chain.

This technology has matured and it has become necessary to extend the IPMP framework into a system, which can support flexible and secure protection systems. This document explains the current IPMP 'hooks' implementation, the reasons for the proposed IPMP Extensions and how this will be achieved.

This paper contains the following sections:

- The MPEG-4 IM-1 IPMP 'hooks'
  A short description of the current IPMP 'hooks' implementation. It examines how they provide an interface between proprietary IPMP systems and the player through a normative interface.

T. Sander (Ed.): DRM 2001, LNCS 2320, pp. 126–140, 2002.

- Why the 'hooks' need to be extended?
  An explanation of what is missing from the current implementation. This section contains a section from the call of proposals stating the exact nature of the problem.

- How the IPMP Extensions work?
  This contains a short walkthrough of a typical scenario involving the IPMP Extensions and the sequence of events that occur.

- The components involved in the IPMP Extensions
  A short description of each of the new components that will be added as a result of the IPMP Extensions. These involve adjustments to the content and the addition of both an IPMP Tool Manager and a Message Router.

- Messages
  Describes the mechanism that will provide the communications framework of the new IPMP Extensions.

- A comparison with an implementation of Open Platform Initiative for Multimedia Access (OPIMA)
  Compares the new IPMP Extensions with the OCCAMM implementation of OPIMA. The Open Components for Controlled Access to Multimedia Materials (OCCAMM) is a specific implementation of the OPIMA specification.

2   The MPEG-4 IM-1 IPMP 'hooks'

MPEG-4 version 1 saw the introduction of Intellectual Property Management Protection framework into the IM-1 player. An extensible framework was provided that allowed developers to integrate protection systems into the IM-1 project.

The developer derives their own IPMP system from this framework. This proprietary IPMP system communicates with the IM-1 player through a normative interface known as the IPMP 'hooks'. Each IPMP system is allocated an objectTypeIndication value. The objectTypeIndication is used as an index into the registry to find the corresponding IPMP dll location. Once located the IM-1 player creates the IPMP system and begins deciphering the content.

The IM-1 player provides 'hooks' into the content at different points in the decoding chain, as shown by Figure 1. This allows a multitude of different protection mechanisms access through a generic interface to content in the state they require.

In Figure 1 each oval represents a point at which the IPMP system can process content in its current state. Currently only the pre- and post-decode 'hooks' (control points) are implemented. Pre-decoded data would be used for encryption, digital signatures and bitstream watermarking.

Post-decoded data would be used for raw Audio and Video watermarking. Pre- and post- decoding systems can be used in conjunction, this allows for in the case of audio, protection in the digital domain through encryption and protection in the analogue domain through watermarking.

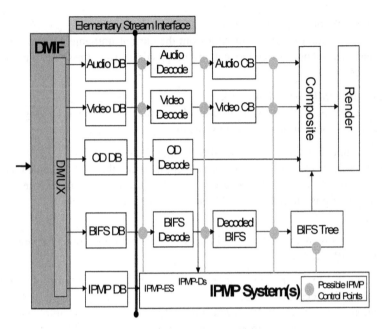

Fig. 1: The MPEG-4 IM-1 IPMP hooks [3]

In MPEG-4 Elementary Streams deliver content to the terminal. Each Elementary Stream provides a distinct part of the content such as an audio track. Each Stream is delivered to the terminal in terms of Access Units (AUs). Each Access Unit should be a self-contained entity that can be decoded without need for the previous or next AU being present. The size of each AU is arbitrary and decided by the properties of the content.

Elementary Streams are grouped into entities known as Object Descriptors. An Object Descriptor is made from one or more Elementary Streams delivering a specific piece of media. For instance take scaleable AAC which has two streams, each one adds a layer of quality to the audio. Each one would have its own Elementary Stream but both would be within the same Object Descriptor. Depending on the available bandwidth the user will receive the Elementary Stream(s) as appropriate.

Access Units are synchronised using timestamps for decoding and for composition. Extra data can be associated with the media called IPMP Information. This allows information such as encryption keys to be passed to the IPMP tool for initialisation. This data is transmitted in an IPMP Elementary Stream providing the data in Access Units to the IPMP System.

IPMP Elementary Streams are associated with the media they protect by IPMP Descriptors pointers or via declaration within the same Object Descriptor. An IPMP Descriptor pointer is placed within the Object Descriptor it is to protect. The actual IPMP Descriptor is declared outside of the protected Object Descriptor. The other case is where they are associated by declaration of the IPMP Elementary Stream within the protected Object Descriptor.

MPEG-4 IM-1 is a collaborative project involving many different entities. As with any standard there will be many implementations of both players and protection systems. Therefore it is important that to provide a usable system to the consumer the protection systems from multiple companies are interoperable and in some cases interchangeable.

3   Why the 'hooks' Need to Be Extended?

The following extract is taken from the 2000 IPMP Extensions call for proposals [7]:

"In 1997, MPEG issued a Call for Proposals for technology in the area of Intellectual Property management and Protection (IPMP). After receiving the proposals and the ensuing discussions, MPEG and the experts drawn to MPEG by the Call decided, in 1998, that it would not be appropriate to standardise complete systems, but that just providing the right interfaces (or 'hooks') would be were standardisation should stop. In 1998 and 1999, technology has matured, requirements for these systems have become clearer, and also MPEG's understanding of the role of IPMP technologies in building interoperable devices and services has evolved. Also, it became clear that not all parties represented in MPEG were convinced that only providing the interfaces would be enough. Particularly, some parties were concerned about interoperability between different products, often for similar services, as developed within the IPMP framework of the MPEG-4 Standard. Also, with convergence becoming a reality, e.g. through the deployment of broadband Internet access and the start of new services on mobile channels, interworking between different types of devices and services becomes a more important requirement. It is the belief of these parties, that the current MPEG-4 IPMP Framework does not provide the necessary infrastructure to meet their interoperability requirements. It is MPEG policy to support legitimate requests to standardise on a technology, knowing that those not interested in that particular standard technology have no obligation to adhere to it because of conformance obligations.

This Call requests submission of proposals that would allow interworking between different devices and services designed to play secure digital MPEG-4 content from multiple sources in a simple way, e.g. without the need to swap physical modules."

4   How the MPEG-4 IPMP Extensions Work?

4.1 User Requests Specific Content

The manner in which content is requested is out of scope of this standard. However, the following recommendations are made for the order in which different parts of the content are received and used:

1. IPMP Requirements on the Terminal should be placed with or before media requirements on the Terminal.
2. Access Information and/or restrictions should precede Content Stream download information.

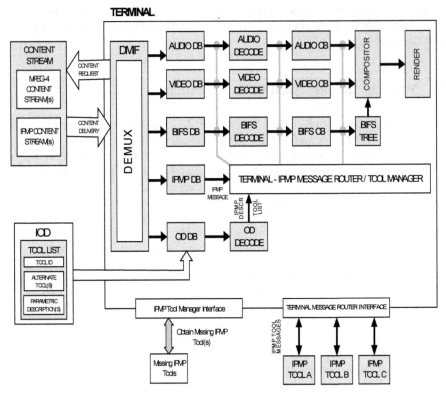

Fig. 2: The MPEG-4 IPMP extensions [2]

4.2 IPMP Tools Description Access

1. The terminal accesses the IPMP Tool List.
2. Using the IPMP Tool List, the Terminal determines the IPMP Tools required to consume the content.

4.3 IPMP Tools Retrieval

1. If the tools are available locally at the terminal, proceed to section 4.4.
2. The terminal attempts to obtain the Missing IPMP Tools. Some Missing Tools may be carried in the Content itself. Otherwise, the Tool must be obtained remotely. The following procedure may be followed for such retrieval:
   1. The terminal accesses an implementation specific database for a location for the missing Tool.
   2. A communication channel is set-up between the terminal and the Tool location.
   3. The terminal implementation provides information about its platform and the Tool database identifies a compatible Tool implementation.
   4. The IPMP Tool Manager accesses/acquires the missing IPMP Tools.
   5. The newly acquired tools are made available for use by the terminal.

4.4 Instantiation of IPMP Tools

1. The Terminal instantiates the IPMP Tool(s) locally or remotely.
2. The instantiated Tools are provided with initial IPMP Information from the Content.
3. One or more Tools, identified in the Content, may use IPMP Information to determine security requirements for content access, and monitor and facilitate the establishment and maintenance of these security requirements in inter-Tool communication.

4.5 IPMP Initialisation and Update – In Parallel with Content Consumption

1. The Message Router routes IPMP Information to the IPMP Tools.
2. The terminal consumes the content if allowed by the requisite IPMP Tool.
3. During content consumption, the complete walkthrough can be requested again. Requests for content consumption are implicit within the process, or are requested by the User.

Specific IPMP Information can be made normative outside this architecture. This architecture supports both transparent and opaque IPMP Information. An IPMP Information ID will be part of the IPMP Information, such ID will be assigned by a Registration Authority.

5   The IPMP Extension Components

5.1 The Content

5.1.1   class IPMP_ToolListDescriptor

The content contains the list of tools required for the presentation of the content. The tool list contains the unique identifiers of the required tools. This contains an 8 bit identifier which is unique within its namespace. An 8 bit field containing the number of tools in the list and the list of tools themselves.

5.1.2   class IPMP_Tool

Describes a tool that may be used to decode this content. This contains the unique identifier for the IPMP Tool. It also contains bit flags that identify whether it is an alternate tool or a parametric tool. These are explained in the following sections.

5.1.3   Alternate Tools

There may be instances where several tools can be used to decode a particular piece of content. If this is the case a set of descriptors can be provided in the IPMP_ToolListDescriptor. Anyone of these can be used depending on their availability.

5.1.4   Parametric Tools

There are cases where a more flexible approach to tool selection is required. For instance in the case of an encryption algorithm such as Rijndael where there are potentially many implementations on many different platforms.

There may also be the case where sets of tools can be used in tandem to render the content. This process is known as parametric aggregation and allows for flexible complex groups of IPMP tools to be established.

The parametric tools need a well known set of standard interfaces so they can be used transparently. A simple language will be used to query the fitness of a tool for the required purpose. Then the parametric configuration would be used to initialise the tool.

5.1.5   Parametric Aggregation

The grouping of several tools, known as aggregation units, requires them to be linked in the correct sequential order. This is achieved by using input and output codes, tools with matching input and output codes are linked together to form the decoding chain. Tools may have multiple inputs and outputs. The first tool in the chain is known as the entry point and is identified as such.

Two distinct types of tools can be identified in the role of Parametric Aggregation. The content management tools and the utility tools. The content management tools would be used to co-ordinate and instantiate the utility tools. They would also be responsible for making a decision as to the users privileges to use the content.

The utility tools would be much simpler, providing a service using a particular algorithm, for instance a DES decoder. These would be similar to the IPMP systems in use with the current IM-1 'hooks'.

5.1.6   Parametric Description

The information about the parametric configuration will be stored in IPMP_ParametricDescriptors. The data stored will be generic and non-specific to allow for transparent usage. A simple schema would follow the following model:

Version	1,2,3 etc…
Tool Class	Watermarking, Decryption, Digital Signature
Sub Class	RSA, Rijndael
Specific information	block size, CBC, ECB

5.1.7   IPMP Information

This can come from a number of sources:

The content stream	Data carried in the IPMP Elementary Stream associated with the protected Media. This is the only means to provide IPMP information in the current IPMP hooks design.
The terminal	Data from the terminal the content is being rendered on.
Remote resources	A remote location.
A fellow IPMP tool	Allows inter-communication between tools to allow for complex interactions.

Two categories of IPMP information will be specified. Generic information that can be understood by both the terminal and the tool, and information specific to the tool receiving it.

5.2 IPMP Tool Manager

5.2.1   Overview

The Tool Manager is responsible for selecting and instantiating the IPMP tools from the given tool list, whether normal, parametric or alternative tools.

5.2.2   Acquiring Tools via Content

The packaging of tools with the content gives a means of delivering the appropriate tools the terminal is missing. The tool would be carried in a new type of associated Elementary Stream, IPMPToolStream. The downloading of tools is handled by the Tool Manager.

The descriptor for the tool stream should be placed in the Initial Object Descriptor to ensure all the tools are present before decoding begins.

The tool would be described in terms of an identifier unique to that class of tool. It would also have a field that identifies the binary form of the tool. ie. .dll, jar file, unix shared library. The final field would describe how the tool is packaged, for instance in zip format.

Missing tools can also be downloaded from a remote source when they are not sent with the content.

5.2.3   Tool Creation

Tools can be created by one of two methods. The first is by a piece of protected content, this is the scenario that occurs in the current IPMP 'hooks' design. Secondly a tool may be instantiated by another tool. This gives the possibility of creating complex protection systems.

Because of the inter-dependant possibilities tools may register themselves for notification on the creation of another specific tool. Each instance of a tool must register the context and scope of protection they will offer. This is the first action for a tool on creation.

Tools will use messages to communicate with one another, so on creation they must first register themselves with the Message Router.

5.3 Message Router

5.3.1   Authentication

One of the missing components of the current IM-1 'hooks' implementation is the ability to ensure that an IPMP system is authentic. To ensure that security is not compromised, tools and the terminal require the ability to authenticate one another. This mechanism should allow varying levels of trust to be established between tools and between tools and the terminal.

The level of trust is indicated by the tool initiating the authentication process, it is likely that this is one of the more complex management systems rather than a utility IPMP system. The two systems involved in the authentication process then agree common protocols and parameters dependent on the trust level.

5.3.2   Certification

IPMP tools and terminals can use certificates such as X.509 to provide information about themselves and also use trust and security metadata to authenticate themselves. There is an interface called TrustSecurityMetadata, which can be sub-classed to provide this functionality.

5.3.3   Routing

To ensure the delivery of the IPMP Information an entity called a Message Router will provide the transport layer. Clearly the Message Router interfaces need to be normative to ensure compatibility.

Each message will contain the source and destination Ids of the tools. A timestamp indicating when the data is to be delivered to the target tool. Whether the delivery method is synchronous or asynchronous. The route and sequence of tools the message is being sent to, and the context under which the message is being sent.

It will be necessary to Synchronize IPMP messages with the content using the timestamps field. This will be important for security methods like encryption that will require synchronized key changes. This synchronization will be specified in the future.

6   Messages

6.1 Function Structure [1]

Messages are defined in Interface Descriptor Language (IDL), this allows for a platform independent representation. The message consists of the following fields:

```
IPMP_ReceiveMessage(
[in] short      Sender,              // Tool ID
[in] short      Recipient,           // Tool ID
[in] long MsgSize,                   // Size in bits
[in] octet      Msg[]                // The message
[in] IPMP_MsgMode      MsgMode,      // Async/Sync
[in] long MsgID )                    // ID of msg

return IPMP_ToolMsgStatus ;          // OK or Error

enum IPMP_ToolMsgStatus
{
IPMP_MSG_STATUS_MSG_POSTED = 0,
IPMP_MSG_STATUS_INVALID_SENDER_ID,
IPMP_MSG_STATUS_INVALID_RECIPIENT_ID,
IPMP_MSG_STATUS_MSG_MODE_NOT_SUPPORTED,
IPMP_MSG_STATUS_GENERIC_ERROR
};
```

```
enum IPMP_MsgMode
{
IPMP_MSG_MODE_SYNC = 0,
IPMP_MSG_MODE_ASYNC
};
```

The receive message method is called by the message router on the IPMP tool when a message is passed to it from the sender IPMP tool. The return value of the method indicates the result for synchronous methods. For asynchronous messages the MsgID can be used to identify the response for a particular message.

6.2 Creation and Notification Messages

This group of messages provides the ability to create and be notified about the creation of tools. Used by tools to gain access to one another and for tools to spawn other tools.

IPMP_CreateNewToolInstance	Signals the creation of a specified new tool
IPMP_RequestInstTools	Returns a list of all tools running on the terminal
IPMP_AddToolInstNotificationListener	Register for notification of tool creation
IPMP_RemoveToolInstNotificationListener	Remove registration for tool creation notification
IPMP_ToolInstNotification	Notification message containing details of tool created, is passed to registered listeners
IPMP_RequestToolContextID	Requests ID's of other tools in the same protection chain
IPMP_SupplyToolContextID	Replies to above with ContextID

6.3 IPMP Information Delivery Messages

Provides the tool with information about its bit stream. Includes messages to provide IPMP information to the tool and decoder information .

IPMP_ DecConfigFromBitstream	Delivers the decoder information from the ES to the tool
IPMP_ DecConfigFromBitstream	Delivers the decoder information from the ES to the tool
IPMP_DescriptorFromBitstream	Delivers the IPMP Descriptor to the tool
IPMP_DataTerminate	Updates or deletes a descriptor when an update or remove is read from the stream

6.4 Processing Messages

The messages providing the tool with the content to be deciphered. Content is processed and then passed back to the terminal in a reply message.

IPMP_ProcessData	Delivers data in a similar fashion to the current IPMPManagerImp::Decrypt() method.
IPMP_ProcessDataReturn	Returns the data processed by above message.

6.5 Intent Messages

The tool uses these messages to notify the terminal that they wish to process a piece of content. The message destination signals its authorisation or rejection in its reply.

IPMP_IntentRequest	Declares an intent to process some data
IPMP_IntentResponse	Yes/No response to above message
IPMP_IntentTerminate	Terminate intent
IPMP_IntentRevoke	Deny access to a part of the content

6.6 User Messages

These messages provide a way for the IPMP tool to query the user. A variety of responses can be made and are sent back to the IPMP tool via a reply message.

ToolToUserMessage	Displays a message and can ask for a response from the user
UserToToolMessage	Contains the reply text from the user or the result of options offered to the user

6.7 Authentication Messages

A normative message interface for authentication between tools and the terminal.

IPMP_InitAuthentication	Initiates an authentication process with the tool specified in the context ID. Different levels of security can be specified

7 A Comparison with OPIMA (Open Platform Initiative for Multimedia Access)

This section provides a comparison with a specific implementation of OPIMA namely the Open Components for Controlled Access to Multimedia Materials (OCCAMM)[6]. This is one of the first implementations of OPIMA and the reader should be aware that other alternatives may exist. Many of the concepts behind the IPMP Extensions can be seen in the OCCAMM implementation of OPIMA.

7.1 Message Routing vs. Scheduler

In OCCAMM operations are handled by the Scheduler, which spawns a thread to handle each individual message. The proposed IPMP extensions use a message-based scheduler called the Message Router, which passes messages between the IPMP tools and terminals.

Both methods allow for asynchronous and synchronous operation, however OCCAMM uses interfaces whereas the IPMP Extensions use messages.

7.2 IPMP Tools vs. OPIMA IPMPS

The OCCAMM IPMPS provides the decision making engine of the OCCAMM platform. Importantly it contains no algorithms, the separation of algorithms and decision making is a fundamental aim of OCCAMM for reasons of security.

OCCAMM provides algorithms fixed within the OPIMA Virtual Machine (OVM), when the algorithms change a new OVM must be downloaded. This is done for security and to limit the complexity of having large amounts of algorithms code in use. OCCAMM specifies the algorithms a terminal supports in terms of compartments. Each compartment supports a certain set of algorithms. This allows for different classes of terminal, there could be a compartment for PDA's, a compartment for PC's etc.

In the IPMP Extensions IPMPS tools can be a decision maker like the IPMPS in OCCAMM and they can also be algorithms. The decision making IPMP tools then spawn and use the algorithm tools to process the content. Unlike OCCAMM both of these components can be downloaded, the security mechanism is provided by mutual authentication. Therefore the IPMP Extensions rely heavily on the fact that this mutual authentication is secure.

In OCCAMM the IPMPS can get IPMP information from the content, which is passed by the MPEG-4 player. And it can also access a remote server through a Secure Access Channel (SAC). It can use this SAC to gain extra usage rules about the user.

7.3 Manufacturer and Consumer-Interoperability vs. Limited Complexity

OCCAMM ensures interoperability with vendors by limiting the amount of algorithms in use. IPMPS decision engines can be downloaded for the specific vendor to enforce their usage rules. In the IPMP Extensions consumer interoperability is more complex as both algorithms and decision engines can be downloaded and these can be combined in many different configurations. This extra complexity can be alleviated slightly by combining the IPMP tools with the content thus ensuring the user has the correct tools.

Manufacturer interoperability is enforced in OCCAMM by pre-defining the algorithms of the OVM, thereby ensuring that the IPMPS can always use the algorithms provided. A balance between interoperability for both the user and manufacturer whilst limiting complexity to a manageable level is a key aim of OCCAMM.

In the IPMP Extensions alternative and parametric tools give a greater amount of interoperability for both the vendor and consumer than tools selected by unique ID. Tools already in local storage can be selected over those requiring download. Similarly parametric tools may give a greater chance of a suitable tool already being present on the terminal.

7.4 Similarities and Differences

OCCAMM provides an example of how a system similar to the IPMP Extensions can and does work. Although the implementations differ in the way they are assembled, the system architecture remains similar even at object level.

OCCAMM	MPEG-4 IPMP Extensions
Scheduler	Message Router
IPMPSDownloadManager	IPMP Tool Manager
IPMPS	IPMP Tool (Decision making)
Algorithm	IPMP Tool (Utility)

In OCCAMM these components, with the exception of the IPMPS, are statically linked into the OVM for security. Whereas the MPEG-4 IPMP Extensions are comprised of distributed objects that use authentication for security and verification.

Importantly, OCCAMM provides the OVM for use by multiple applications rather than the MPEG player, which is a stand-alone application. This allows application developers to use the features of the OVM within their own software.

7.5 Interoperability between OCCAMM and the IPMP Extensions

Within OCCAMM an MPEG-4 player provides the content rendering capabilities. This means that in essence all the functionality in the MPEG-4 player is also available to OCCAMM platform. Therefore OCCAMM can be seen as a value added system.

OCCAMM interfaces with the MPEG-4 player using two IPMP tools, the opima.dll for pre-decoded content and the postwrap.dll for post-decoded content. Instead of containing algorithms, these are proxy dlls, which pass content to the OVM for secure processing.

The opima and postwrap tools contain no algorithms of their own. They are loaded by the player when specified in the IPMP Tools List. They then pass the OVM content as it is passed through the decoding chain to them. The OVM then processes the content and places it into the buffers given by the opima and postwrap tools.

There are two key areas where compatibility is required, the algorithms used to protect the content, and the IPMP information that contains the content rules. If both systems can interchange these then there is no problem with interoperability.

Most algorithms in use are standardised so as long as the same one is present in the OVM and in MPEG-4 IPMP Extensions there will be no incompatibility. The OVM compartment can be periodically updated to take into account any algorithm updates or changes.

IPMP information could be standardised into a universal content management language. This could express both the rules under which the content is to be used, and algorithm parameters.

It could even be possible to have OCCAMM interact with other MPEG-4 IPMP tools through IPMP Information passed to and from the opima and postwrap dlls.

7.6 A Walkthrough in an OCCAMM System Using MPEG-4 IPMP Extension Capable Player

The following walkthrough shows how content aimed at an MPEG-4 IPMP Extension player can be played through the OVM. This is done by adding the opima and postwrap tools to the IPMP Tool List, in this case as alternatives. The content could easily have the postwrap and opima tools as the main tools in the IPMP Tool List.

1. User loads the application of their choice
2. The application requests the OVM to open the content
3. The OVM requests the MPEG-4 player to load the content
4. In the MPEG-4 player the IPMP Tool List is loaded
5. From the alternative tools – opima tool and postwrap tool selected
6. Terminal loads opima and postwrap tools
7. Authentication of opima tool, postwrap tool and terminal
8. IPMP Information routed to the corresponding opima and postwrap tools
9. Tools pass IPMP Information to the OVM
10. OVM instantiates the appropriate OCCAMM IPMPS
11. OVM passes IPMP Information to the OCCAMM IPMPS
12. OCCAMM IPMPS initialises the algorithms according to the IPMP Information
13. The tools pass the incoming media data to the OVM for processing and the results are passed to the OCCAMM IPMPS for evaluation
14. Decoding continues

The walkthrough above shows how content can be shared by both, a stand-alone IPMP Extension compliant MPEG-4 player, or a system using OPIMA/OCCAMM. By using the alternative tools list the opima and postwrap tools can be loaded, passing control of the content to the OVM.

8   Conclusions

MPEG has further progressed its specification for interoperable Intellectual Property Management and Protection (IPMP) to Committee Draft. The term IPMP is used by MPEG to describe Digital Rights Management. This paper has described the MPEG IPMP Extensions as a mapping into an MPEG-4 player. In the future there will be mappings to both MPEG-7 and MPEG-2. The concepts explained in this paper are to be the basis for content protection throughout the whole of the MPEG family of standards.

References

1. ISO/IEC JTC1/SC29/WG11 MPEG, Text of ISO/IEC 21000-4/CD, N4269, (MPEG-21 Part-4: IPMP), Sydney, July 2001.
2. ISO/IEC JTC1/SC29/WG11 MPEG, Text of ISO/IEC 14496-1/PDAM3, N4270, (MPEG-4 Part-1: Systems), Sydney, July 2001.
3. ISO/IEC JTC1/SC29/WG11 MPEG, "MPEG-4 Intellectual Property Management & Protection (IPMP) Overview & Applications", N2614, Rome, Dec. 1998.
4. ISO/IEC JTC 1/SC 29/WG11 MPEG, International Standard ISO/IEC 14496-1. Information Technology – Generic Coding of Moving Pictures and Associated Audio, Part 1: Systems, 2001.
5. "Open Platform Initiative for Multimedia Access (OPIMA) specification 1.1", http://www.cselt.it/opima/
6. OCCAMM EC project http://sharon.cselt.it/projects/occamm/publicmaterial.htm
7. ISO/IEC JTC1/SC29/WG11 MPEG, "Call of Proposals for IPMP solutions", N3543, Beijing, July 2000.

Dynamic Self-Checking Techniques for Improved Tamper Resistance

Bill Horne, Lesley Matheson, Casey Sheehan, and Robert E. Tarjan

STAR Lab, InterTrust Technologies
4751 Partick Henry Dr., Santa Clara, CA 95054
{bhorne,lrm,casey,ret}@intertrust.com

Abstract. We describe a software self-checking mechanism designed to improve the tamper resistance of large programs. The mechanism consists of a number of *testers* that redundantly test for changes in the executable code as it is running and report modifications. The mechanism is built to be compatible with copy-specific static watermarking and other tamper-resistance techniques. The mechanism includes several innovations to make it stealthy and more robust.

1 Introduction

There are many situations in which it is desirable to protect a piece of software from malicious tampering once it gets distributed to a user community. Examples include time-limited evaluation copies of software, password-protected access to unencrypted software, certain kinds of e-commerce systems, and software that enforces rights to access copyrighted content.

Tamper resistance is the art and science of protecting software or hardware from unauthorized modification, distribution, and misuse. Although hard to characterize or measure, effective protection appears to require a set of tamper resistance techniques working together to confound an adversary.

One important technique is *self-checking* (also called self-validation or integrity checking), in which a program, while running, checks itself to verify that it has not been modified. We distinguish between *static* self-checking, in which the program checks its integrity only once, during start-up, and *dynamic* self-checking, in which the program repeatedly verifies its integrity as it is running.

Self-checking alone is not sufficient to robustly protect software. The level of protection from tampering can be improved by using techniques that thwart reverse engineering, such as customization and obfuscation, techniques that thwart debuggers and emulators, and methods for marking or identifying code, such as watermarking or fingerprinting. These techniques reinforce each other, making the whole protection mechanism much greater than the sum of its parts.

In this paper we describe the design and implementation of a dynamic self-checking mechanism that substantially raises the level of tamper-resistance protection against an adversary with static analysis tools and knowledge of our algorithm and most details of our implementation. Our threat model is described

T. Sander (Ed.): DRM 2001, LNCS 2320, pp. 141–159, 2002.

in detail in Section 3. Our overall goal is to protect client-side software running on a potentially hostile host.

We begin in Section 2 with a brief discussion of related work. In Section 3 we address our threat model and the design objectives we used to create techniques to oppose these threats. Section 4 presents an overview of our self-checking mechanism and its components. Section 5 describes the design, performance and placement of the testing mechanism. Section 6 discusses the design and interconnection of the tested intervals of code. Finally, Section 7 concludes with a summary and a brief discussion of directions for future improvements.

The authors of this document were primarily responsible for the design and implementation of the self-checking technology. Throughout its evolution, however, many important contributions came from others, including Ann Cowan, Chacko George, Jim Horning, Greg Humphreys, Mike MacKay, John McGinty, Umesh Maheshwari, Susan Owicki, Olin Sibert, Oscar Steele, Andrew Wright, and Lance Zaklan.

2   Related Work

There has been a significant amount of work done on the problem of executing untrusted code on a trusted host computer [10,11,12]. The field of tamper resistance is the dual problem of running trusted code on an untrusted host. Although of considerable practical value, there has been little formal work done on this problem. Most of the work reported in the literature is ad hoc. It is not clear that any solutions exist that have provable security guarantees. In addition, the field suffers from a lack of widely recognized standards to measure effectiveness. With these disclaimers in mind, we present a brief survey of some important work related to our self-checking technology.

Obfuscation attempts to thwart reverse engineering by making it hard to understand the behavior of a program through static or dynamic analysis. Obfuscation techniques tend to be ad hoc, based on ideas about human behavior or methods aimed to derail automated static or dynamic analysis. Collberg, et al. [5,7,8] presented classes of transformations to a binary that attempt to confuse static analysis of the control flow graph of a program. Wang, et al. [15,16,17] also proposed transformations to make it hard to determine the control flow graph of a program by obscuring the destination of branch targets and making the target of branches data-dependent. Wang, et al. present a proof that their transformations make the determination of the control graph of a transformed program NP-hard. Theoretical work on encrypted computation is also related to obfuscation. For example, Sander and Tschudin [14] propose a theoretical obfuscation method that allows code to execute in an encrypted form for a limited class of computations. Other work on obfuscation appears in [6,13].

Customization takes one copy of a program and creates many very different versions. Distributing many different versions of a program stops widespread damage from a security break since published patches to break one version of an executable might not apply to other customized versions. Aucsmith uses this type of technique in his IVP technology [ ]. Each instantiation of a protected program is different.

Software watermarking, which allows tracking of misused program copies, complements both obfuscation and customization by providing an additional deterrent to tampering. Many software watermarking methods have been proposed, but none of them appear to be in widespread use. Collberg and Thomborson [ ] classify software watermarks as either static or dynamic and provide a survey of research and commercial methods. They make the distinction between software watermarking methods that can be read from an image of a program and those that can be read from a running program. Static methods include a system described by Davidson and Myhrvold [ ] in which a program's basic blocks are shuffled to create a unique ordering in the binary, which serves as a unique identifier for that version of the program.

Self-checking, also referred to as tamper-proofing, integrity checking, and anti-tampering technology, is an essential element in an effective tamper-resistance strategy. Self-checking detects changes in the program and invokes an appropriate response if change is detected. This prevents both misuse and repetitive experiments for reverse engineering or other malicious attacks. Aucsmith [ ] presents a self-checking technology in which embedded code segments verify the integrity of a software program as the program is running. These embedded code segments (Integrity Verification Kernels, IVK's) check that a running program has not been altered, even by one bit. Aucsmith proposes a set of design criteria for his self-checking technology including interleaving important checking-related tasks for stealth (partial computation of the check sum), obfuscated testing code, non-deterministic behavior, customization of testing code (non-unique installations) and distributed secrets. We adhere to similar design criteria.

Chang and Atallah [ ] propose a method in which software is protected by a set of *guards,* each of which can do any computation. In addition to guards that compute checksums of code segments (analogous to our testers), they propose the use of guards that actually repair attacked code. Their emphasis is on a system for automatically placing guards and allowing the user of the system to specify both the guards and the regions of the program that should be guarded. In emphasizing these issues, their results are somewhat complementary to ours.

Collberg and Thomborson [ ] provide a view of the nature of these classes of tamper-resistance technologies. Unfortunately, little research into the complementary aspects of these kinds of technologies can be found.

3   Design Objectives and Threat Model

The fundamental purpose of a dynamic program self-checking mechanism is to detect any modification to the program as it is running, and upon detection to trigger an appropriate response. We sought a self-checking mechanism that would be as robust as possible against various attacks while fulfilling various non-security objectives. In this section we summarize our threat model and design objectives.

3.1 Functionality

- **Comprehensive and Timely Dynamic Detection** The mechanism should detect the change of a single bit in any non-modifiable part of the program, as the program is running and soon after the change occurs. This helps to prevent an attack in which the program is modified temporarily and then restored after deviant behavior occurs.
- **Separate, Flexible Response** Separating the response mechanism from the detection mechanism allows customization of the response depending upon the circumstances, and makes it more difficult to locate the entire mechanism having found any part.
- **Modular Components** The components of the mechanism are modular and can be independently replaced or modified, making future experimentation and enhancements easier, and making extensions to other executables and executable formats easier.
- **Platform Independence** Although the initial implementation of our self-checking technology is Intel x86-specific, the general mechanism can be adapted to any platform.
- **Insignificant Performance Degradation** The self-checking mechanism should not noticeably slow down the execution of the original code and should not add significantly to the size of the code. Our goal is to have no more than a 5% impact on performance.
- **Easy Integration** We designed our self-checking technology to work in conjunction with copy-specific static watermarking and with other tamper-resistance methods such as customization. Embedding the self-checking technology in a program relies on source-level program insertions as well as object code manipulations.
- **Suitable for a Large Code Base** Our test-bed executable was several megabytes in length.

3.2 Security

The two general attacks on a software self-checking mechanism are *discovery* and *disablement*. Methods of discovering such a mechanism, and our approaches for preventing or inhibiting these methods, follow.

Discovery

- **Static Inspection** We made the various components of the self-checking mechanism as stealthy and obfuscated as we could, to make detection by static inspection, especially automated inspection (by a program) hard.
- **Use of Debuggers and Similar Software Tools** Off-the-shelf dynamic analysis tools such as debuggers and profilers pose a significant threat to our self-checking technology. Self-checking requires memory references (reads) into executable code sections. These can be detected with a debugger, although any debugger that relies on modifying the code will be defeated by

the self-checking mechanism. Our mechanism is enormously strengthened by the addition of a mechanism that detects standard debuggers and responds appropriately. (The design of such a mechanism is beyond the scope of this paper.) Homemade debuggers also pose a threat but require a substantial investment by an attacker.

– **Detection of Reads into the Code** We attempted to thwart both static and dynamic detection of reads into the code sections by obfuscating the read instructions, so that the code section addresses targeted by such reads were never in single registers. Detection of such reads thus requires noticing that such a read has actually occurred; inspecting the code or monitoring the registers will not reveal this fact.

– **Generalization** The self-checking mechanism consists of a large number of lightweight code fragments called *testers*, each testing a small contiguous section of code. An attacker, having discovered one such tester, could look for others by searching for similar code sequences. We customized the testers, so that generalizing from one to others is difficult: not only are there multiple classes of testers, each class performing a different test (computing a different hash function), but within each class the testers use different code sequences to do the same job.

– **Collusion** Our self-checking mechanism is designed so that it can be used on statically-watermarked code. If copy-specific watermarks are used, an attacker might be able to locate the tester mechanism by obtaining two differently marked copies of the code and comparing them. The differences might reveal not only the watermarks but also any changes needed in the self-checking mechanism to compensate for different watermarks. In our mechanism, the bits that vary in order to compensate for the watermarks are called *correctors*. These correctors are separated from the testers and the response mechanism. Therefore, neither the testers nor the response mechanism can be detected by collusion. In addition, detection of the correctors by collusion provides an attacker with very little information. Knowing the correctors and their values does not facilitate discovering or disabling the rest of the mechanism. The use of customization, in which there are many radically different copies of the code, would also foil this kind of attack since everything in the program looks different in every copy.

– **Inspection of Installation Patches** The final step of the watermarking and self-checking initialization process that we propose here relies on using a patch file to modify a previously obfuscated, non-functional executable. Inspection of the patch file might reveal some parts of the self-checking mechanism. With our method, the only parts of the self-checking mechanism that are in the patches are the correctors, not the testers or the response mechanism. If copy-specific watermarking is not used, this patching process is not required.

Disablement In general, our goal was to eliminate single points of failure and to require discovery and modification of all or most of the self-checking mechanism for an attacker to succeed.

- **Modifying the Testers** One possible disabling attack is to modify one or more testers so that they fail to signal a modification of the tested code section. Our testers are designed to provide redundant, overlapping coverage, so that each tester is tested by several others. Disabling one or more of the testers by modifying them will produce detection of these changes by the unmodified testers. All or almost all of the testers must be disabled for this kind of attack to succeed.
- **Modifying the Response Mechanism** Another disabling attack is to modify the response mechanism. Again, because of the redundant testing mechanism, substantially all of the response functionality must be disabled for such an attack to succeed. In our current implementation we used direct calls to a tamper-response mechanism. Future possible work is to build a stealthier, more robust tamper-response mechanism, including variably delayed response and multiple paths to the response code.
- **Modifying Correctors** Another possible attack is to modify the code so that it behaves incorrectly and still does not trigger the testers. With our use of multiple overlapping hash computations, such an attack is unlikely to succeed without discovery of all or most of the testers. Such discovery would allow a successful tester-disabling attack. Thus, the former attack is no greater a threat than the latter.
- **Temporary Modifications** A dynamic attack might modify the code so that it behaves anomalously and then restore the code to its original form before the self-checking mechanism detected the change. Our use of dynamic, redundant self-checking minimizes this threat.

4   Algorithm Design

In this section we provide an overview of our self-checking mechanism, including some discussion of our design decisions and possible alternatives and extensions. In subsequent sections we discuss various aspects of the mechanism in more detail.

4.1   Components and Embedding Process

The self-checking mechanism consists of a collection of two kinds of components, *testers* and *correctors*, discussed in Sections 4.2. and 4.4, respectively. These components are embedded into an executable in a three-step process:

Step 1 Source-code processing Insert a set of testers, coded in assembly language, into the source code of the executable.

Step 2 Object-code processing

  Step 2A Shuffle groups of basic blocks of the object code, thereby randomizing the tester distribution.

Step 2B Insert correctors, at least one per tester, into the object code.

Step 2C Associate a corrector and a tester interval with each tester, in such a way as to provide redundant coverage of the executable and so that the correctors can later be set in an appropriate order to make the testers test correctly.

Step 3 Installation-time processing

Step 3A Compute watermark values.

Step 3B Compute corrector values given the watermark values.

Step 3C Form patches containing the watermark and corrector values.

Step 3D Install the program by combining the patches with a pre-existing, non-functional executable to prepare a watermarked, self-checking, fully functional executable.

Testers are inserted into source code instead of object code. If instead we were to insert the testers into the object code it would be difficult to insure that the registers used by the testers do not conflict with the registers being actively used by the object code at the insertion point. By inserting the testers in the source code, the compiler will do the appropriate register allocation to avoid any conflicts. This insertion method also affords us more control over the run-time performance of the self-checking mechanism, since we can more easily place testers in code segments with desired performance characteristics. On the other hand, we do not have fine-grained control over the placement of testers in the executable. Object-level placement of the correctors gives us great control over their static distribution, which is their most important attribute. The issues of where and when to insert the testers, correctors and other security components deserve further study.

Our self-checking method is designed to work in combination with watermarking. Since copy-specific watermarking must be done at installation time, the self-checking mechanism must either avoid checking the watermarks or must be modified at installation time to correct for the watermark values. We chose the latter course as being more secure. Our installation mechanism uses an "intelligent patching" process, in which both watermarks and correctors for the self-checking mechanism are placed into a set of patches on the server side. These patches are sent to the client, which patches the code to produce a working executable. The patches contain no information about the code outside the patches. This minimizes security risks on the client, time and space transferring the patch lists, and time and space on the server, for maintaining and computing patch lists. This design led to a choice of linear hash functions for the self-checking mechanism. If copy-specific watermarking is not used, or an entire copy of the executable can be delivered at installation time, then the patching mechanism is not needed.

4.2 Testers

The heart of the self-checking mechanism is a collection of *testers*, each of which computes a hash (a pseudo-random many-one mapping) of a contiguous section of the code region and compares the computed hash value to the correct value. An incorrect value triggers the response mechanism.

To set the testing frequency and the size of the code tested by each tester, we need to balance performance, security, and stealth objectives. Experiments on a set of Pentium processors for a variety of linear hashes suggested that performance is relatively invariant until the size of the code interval being tested exceeds the size of the L2 cache. With our Pentium II processors we observed a marked deterioration of performance when the code interval size exceeded 512 kilobytes. Breaking the computation into pieces also addresses our threat model and meets our design objectives. It makes the self-checking mechanism stealthier. The testers execute quickly, without observable interruption to the program execution. Each of our testers, therefore, tests a contiguous section that is a few hundred kilobytes long.

A single tester, when executed, completely computes the hash value for its assigned interval and tests the result. We considered more distributed alternatives, in which a single call of a tester would only partially compute a hash value. Aucsmith promotes this type of design in his Integrity Verification Kernel, a self-checking mechanism proposed in [ ]. He promotes the use of *interleaved tasks* that perform only partial checking computations. With such an alternative, either a single tester or several different testers are responsible for the complete computation of the hash of an interval. We rejected such alternatives as being more complicated and less stealthy, in that they require storage of extra state information (the partially computed hash function).

An important design decision was where to store the correct hash values. One possibility is with the testers themselves. This poses a security risk. Because the self-checking mechanism tests the entire code and watermarks differ among different copies of the code, many of the hash values will differ among copies. In the absence of code customization (which creates drastically different versions of the code), the hash values can be exposed by a collusion attack, in which different copies of the code are compared. Storing the hash values with the testers thus potentially exposes the testers to a collusion attack. Another difficulty is the circularity that may arise if testers are testing regions that include testers and their hash values: there may be no consistent way to assign correct hash values, or such an assignment may exist, but be very difficult to compute.

Another possibility that avoids both of these problems (revealing the testers by collusion and circularity of hash value assignments) is to store the hash values in the data section. But then the hash values themselves are unprotected from change, since the self-checking mechanism does not check the data section. We could avoid this problem by dividing the data section into fixed data and variable data, storing the hash values in the fixed data section, and testing the fixed data section, but this alternative may still be less secure than the one we have chosen.

We chose a third alternative, in which each hash interval has a variable word, called a *corrector*. A corrector can be set to an arbitrary value, and is set so that the interval hashes to a fixed value for the particular hash function used by the tester testing the interval. Collusion can reveal the correctors, but does not reveal the testers. Since the correctors are themselves tested, changing them is not an easy job for an attacker. Each tested interval has its own corrector, and is tested by exactly one tester. Aucsmith's testers (IVK's), although encrypted, are vulnerable to discovery by collusive attacks because the testers themselves are unique in each different copy of the protected software.

We experimented with multiple testers testing the same interval but rejected this approach as being overly complicated and not providing additional security.

Another important design decision is how to trigger the execution of the testers. We chose to let them be triggered by normal program execution, sprinkling them in-line in the existing code. Alternatives include having one or more separate tester threads, or triggering testers by function calls, exceptions, or some other specific events. We rejected the latter mechanisms as being insufficiently stealthy. Having separate tester threads in combination with an in-line triggering mechanism deserves further study, as it may provide additional security through diversity.

A third design decision was the choice of hash functions. We used chained linear hash functions: linearity was important to make installation easy. Because the actual hash values are not known until installation time, partial hash values had to be pre-computed and later combined with the values of the software watermarks. We chose to use multiple hash functions, so that knowing a hash interval and a corrector site is still not enough information to set a corrector value to compensate for a code change.

4.3   Testing Pattern

We cover the entire executable code section with overlapping intervals, each of which is tested by a single tester. The overlap factor (number of different testing intervals containing a particular byte) is six for most bytes. The testers are randomly assigned to the intervals. The high overlap plus the random assignment provide a high degree of security for the testing mechanism: changing even a single bit requires disabling a large fraction of the testers to avoid detection, even if some of the testers are ineffective because they are executed infrequently.

4.4   Correctors and Intervals

Each interval requires its own corrector, whose value can be set so that the interval hashes to zero. In our current implementation, each corrector is a single 32-bit unsigned integer. We place correctors in-between basic code blocks using post-compilation binary manipulation. Everything between basic blocks is dead code; control will never be transferred to the correctors. An alternative would be to insert correctors as live code no-ops. We chose the former approach as being simpler and possibly stealthier, but this issue deserves further study.

Correctors are inserted as uniformly as possible throughout the code. Intervals are then constructed based on the desired degree of interval overlap, using randomization to select interval endpoints between appropriate correctors. This construction is such that it is possible to fill in corrector values in a left-to-right pass to make each of the intervals hash to zero. That is, there are no circular dependencies in the equations defining the corrector values. Since our hash functions are linear, an alternative approach is to allow such circularities and to solve the resulting (sparse) system of linear equations to compute corrector values. This alternative deserves further study.

Computing corrector values requires invertible hash functions, since we must work backwards from the desired hash value to the needed corrector value. This issue is discussed further below.

4.5   Tamper Response

A final component of our self-checking technology is the mechanism that invokes action if tampering is detected. In our current implementation each tester calls a tamper response mechanism directly via a simple function call.

We considered several alternative, indirect response mechanisms that appear to be promising. One of our primary objectives for the response mechanism is to avoid passing the execution of a response through a single point of failure. One of our primary integration objectives, however, was to make our mechanism easy to combine with other software protection mechanisms. Thus in our initial implementation we opted to use a simple direct response mechanism. Stealthier, more robust response mechanisms would use multiple access paths with a variable number of steps and running time. Such mechanisms are a subject of future work.

5   Tester Design and Placement

The function of a tester is to map a large interval of the executable (several hundred kilobytes) into a relatively small set of values (32 bits) by an easy-to-compute but "scrambling" map, a hash function. The idea is that any change to the interval being hashed will change the value returned by the tester and hence result in detection if the tester output is compared to the correct hash value. Of course, there is some probability of a changed interval mapping to the correct value, but with a good choice of hash function this chance will be vanishingly small (2^{-32}).

In this section we describe the design of our testers, including the objectives that went into the design. We also describe the approach we used to place the testers in the code.

5.1   Design Objectives

Our tester design was based on the following objectives.

- **Lightweight Hash Functions** Part of our design goal was that executing the tester mechanism should not have a substantial impact on program performance. This suggested the use of lightweight hash functions, combining an additive chaining mechanism with a simple 32-bit mapping that uses a few arithmetic or logical operations. In addition to being fast, simple hash functions were judged to be stealthier than standard hash functions such as CRC32 or SHA, since they consist of very short sequences of instructions.
- **Multiple Hash Functions** As a defense against an attack based on knowing the hash function, we thought it valuable to have multiple hash functions, randomly selected. A multiplicity of lightweight hash functions was judged to be sufficiently secure for our needs; cryptographically strong hash functions buy us little or nothing here.
- **Summarizable Hash Functions** Because watermark values and corrector values are computed in a final pass, at installation time, performance considerations dictated that partial hash functions be easily summarizable. This issue, which arose because of installation constraints, is discussed in more detail in Section 5.2.
- **Stealthy Testers** We wanted the testers to be hard to find by manual or automatic code inspection. In particular, they should look like any other part of the executable. Obfuscation techniques applied to the executable could conceivably help hide the testers. Short testers were judged to be stealthier than long testers.
- **Resistance to Auto-collusion** In an auto-collusion attack, the finding of one tester is used to help find others, based on their similarity to the first. To make an auto-collusion attack harder, we favored short customized testers. Ideally, each tester should be as different from the others as possible.
- **Obfuscated Address Calculation** A vulnerability of testers is that they load bytes from the code, which "normal" code does not do. We required that code-section addresses never appear in any general-purpose register during the calculation, thus complicating a "sampling" attack, in which the contents of the registers and the stack are monitored for suspicious values such as code-section addresses. Complex addressing modes provide one way of implementing this idea.
- **Harmless to Development** Testers are inserted into the source code and later (post-compilation) "stamped" with the start and end addresses of the intervals to be hashed. Unstamped testers should not trigger the response mechanism, so that unstamped testers are harmless to program development.

5.2   Linear Hash Functions

We did performance-testing with several lightweight hash functions built from one or more arithmetic or logical operations. We compared the performance of each hash function with CRC32, a standard 32-bit chained hash function. Our sample hash functions ran 8-10 times faster than CRC32. We built "debug" testers using an "exclusive-or" chained hash function. The debug testers ran in 1-2 milliseconds per 128k bytes on a 200 Mhz Pentium. This is an upper bound on the expected performance of production testers, since the debug testers gathered extra information for use in our development. The debug testers were certainly fast enough that adding our self-checking mechanism to a program would not significantly impact its performance.

The requirements of invertibility and summarizability led us to the use of chained linear hash functions. In particular, given an interval of data d, consisting of the words $d_1, d_2, \ldots d_n$, the value $h_n(d)$ of the hash function on d is defined recursively by $h_0(d) = 0, h_i(d) = c * (d_i + h_{i-1}(d))$ for $0 < i \leq n$, where c is a suitably chosen non-zero multiplier that defines the hash function. Such a hash function is easily invertible, since we have $h_{(i-1)}(d) = h_i(d)/c - d_i$ for $0 < i \leq n$,which can be used recursively to compute $h_i(d)$ for any value of i, given $h_n(d)$.

Furthermore, the hash function is easily summarizable in the following sense. If we generalize the recurrence defining h to $h_0(x, d) = x, h_i(x, d) = c * (d_i + h_{i-1}(x, d))$, and view d as a constant vector and x as a variable, then $h_n(x, d)$ is a linear function of x. Namely, $h_n(x, d) = a_n(d)x + b_n(d)$, where a_n and b_n are defined recursively by $a_0(d) = 1, b_0(d) = 0, a_i(d) = c * a_{i-1}(d), b_i(d) = c * (d_i + b_{i-1}(d))$, for $0 < i \leq n$. Finally, the inverse function of h_n is also linear, and can be defined recursively in a similar way.

Invertibility and summarizability mean that, given an interval that is mostly constant but has certain variable words (watermark slots) and a single "corrector" word, we can precompute a representation of the hash function that requires space linear in the number of watermark slots. Given values for the watermark slots, we can then compute a value for the corrector that makes the entire interval hash to zero, in time proportional to the number of watermark slots. The precomputation time to construct the summary of the hash function is linear in the length of the interval. This computation is the final step in activating the testers. One problem in the actual corrector computation for Intel x86 executables is that the corrector is not necessarily aligned on a word boundary relative to the start and end of the hashed interval. This can, however, be handled, at a cost of complicating the calculation. Another possibility, which we did not choose, is to explicitly align the correctors, if necessary by providing 7-byte corrector slots rather than 4-byte slots.

The constant multipliers used to define our hash functions were chosen from a small set that allowed the hash computation to be performed without an explicit multiply instruction. Our particular construction resulted in a collection of 30 possible hash functions, corresponding to different multipliers. To expand the set of possible hash functions, we could have included an additive constant in the hash function (either by redefining the initial condition to be $h_0(d) = r$ or by redefining the recurrence to be $h_i(d) = c * (d_i + h_{i-1}(d) + r)$, for $0 < i \leq n$). This would increase the set of possible hash functions to $30 * 2^{32}$ and might be something to explore in the future. For now, having 30 different hash functions was judged to be sufficiently secure, because an attacker must know not only the hash function but the start and end of the hashed interval, which seems as hard to determine as finding the tester itself.

5.3   Tester Construction and Customization

To help make our testers stealthy, we implemented a tester prototype in C and compiled it to get an assembly-language tester prototype. By doing this, we hoped to minimize the presence of unstealthy assembly-language constructs, specifically those that would not be generated by a compiler. However, in order to make the resulting testers practical, we made three modifications to this compiled tester prototype. First, we modified the prototype so that an unstamped tester would not call the response mechanism. Second, we added an obfuscation variable to the address calculations to guarantee that no code-section address would ever appear in a general-purpose register during the running of a tester (indicating a read of a code-section address). Third, we simplified the tester slightly.

Then, we applied a variety of customizations to guarantee that each tester had a unique code sequence, thus increasing the difficulty of an auto-collusion attack. These customizations included changing the multiplier defining the hash function and the exact instructions used to compute the hash function, shuffling the basic blocks of the tester, inverting the jump logic of conditional jumps, reordering instructions within basic blocks, permuting the registers used, and doing customization of individual instructions. The result was a set of 2,916,864 distinct tester implementations, each occupying less than 50 bytes.

5.4   Tester Placement

As discussed in Section 4.2, we chose to place testers in-line in the code and have them fire as they are reached during normal execution. Our goal for tester firing is that testers execute frequently enough that most or all of the code is tested often during normal execution, but not so often that tester firing causes a significant efficiency degradation. In order to place testers most effectively to realize these conflicting performance goals, we used source-level tester placement. Our tester placement strategy required significant manual effort. With more advanced software tools, the process could become more automated.

Our goal was to insert the various individual testers in source program functions so that the testers executed to meet coverage objectives in what we deemed to be typical program runs. To achieve this we used profiling tools to count function executions during runs of a several-megabyte test executable. We discarded functions not run at least once during start-up and at least once after start-up. We ordered the remaining functions in increasing order by execution frequency, and inserted testers into the functions in order, one tester per function, until the desired number of testers, around 200, were inserted.

This placement of testers, when combined with our method of interval construction and tester-to-interval connection, resulted in acceptable dynamic testing coverage, as we discuss in Section 6. A significant drawback, however, is that the testers are bunched in the executable, because they tend to be inserted into library functions that appear together in the executable. To overcome this problem, we relied on block-shuffling of the executable to disperse the testers more uniformly.

A straightforward analysis, which we omit here, shows that random shuffling of code blocks, assuming uniform block size and at most one tester per block, results in a maximum gap between testers that exceeds exactly equal spacing by a logarithmic factor. We deemed this adequate to provide the desired amount of testing robustness. (See Section 6.) We could achieve much more uniform spacing of testers by taking the location of the testers into account when doing the shuffling, or inserting the testers into the object code instead of the source code. This is a subject for future investigation.

6   Interval Construction

In addition to the testers, the other component of the self-checking mechanism is the code intervals over which the testers compute hash functions. Recall that we desire these intervals to provide uniform, redundant coverage of the entire executable and to be hard to discover. Also, each interval requires its own corrector, which must be able to be set so that the interval hashes to zero. Finally, there must be a global ordering of the correctors that allows them to be set sequentially, without circular dependencies.

We chose to base the interval construction on corrector placement. With this approach, interval construction consists of three steps: corrector placement, interval definition, and assignment of testers to intervals. We discuss these three steps in Sections 6.1–6.3. In Section 6.3 we also discuss the robustness of the resulting overlapping checking mechanism. In each section, we discuss alternatives to our current approach, both those we did and those we did not try.

6.1   Corrector Placement

We need one interval, and hence one corrector, per tester. Since we want the intervals to be approximately of equal size and approximately uniformly spaced, we want the correctors to be approximately uniformly spaced as well. Our current method of corrector placement is a second-generation design that inserts correctors as dead code (between basic blocks) once basic block shuffling is completed.

It is illuminating to consider our original design, which used source-code insertion, to understand the virtues of the current method. In our original design, and our original implementation, a very large number of correctors, consisting of obfuscated NOPs, were inserted into the source code by including them in appropriately chosen source-language functions. In the absence of basic-block shuffling, the distribution of these correctors is extremely non-uniform; indeed, the correctors are often clumped closely together. We therefore relied on shuffling of basic blocks to provide a much more uniform distribution of correctors in the executable. Even random shuffling does not produce uniformly spaced correctors; the corrector gaps have a Poisson distribution, which implies that the expected maximum gap size is a logarithmic factor greater than the average gap size. To overcome this problem we inserted many more correctors than needed (at least a logarithmic factor more) and used a "pruning" step to select a small subset of correctors that we actually used.

Although we implemented this method and demonstrated its effectiveness in practice, it has at least three drawbacks: the insertion of many more correctors than needed, the extra computation step of corrector pruning, and the need to carefully place correctors in replicated functions in the source code to make sure there are enough correctors in the executable. It was the last drawback that made us replace this corrector insertion method with the one described below. In the course of our experiments, we discovered that the correctors were being inserted into code that was never executed. Eliminating this dead code significantly shrank the size of our test executable but left us with no convenient place in the source code to put the correctors.

We therefore replaced our corrector insertion method with an executable-based insertion method. Specifically, the correctors are inserted after the blocks are shuffled. This approach has some significant advantages over the source-code-based insertion scheme. It gives us fine-grained control over the positioning of the correctors in the executable. We can insert correctors as dead code (between basic blocks) instead of, or in addition to, as obfuscated NOPs. Dead-code correctors can consist just of the 32 correction bits, rather than forming valid instructions or instruction sequences. We also can dispense with the corrector pruning step (although we left this step in our current implementation: it provides possibly redundant smoothing of the corrector distribution).

In detail, the corrector placement process works as follows. Word-length (32 bit) corrector slots are inserted at the end of basic blocks (after unconditional jump instructions). We chose a gross number of corrector slots to insert (before pruning). To determine where to insert the correctors, we count the total number of usable basic blocks for insertion and divided by the number of correctors. If the result is k, we insert a corrector after each k basic blocks.

We then prune the correctors down to the set actually used, as follows. While we have too many correctors, we apply the following step to remove a corrector: find the two adjacent correctors closest together (in bytes) and eliminate the one whose removal creates the smallest new gap. This algorithm can be implemented efficiently using a heap (priority queue) data structure to keep track of the gap sizes, at a logarithmic cost per deleted corrector. In our current performance run, we use 1000 as the gross number of correctors and about 200 as the number of testers and net number of correctors.

An improved design, which we leave for future work, is to space the correctors using a byte count (instead of a block count) and to eliminate the pruning step entirely. We also would like to investigate whether insertion of testers inside basic blocks, rather than just between basic blocks, provides sufficient additional uniformity as to be worthwhile. (Since basic blocks are extremely small compared to interval lengths, we doubt it.) An interesting research question is to devise an efficient algorithm to insert k correctors among n basic blocks so as to minimize the maximum gap (in bytes) between correctors (assuming dummy correctors exist at the start and end of the code).

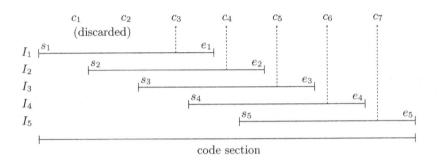

Fig. 1. Illustration of interval construction for n=5 and k=3

6.2   Interval Definition

We define the intervals to be tested based on the placement of the correctors, using random choice of interval endpoints between appropriate correctors to help make it hard for an attacker to determine these endpoints. In addition we use a *overlap factor* $k \geq 1$, such that most bytes in the executable will be covered by k intervals. Currently, we use an overlap factor of 6.

Suppose we desire n test intervals $I_i, 1 \leq i \leq n$. Then we will use $n + k - 1$ correctors, of which $k - 1$ will be discarded. Label the correctors $c_1, c_2, ..., c_{n+k-1}$ in the order they occur in the executable. We choose a start s_i and end e_i for each of the intervals, as follows. Start s_1 is at the beginning of the code section, and end e_n is at the end of the code section. For i in the range $1 < i \leq k$, we choose s_i uniformly at random between c_{i-1} and c_i and e_{n-i+2} uniformly at random between c_{n+k-i} and $c_{n+k-i+1}$. For i in the range $k < i \leq n$, we choose two points uniformly at random between c_{i-1} and c_i. The smaller point is s_i and the larger point is e_{i-k}. We then associate corrector c_{k+i} with interval I_i, and discard the first $k - 1$ correctors. The construction is illustrated in Figure 1.

This choice of intervals has two important properties. Except near the beginning and end of the code section, every byte of the code is contained in k (or possibly $k+1$) test intervals. The first corrector in test interval I_i is c_{i+k-1}, which means that we can set corrector values in the order $c_k, c_{k+1}, \ldots c_{n+k-1}$ to make successive intervals $I_1, I_2, \ldots, I_n$ hash correctly without having later corrector settings invalidate earlier settings. That is, there are no circular dependencies.

The ends of the code section are not covered as redundantly as the rest of the code. We do not think this affects the robustness of the testing mechanism in any significant way. It is easy to modify the interval construction scheme so that the corrector setting works from the two ends of the code toward the middle, so that the non-redundant coverage occurs in the middle. We could choose the region of non-redundant coverage randomly, or to be unimportant code. Also, as noted in Section 4.4, we could modify the interval construction to allow circularities and solve the resulting system of linear equations to get corrector values. Such a method would be even more robust. Modifying our scheme along these lines is a topic for future research.

6.3   Assignment of Testers to Intervals

Once intervals are constructed, the next step is to assign testers to the intervals. The objectives of this assignment are coverage and security. We want each byte to be tested often as the code is running, and we want to force an attacker to disable many or most testers to successfully modify even a single byte of the program without detection. Our approach to accomplishing these goals is to harness the power of randomization: we assign each tester to a different interval using a random permutation to define the assignment.

Both experimental and theoretical evidence suggest that a random assignment is a good one. Our theoretical evidence is based on our intuition and on theorems about random graphs in the literature. An interesting area for future research is to develop a mathematical theory, with proofs, about the performance of random tester assignment. For now, we rely on the following observations.

First, almost every byte in the code is covered by k testing intervals and hence tested by k testers. With random assignment, the most important bytes will be redundantly tested, even if a significant fraction of the testers are ineffective because of infrequent execution.

Our second and third observations concern a graph, *the tester graph*, that models the pattern of testers testing other testers. The vertices of the graph are testers. The graph contains an edge from tester A to tester B if tester B is contained in the interval tested by tester A. (Our construction of intervals allows the possibility that an interval boundary might be in the middle of a tester. In such a case the graph would not contain the corresponding edge. We could easily modify our interval construction to move interval boundaries outside of testers. Whether this is worth doing is a subject for future research.)

Suppose that all testers are effective (i.e., they execute frequently when the program is running normally). Suppose further that an attacker modifies a byte of the program that is in an interval tested by tester X. Then, to avoid detection, the attacker must disable every tester Y such that there is a path from Y to X in the tester graph. Suppose the tester graph is *strongly connected*; that is, there is a path from every vertex to every other vertex. Then a successful attack, changing even a single byte, would require disabling *every* tester.

We thus would like the tester graph to be strongly connected. With our method of interval construction and random tester assignment, the tester graph is strongly connected with high probability. This is true as long as the intervals are sufficiently uniform and the redundancy factor k is sufficiently high. Experiments confirmed that the number of components drops rapidly as k increases. For small values of k, there is one large component and a small number of single node components. (Thus it is close to strongly connected.)

If strong connectivity were the only desired property of the tester graph, random assignment would not be necessary. We could, for example, guarantee strong connectivity by embedding a large cycle in the tester graph. Strong connectivity is not enough to guarantee the robustness of the testing mechanism, however. For example, if the tester graph consists only of one big cycle and some testers are ineffective (meaning they are in parts of code that do not get executed during an attack), then the effective tester graph consists of disconnected pieces, and (hypothetically) certain parts of the program may be attacked by disabling only a few testers.

A stronger connectivity property is that, even if a fraction of the testers are ineffective, a single byte change would require disabling many or most of the effective testers to avoid detection. This kind of robust connectivity is related to the expansion property, which is possessed by certain random graphs. "Expansion" means that there is a constant factor $\alpha > 1$, such that for any subset X of at most a constant fraction of the vertices, at least $\alpha|X|$ other vertices have edges into X. Expansion implies both strong and robust connectivity, depending on α. The possession of this property by random graphs is the main reason we used random tester assignment. The expansion property is hard to test empirically (doing so takes exponential time), so we have not verified that our tester graphs possess it. Nor have we done a careful theoretical analysis (which would yield very conservative constant factors). This is future research. We are confident, however, that our tester graphs possess sufficiently robust connectivity, and we hope to investigate this issue further.

7 Summary and Future Work

We have designed and built a dynamic software self-checking mechanism suitable to protect client-side software running in a potentially hostile environment. It is designed to be used in conjunction with other tamper-resistance techniques, and integrated with static copy-specific software watermarking.

Directions for future research include building a stealthier response mechanism that would add an additional layer between response detection and response reporting, doing further experimental and theoretical work on the coverage and robustness of the self-checking mechanism, modifying and simplifying the corrector insertion step, and developing additional hash functions, customizations, and obfuscations for the testers. A more speculative but potentially interesting direction is to investigate non-hash-based checking, in which, for example, the testing mechanism checks that correct values are stored in certain registers at certain times. Other directions include exploring other triggering mechanisms for the testers, e.g., executing some of them as separate threads, investigating temporally-distributed testers, and studying hash-based methods that do not use correctors.

References

1. D. Aucsmith. Tamper resistant software: An implementation. In R. J. Anderson, editor, *Information Hiding, Lecture Notes in Computer Science 1174*, pages 317–333. Springer-Verlag, 1996. 143, 148

2. H. Chang and M. Atallah. Protecting software by guards. This volume. 143

3. S. T. Chow, Y. Gu, H. J. Johnson, and V. A. Zakharov. An approach to the obfuscation of control–flow of sequential computer programs. In G. I. Davida and Y. Frankel, editors, *ISC 2001, Lecture Notes in Computer Science 2200*, pages 144–155. Springer-Verlag, 2001. 142

4. C. Collberg and C. Thomborson. Software watermarking: Models and dynamic embeddings. In *Principles of Programming Languages, San Antonio, TX*, pages 311–324, January 1999. 143

5. C. Collberg and C. Thomborson. Watermarking, tamper-proofing, obfuscation – Tools for software protection. Technical Report 2000–03, University of Arizona, February 2000. 143

6. C. Collberg, C. Thomborson, and D. Low. A taxonomy of obfuscating transformations. Technical Report 148, University of Auckland, 1997. 142

7. C. Collberg, C. Thomborson, and D. Low. Breaking abstractions and unstructuring data structures. In *IEEE International Conference on Computer Languages, Chicago, IL*, pages 28–38, May 1998. 142

8. C. Collberg, C. Thomborson, and D. Low. Manufacturing cheap, resilient and stealthy opaque constructs. In *Principles of Programming Languages 1998, San Diego, CA*, pages 184–196, January 1998. 142

9. R. Davidson and N. Myhrvold. Method and systems for generating and auditing a signature for a computer program, September 1996. US Patent 5,559,884. Assignee: Microsoft Corporation. 143

10. G. Morrisett, D. Walker, K. Crary, and N. Glew. From system F to typed assembly language. *ACM Transactions on Programming Languages and Systems*, 21(3):528–569, May 1999. 142

11. G. C. Necula. *Compiling with proofs*. PhD thesis, Carnegie Mellon University, September 1998. 142

12. G. C. Necula and P. Lee. Safe kernel extensions without run–time checking. In *Proceedings of the Second Symposium on Operating Systems Design and Implementation, Seattle, WA*, pages 229–243, October 1996. 142

13. J. R. Nickerson, S. T. Chow, and H. J. Johnson. Tamper resistant software: extending trust into a hostile environment. In *Multimedia and Security Workshop at ACM Multimedia 2001, Ottawa, CA*, October 2001. 142

14. T. Sander and C. Tschudin. Protecting mobile agents against malicious hosts. In *Mobile Agents and Security, Lecture Notes in Computer Science 1419*. Springer-Verlag, 1998. 142

15. C. Wang. *A security architecture of survivable systems*. PhD thesis, Department of Computer Science, University of Virginia, 2001. 142

16. C. Wang, J. Davidson, J. Hill, and J. Knight. Protection of software–based survivability mechanisms. In *IEEE/IFIP International Conference on Dependable Systems and Networks, Goteborg, Sweden*, July 2001. 142

17. C. Wang, J. Hill, J. Knight, and J. Davidson. Software tamper resistance: Obstructing the static analysis of programs. Technical Report CS–2000–12, Department of Computer Science, University of Virginia, 2000. 142

Protecting Software Code by Guards*

Hoi Chang and Mikhail J. Atallah

[1] CERIAS, Purdue University
1315 Recitation Building, West Lafayette, IN 47907, USA
[2] Arxan Technologies, Inc.
3000 Kent Ave., Suite 1D-107, W. Lafayette, IN 47906, USA
{changh,mja}@cerias.purdue.edu

Abstract. Protection of software code against illegitimate modifications by its users is a pressing issue to many software developers. Many software-based mechanisms for protecting program code are too weak (e.g., they have single points of failure) or too expensive to apply (e.g., they incur heavy runtime performance penalty to the protected programs). In this paper, we present and explore a methodology that we believe can protect program integrity in a more tamper-resilient and flexible manner. Our approach is based on a distributed scheme, in which protection and tamper-resistance of program code is achieved, not by a single security module, but by a network of (smaller) security units that work together in the program. These security units, or *guards*, can be programmed to do certain tasks (checksumming the program code is one example) and a network of them can reinforce the protection of each other by creating mutual-protection. We have implemented a system for automating the process of installing guards into Win32 executables[1]. It is because our system operates on binaries that we are able to apply our protection mechanism to EXEs and DLLs. Experimental results show that memory space and runtime performance impacts incurred by guards can be kept very low (as explained later in the paper).

1 Introduction

Software cracking is a serious threat to many in the software industry. It is the problem in which a *cracker*, having obtained a copy of the software he wants to attack, succeeds in breaking the protection that comes built into it. Typically, crackers would create modified versions of the software, or *crackz*, whose copy protection or usage control mechanisms have been disabled. Cracked software can then be illegally redistributed to the public, exacerbating the software piracy problem. With commerce and distribution of copyrighted multi-media rapidly moving online, the need for software protection is even more urgent than before:

---

* Portions of this work were supported by sponsors of CERIAS and the Purdue Trask fund.
[1] A US patent on the technology has been filed by Purdue University and licensed to Arxan Technologies, Inc.

T. Sander (Ed.): DRM 2001, LNCS 2320, pp. 160–175, 2002.
© Springer-Verlag Berlin Heidelberg 2002

client software code running on untrusted machines has to be secured against tampering.

What makes software cracking so widespread is in part caused by the simplicity of direct inspection and modification of binary program code with existing software debugging and editing tools. Here is an example of how a program requiring online registration can typically be cracked. The program would normally go through a long sequence of procedures asking for a registration serial number from its user, and then in a stealthy manner, comparing a function of the true serial number with the same function of the entered one. After comparing these two items, however, the program then ends up deciding the authenticity of the software user with one single instruction, typically a conditional branch that decides whether the software can henceforth be used. To defeat the entire registration scheme, one only needs to replace that single instruction in the binary file with an unconditional jump (that jumps to a desired location), or by a sequence of smaller no-ops (that do nothing except letting the execution flow to the desired location naturally). The problem with this protection scheme is that the branch instruction is a single point of failure. With sophisticated program debuggers and hex editors (such as SoftICE [ ] and HIEW), attackers are able to trace targeted parts of the program, pinpoint the code they need to compromise, and finally apply changes to the program files.

Many commercial protection schemes employ what we call monolithic protection schemes, in which protection is enforced by a single code module in the program but which is loosely attached to the program and thus can be disengaged easily (using methods similar to the above example).

How can software be perfectly secured against cracking? This looks like an impossible task *if* one interprets "cracking" as "eventually cracking", i.e., after a long time. The fact that crackers have huge cracking resources makes successful attacks possible after a long enough time (because they could rewrite the software from scratch after sufficient analyses of the code). However, it is possible to "raise the bar" for attackers and make it *sufficiently secure*. Because many software developers only hope for a minimum length of time during which they could sell a large enough number of a newly released product, securing software code until the end of the period is cost-effective.

Protection mechanisms that can effectively protect software running in untrusted environments should have the following properties:

- **Resilience**: The protection has no single points of failure and is hard to disable.
- **Self-defense**: Able to detect and take actions against tampering (i.e., code modification).
- **Configurability**: Protection is customizable and can be made as strong as one needs.
- **White-box security**: Because any scheme for protection is likely to become publicly known over time, its strength should not be based on its secrecy but rather on the knowledge of a secret key used at protection-install time (but not stored anywhere within the protected program).

This paper describes a security framework and system (having the above desirable properties) for protecting program code against tampering. We extend the traditional ideas of having code check and modify itself to a general setting, in which a program is protected by a multitude of such functional units (called guards) integrated with the program. To defend themselves against attacks, guards form a network by which they protect each other in an interlocking manner. The network of guards is harder to defeat because security is shared among all the guards, and each of them is potentially guarded by other guards. The fact that there are many ways to form a guards network, makes it hard for attackers to predict its form. Furthermore, more guards can always be added to the program if a greater level of protection is desired.

We believe that this guarding framework can advance the state of software protection by making protection schemes derived from it more sophisticated than existing schemes, and easier to apply. Using our system, we show that protecting programs using this guarding framework is possible. Also, we show that the guarding process can be automated (so that it will become unnecessary for one to go through a laborious and error-prone process of manually guarding the program code).

The paper is organized as follows. Section 2 provides some related work in this field. In section 3, we describe the protection framework and discuss its security issues. In section 4, we introduce the system we built. This is then followed by experimental results in section 5. The final section concludes and describes enhancements to the system that are currently being implemented.

2   Related Work

The protection mechanisms for software protection involve two main approaches to the problem: hardware-based protection (which relies on secured hardware devices for protection), and software-based protection (which only relies on software mechanisms for protection).

One hardware solution is the use of secure coprocessors (or processors) [18,19,15]. In secure coprocessors, programs or portions of them can be run encrypted, so their code is never revealed in untrusted memory. Thus secure coprocessors can provide the programs isolated execution environments that are difficult to tamper with. Although tamper-resistant, this approach requires the use of special hardware for executing programs, which may not be cost-effective for widespread use (say, in typical home-user environments).

Using smart cards for software protection is another solution [2,10]. Since smart cards contain both secure storage and processing power (although some only provide secure storage), security-sensitive computations and data can be processed and stored inside the cards. A major difference between smart cards and secure coprocessors is that the former are resource-tight (i.e., limited storage space and processing power), and can be used to protect only small fragments of code and data.

Dongles have long been in use by the industry for software protection. They are the hardware keys plugged in the computer, without which the programs that came with the dongles cannot execute. The major drawback of dongles is that each dongle-enabled software usually requires a different dongle. Moreover, the protection can often be bypassed because the communication traffic between dongles and their programs can be intercepted and modified.

One software-based approach for protection is code obfuscation, which "scrambles up" program code so that it results in some executable code that has the same functionality as the original but is difficult to understand and analyze [11,5,8,4,12,13,7,17]. This form of protection is more flexible than the hardware-based one because it does not require special execution environments. But exactly how secure it is is still a matter of debate [ ].

There are other software-based approaches to the problem as well. These include the use of self-modifying code [ ] (code that generates other code at run-time) and code encryption and decryption [ ] (partially encrypted code self-decrypting at run-time). A hybrid approach of the above has been proposed by Aucsmith [ ], which involves the use of cryptographic means to decrypt and encrypt a window of security-sensitive program instructions before and after each execution round of those instructions. One of the problems with this approach is that it does not scale well as the size of the above-mentioned "window" gets large (because of the time taken by encryption and decryption).

3   The Guarding Framework

In this section, we describe our guarding framework and explore some of its security issues on an informal basis.

3.1   Guards

In our guarding framework, protection is provided by a network of execution units (or *guards*) embedded within a program. Each guard is a piece of code responsible for performing certain security-related actions during program execution. Guards can be programmed to do any computations, and the following are two useful ones:

- **Checksum code** [2]: Checksum another piece of program code at runtime and verify its integrity (i.e., check if it has been tampered with). If the guarded code is found altered, the guard will trigger whichever sequence of actions is desired for the situation, ranging from the mildest of silently logging the detection event, to the extreme of making the software unusable (e.g., by halting its execution, or better yet, causing an eventual crash that will be hard to trace back to the guard). If no code changes are detected, the program execution proceeds normally. Programs guarded by checksumming guards are made, in some sense, "self-aware" of their own integrity.

---

[2] In this paper, "code" refers to both the runtime data and executable code of a program.

– **Repair code**: Restore a piece of damaged code to its original form before it is executed or used (as data). One way to achieve code repairing is to overwrite tampered code with a clean copy of it stored elsewhere. This repairing action effectively eliminates the changes done to the code by an attacker, and allows the program to run as if unmodified. Repairing guards provide a program with "self-healing" capabilities.

3.2   Guards Network

A group of guards can work together and implement a sophisticated protection scheme that is more resilient against attacks than a single guard. For example, if a program has multiple pieces of code whose integrity needs to be protected, then it can deploy multiple checksumming guards for protecting the different pieces. Besides sharing the load of protection, guards have the flexibility to protect one another. Figure 1 shows a possible guarding scenario in which two security-sensitive regions of a program, C_1 and C_2, are protected by both checksumming and repairing guards. Figure (a) shows the memory image of the guarded program, in which C_1 and C_2 are guarded by guards $G_1, \ldots, G_5$ in an interlocking manner. The corresponding guarding relationships can be more clearly depicted by a *guard graph* in Figure 1 (b), where C_1 is repaired by G_3 before C_1 executes, and the repaired C_1 will subsequently be also checksummed by G_1 and G_5 (but G_2 will repair G_5 before G_5 executes).

In order to perform their duties, a network of guards need to be placed into the program and hooked to its execution flows in an appropriate way. For example, a repairing guard has to be inserted into a point in the control flow that is to be reached first (in execution order) before the guarded code is reached; i.e., a repairing guard has to *dominate* the target code in their control-flow locations. On the other hand, a checksumming guard must be installed at a point at whose execution time the code to be checksummed must be present in the program image. Figure 2 (a) shows a graph that depicts the dominance relationships between different pairs of the nodes in Figure 1 (e.g., $G_3 \rightarrow G_1$ means location of G_3 dominates that of G_1).

Figure 2 (b) shows two possible scenarios in which the network of guards can be installed into the control flow graph of a program without violating the partial ordering of their executions specified in (a). As seen from the figure, the larger a program, the more ways there are to deploy the network of guards.

3.3   Security

Contrary to monolithic protection schemes in which security is enforced by single security modules, protection by guards enjoys the following advantages:

– **Distributedness**. There is no single point of entry (exit) into (out of) the guards network because its individual components (i.e., guards) are invoked at different points at runtime. This makes it much harder for an attacker to detach the network from the program. To defeat the guards, their locations

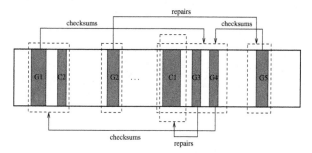

(a) Memory layout of the guarded program

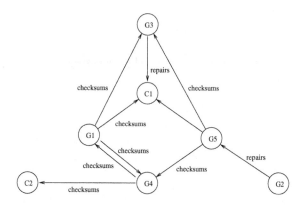

(b) The corresponding guard graph

Fig. 1. Program image guarded by five guards and the corresponding guard graph

and guarding relationships need to be identified (an even more difficult task if the program is large and complex).

- **Multiplicity**. Multiple guards can be used to guard a single piece of code, providing it a variety of protection at different times.
- **Dynamism**. There are many ways in which a guards network can be configured. For example, a group of ten guards can form different types of formations, ranging from simple trees to general directed graphs with cycles. Even if one knows the general mechanism for guarding programs, one is still faced with the actual deployment scheme in the program. Furthermore, a fixed formation can be installed in various ways because parameters such as the physical locations of guards and the exact ranges of code they guard could vary from installation to installation. (Consider that each installation is driven by a different random number.)
- **Scalability**. It is easy for the levels of guarding to be scaled up for larger or more security-critical programs by adding to them more guards.

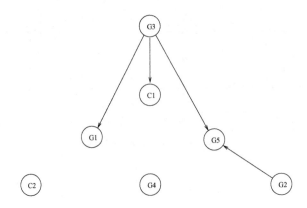

(a) Partial execution ordering of the guards

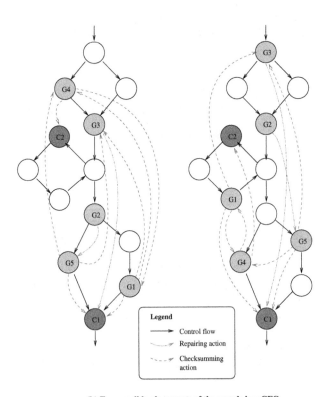

(b) Two possible placements of the guards in a CFG

Fig. 2. Guards network installed into a program CFG

Strengthening the Guards Network A guard cycle is a circular chain of guards each of which protects its next neighbor, forming a cycle of guarding relationships in the guard graph. Such a formation allows each guard in the cycle to be protected without any "loose ends" (i.e., unprotected guards). Defeating a guard cycle requires all of the guards to be disabled at the same time. How to implement checksumming in guard cycles is itself an interesting problem, because the checksumming function should have a 1-way property (we have solved the problem but due to page limitation, we omit the discussion in this paper).

The above property of guard cycles leads to a more general guards strengthening scheme: Connect any disconnected components in a guard graph in such a way that each guard in the graph can be reached by the rest of the guards (i.e., the resulting guard graph is strongly connected). As a result, strong connectivity forces the amount of attack efforts to be scaled up proportionally to the total number of the guards deployed in a program.

Strengthening Individual Guards The level of difficulty in locating guards and understanding their semantics depend on how "stealthy" and tamper-resistant the guards are.

- **Stealthiness**. Guard code should have no recognizable signatures (e.g., fixed set of instructions) that an attacker can statically scan for. Also, their actions should be made as inconspicuous as possible. For example, instead of instantly sounding an alarm upon detection of an attack, guards should delay such an action until a later time when it is unclear why and how it has taken place. To thwart sophisticated runtime program analyzers from identifying the checksumming or repairing actions of guards, logical boundaries between the executable code and runtime data of a program should be blurred. For example, the code sections are made to contain runtime data, and conversely, the data sections are made to contain executable code.
- **Tamper-resistance**. In situations where the location of a guard has been identified, it is important to have the guard protect itself (besides having other guards protect it). One effective way to achieve this is to obfuscate the guard code. There are many ways to do so. A simple way would be to rearrange its instructions and mix them with dummy code [ ]. More aggressive obfuscating transformations are possible and can make the resulting code very difficult to reverse-engineer. Such transformations involve both control and data flow obfuscations. Some particular techniques are discussed in [, , ,].

4   Description of System

We have built Version 1.0 of a system for guarding Win32 executables. It takes an EXE program file as input and inserts into it guards that can perform functions such as checksumming and repairing program code. The guard installation is an automated process guided by a user-provided guarding script that specifies

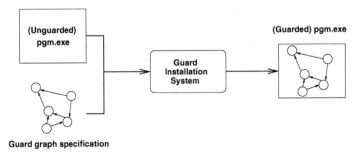

Guard graph specification

Fig. 3. The guarding system

what and how guards will protect the program code and themselves (i.e., the description of a guard graph). Figure 3 gives an overview of our system.

Our system processes binary code directly because high-level code lacks much binary information that guards need (such as memory addresses and binary contents of the program code). Also, manipulating code at the binary level makes it easier to transform program code to whatever form is desired without typical structural restrictions imposed by high-level languages.

Guard installation by our system involves inserting a guard into the program and parameterizing it appropriately. We call this *guard instantiation*, in which guards are instantiated from predefined guard templates, which are object code and stored in a database (of course these are "polymorphic" in the sense that even if two of them have the same functionality they look different; this prevents attacks based on pattern matching techniques). Below is a simple example of a guard template, which is programmed to corrupt stack frame pointer ebp if the computed checksum is different from checksum. [3]

```
guard:
        add     ebp, -checksum
        mov     eax, client_addr
for:
        cmp     eax, client_end
        jg      end
        mov     ebx, dword[eax]
        add     ebp, ebx
        add     eax, 4
        jmp     for
end:
```

During instantiation of the guard, the system initializes client_addr and client_end with the addresses of the target code range that the guard needs to protect. The other parameter, checksum, is later patched to the guard code

---

[3] The sample template is shown in the NASM assembler language [10].

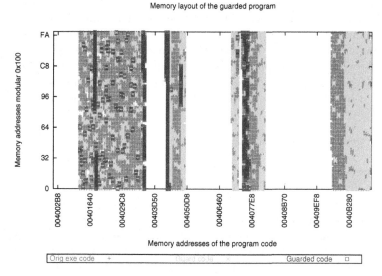

Fig. 4. The memory image of a program heavily guarded by 307 guards

	Before guarding		After guarding (without increasing file size)			
	File size	# instructions	File size	# instructions	# guards installed	Avg guard size
gzip	172 KB	38348	172 KB	38897	25	76 bytes
disasm	376 KB	54931	376 KB	56456	70	75 bytes
avi2mpg	380 KB	51647	380 KB	54913	144	78 bytes

Fig. 5. Statistics of the guarded programs and their guards

when the checksum value of the target range has been obtained by the system. This illustrates why it is convenient to operate at the binary level: Had we attempted this at the source code level, we would not have had the needed address information (because it is not possible for us to precisely predict the effect of the subsequent compilation on that source code).

Figure 4 shows the memory image of a program after it has been installed with 307 guards. (Its linear address space is represented by a two-dimensional space for easy interpretation of the image contents.) Shown in dark colors are the four executable regions of the program. (The white regions are file formatting and data areas of the program.) These four regions include three types of code: original (executable) program code, the inserted guard code, and the code protected by the guards (which includes portions of the program code and guard code).

It is important that guard installations be automated. If done manually, it is a very laborious and error-prone process, as it requires one to deal with binary information in the program files directly (consider implementing by hand a function that checksums its own code). The manual task will become more difficult and time-consuming as the number of guards and complexity of their inter-locking relationships increase. Furthermore, programs with "hand-patched" checksumming guards would be very hard to maintain because one cannot change the code without recomputing checksums of the modified code. Our system streamlines the guarding process by separating the task of software development from that of software protection (which is now done post-compilation).

5   Experimental Results

In this section, we examine how much program resouces guards would need from several software applications. By program resources we mean increases in program size and program execution time. We applied our system to three software applications: disasm, gzip, and avi2mpg. disasm is an Intel x86 disassembler that is branch-intensive; gzip is a GNU file compressing and decompressing tool that has a mixed use of branches and loops; and finally, avi2mpg is a Win32 application which converts an AVI video file into an MPEG one. Our experiments were conducted on a Pentium III 600MHz machine running Windows NT.

5.1   Impacts on Program Size

The amount of program space required for storing guard code is proportional to the number of installed guards and their average size. But sometimes, Win32 executables can accommodate a number of guards without needing more file space. To illustrate this, we ran our system on the test programs and installed into each as many guards (of the same size) as possible (while keeping their file sizes unchanged). Figure 5 shows the maximum numbers of guards that can fit into each program without increasing its size. For the sake of this experiment, the guards inserted into each program were instantiated from the same guard template (of size 62 bytes), which is similar to the one shown previously. The instantiated guards need more bytes because extra instructions are needed to hook their code to the program flows (of course in a "production run" of our system we would use guards having a variety of sizes).

We believe the issue of storage space does not pose a problem to guarding. As storage media such as hard disks are getting more spacious and cheaper, software applications also tend to expand in size (because more functionality can be included). Increasing the size of a program by a few kilobytes (as a result of guarding) does not even show up on the radar screen when compared to the natural increase in the size of software.

5.2   Impacts on Program Performance

In this section we examine how guarding affects program performance. In particular, we want to answer the basic question: Would guards impose prohibitive time-performance penalty on programs?

We tested the performances of disasm, gzip, and avi2mpg as follows. For each program, its original performance (before guarding) was measured. Then we created a set of guarded versions of each program, each version executing a different number of guards. Inserted into the program at random locations, the guards were invoked *every* time the execution flow reached them. All of the guards performed checksumming on some piece of code of 0x50 bytes long using the same checksumming algorithm. The execution times of this set of guarded programs are keyed as "uncontrolled guard invocations" in Figures 6, 7, and 8.

These performance results (and many others that we ran) show that if guards are placed within highly repetitive loops and execute as many times as they iterate, the performance would suffer. But the results also suggest that if the execution frequency of guards is restricted to a small number, then the programs would likely perform well without much degradation in speed. Indeed, in many cases, guards do not need to execute over and over again if all they do is to repeat the same checksumming or repairing actions that they have repeated many times already.

To test how controlled invocations of guards affect program performance, for each test program we created another set of guarded versions of it, which were exactly the same as the set created earlier except that in this case each guard executed once only (no matter where it was located in the CFG). The execution times of these guarded programs are shown in the same figures as "controlled guard invocations." Clearly, the new results indicate only slight increase in execution times, as compared to the previous results.

In situations where one could avoid installing guards within performance-sensitive code, the performance results are expected to be better than those reported here. (Our system includes a graphical user interface that makes it easy to highlight portions of program code where guard-installation is recommended, and portions where it is not recommended, in addition to highlighting which portions of the program code should be guarded.) The reason we decided to not use this facility in our experiments is the difficulty in quantifying what "good guard-placement hints" are, and in accounting for their variability from one test application to the next. Instead, we ran our system in "random guard-installation" mode, because it makes comparisons easier between one protected application and another.

6   Conclusion and Further Remarks

We have explored a software-based methodology for making program code tamper-resilient by using guards. Guards are special code segments in the program which, when deployed collectively, can make the following possible:

- **Distributed protection**. Spreading the load of protection among guards essentially eliminates the "single point of failure" problem.
- **Variety of protection schemes**. There are many ways to group the guards together. As a result, a software developer can have different copies of its

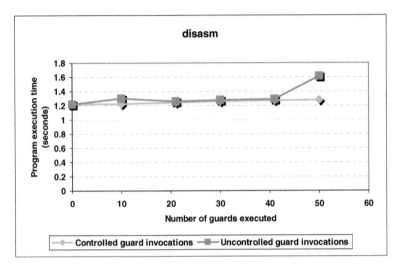

Fig. 6. Comparison between the runtime performances of disasm in two scenarios

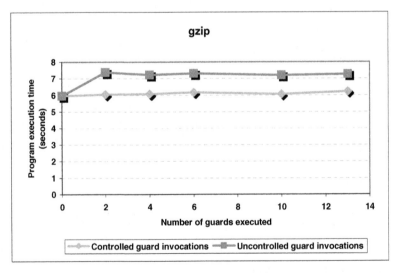

Fig. 7. Comparison between the runtime performances of gzip in two scenarios

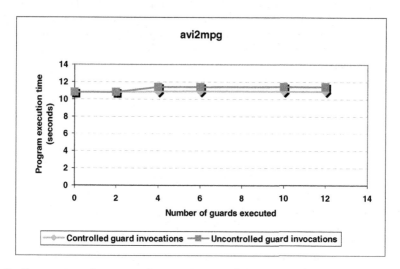

Fig. 8. Comparison between the runtime performances of avi2mpg in two scenarios

gzip						
Total no. of installed guards	0	5	10	15	20	25
No. (%) of guards executed in a typical run	0 (0%)	2 (40%)	4 (40%)	6 (40%)	10 (50%)	13 (52%)
% increase in exe time — Uncontrolled guard invoc. (bad)	0.0%	23.5%	21.2%	22.4%	20.6%	21.7%
% increase in exe time — Controlled guard invoc. (preferable)	0.0%	1.1%	1.6%	3.4%	1.4%	4.1%
disasm						
Total no. of installed guards	0	14	28	42	56	70
No. (%) of guards executed in a typical run	0 (0%)	10 (71%)	21 (75%)	30 (71%)	41 (73%)	50 (71%)
% increase in exe time — Uncontrolled guard invoc. (bad)	0.0%	6.7%	3.3%	4.8%	5.7%	32.2%
% increase in exe time — Controlled guard invoc. (preferable)	0.0%	0.5%	2.1%	3.1%	4.3%	4.9%
avi2mpg						
Total no. of installed guards	0	27	55	82	109	136
No. (%) of guards executed in a typical run	0 (0%)	2 (7%)	4 (7%)	6 (7%)	10 (9%)	12 (9%)
% increase in exe time — Uncontrolled guard invoc. (bad)	0.0%	-0.1%	5.4%	5.5%	5.5%	5.7%
% increase in exe time — Controlled guard invoc. (preferable)	0.0%	0.0%	0.5%	0.6%	0.7%	0.7%

Fig. 9. Increases in execution time under the scenarios of controlled and uncontrolled guard invocations

software applications protected differently so that successful attacks against one of the copies would not work for the others (i.e., no "wholesale" attacks). We have developed techniques for preventing "diff" attacks that would compare two differently protected copies of the same software.
- **Configurable tamper-resistance**. The guarding approach makes it flexible for a software developer to control the levels of protection (e.g., how many guards) its software applications need, allowing configurable tamper-resistance with little performance degradation. That our system works after compilation makes it unnecessary to recompile if we later modify the protection scheme (like the number of guards, the guarding network, etc).

We have implemented a system that automates the process of installing guards in Win32 executables in a configurable manner. Our experiences have convinced us that it is possible to easily guard software which is difficult to "unguard"—i.e., asymmetry in the efforts (small effort to protect, large effort to attack).

Our results show that if configured appropriately, guards cause only slight impacts on the performance of guarded programs. We believe that such impacts are insignificant in most situations, and that they are reasonable tradeoffs for the levels of protection received.

We are currently in the process of completing Version 1.1 of our system. This version has the convenience of a graphical user interface integrated with Microsoft Visual C++ 6.0, and will extend the obfuscation capabilities of the current Version 1.0. Although the paper[ ] gives theoretical evidence of the difficulty of absolute obfuscation, "practical" obfuscation (in the sense of delaying attacks on the software by substantially "raising the bar" for an attacker) are still a worthwhile endeavor in many practical situations. In our case what we really need out of obfuscation is limited to "code entanglement", that is, the binding of guard code with the original program's code so it is hard to disentangle them, that is, difficult to distinguish binary-level guard code from the original binary code (as mentioned in Section 2, there are many ways to achieve such binding, ranging from the use of artificially introduced dependencies and "dummy code", to the use of complex mathematical identities, etc). What we need is more limited, and experiments performed at Purdue and elsewhere lead us to believe that it is achievable in a practical sense. This implies that even if the regions of code containing guards were roughly located by an attacker, it would still be very difficult to "separate" and remove the guard code from the code needed by the program's functionality.

Additional work is also under way to port the system to other platforms, and to develop a facility that allows efficient and safe software patch distributions using the scheme described in this paper; here "efficient" is in the sense that the patch can have a small size compared to the total program, and "safe" in the sense that it is does not compromise the guarding network.

References

1. David Aucsmith. Tamper-resistance software: an implementation. In Ross Anderson, editor, *Information Hiding – Proceedings of the First International Workshop*, volume 1174 of *LNCS*, pages 317–333, May/June 1996. 163
2. T. Aura and D. Gollman. Software licence management with smart cards. In *Proceedings of the USENIX Workshop on Smartcard Technology (Smartcard '99)*, pages 75–85, May 1999. 162
3. Boaz Barak, Oded Goldreich, Russell Impagliazzo, Steven Rudich, Amit Sahai, Salil Vadhan, and Ke Yang. On the (im)possibility of obfuscating programs. In *CRYPTO 2001*, August 2001. 163, 174
4. Clark Thomborson Christian Collberg. Watermarking, tamper-proofing, and obfuscation – tools for software protection. 163
5. Christian Collberg, Clark Thomborson, and Douglas Low. Breaking abstractions and unstructuring data structures. In *IEEE International Conference on Computer Languages, ICCL'98*, Chicago, IL, USA, May 1998. 163, 167
6. Christian Collberg, Clark Thomborson, and Douglas Low. A taxonomy of obfuscating transformations. Technical Report 148, Department of Computer Science, The University of Auckland, Private Bag 92019, Auckland, New Zealand, 1998. 163, 167
7. Cloakware Corporation. Introduction to cloakware tamper-resistant software (trs) technology, March 2001. http://www.cloakware.com/pdfs/TRS_intro.pdf. 163, 167
8. Compuware Corporation. Numega softice. 161 http://www.numega.com/drivercentral-/components/softice/si_features.shtml.
9. H. G. Joepgen and S. Krauss. Software by means of the 'protprog' method. ii. *Elektronik*, 42(17):52–56, Aug. 1993. 163
10. O. Kommerling and M. Kuhn. Design principles for tamper-resistant smartcard processors. In *Proc. USENIX Workshop on Smartcard Technology*, Chicago, IL, May 1999. 162
11. Josh MacDonald. On program security and obfuscation. 163
12. Masahiro Mambo, Takanori Murayama, and Eiji Okamoto. A tentative approach to constructing tamper-resistant software. In *New Security Paradigms Workshop. Proceedings*, pages 23–33, New York, NY, USA, 1998. ACM. 163, 167
13. Landon Curt Noll, Jeremy Horn, Peter Seebach, and Leonid A. Broukhis. The International Obfuscated C Code Contest, 1998. http://www.ioccc.org/. 163
14. A. Schulman. Examining the Windows AARD detection code. *Dr. Dobb's Journal*, 18(9):42,44–8,89, Sept. 1993. 163
15. S. Smith and S. Weingart. Building a high-performache programmable secure coprocessor. *Computer Networks*, 31:831–860, 1999. 162
16. Simon Tatham and Julian Hall. Netwide Assembler. http://www.web-sites.co.uk/nasm. 168
17. Chenxi Wang, Jonathan Hill, John Knight, and Jack Davidson. Software tamper resistance: Obstructing static analysis of programs. Technical Report CS-2000-12, 12 2000. 163, 167
18. Steve R. White and Liam Comerford. ABYSS: An architecture for software protection. *IEEE Transactions on Software Engineering*, 16(6):619–629, June 1990. 162
19. Bennett Yee and J. D. Tygar. Secure coprocessors in electronic commerce applications. pages 155–170, 1995. 162

How to Manage Persistent State in DRM Systems

William Shapiro and Radek Vingralek

STAR Lab, InterTrust Technologies Corporation
4750 Patrick Henry Drive, Santa Clara, CA 95054
bill_shapiro@yahoo.com
radek.vingralek@oracle.com

Abstract. Digital Rights Managements (DRM) systems often must manage persistent state, which includes protected content, an audit trail, content usage counts, certificates and decryption keys. Ideally, persistent state that has monetary value should be stored in a physically secure server. However, frequently the persistent state may need to be stored in a hostile environment. For example, for good performance and to support disconnected operation, recent audit records may be stored on a consumer device. The device's user may have an incentive to alter the audit trail and thus obtain content for free. In this paper we explain the need for persistent state in DRM systems, describe several methods for maintaining persistent state depending on the system requirements, and then focus on the the special case of protecting persistent state in hostile environments.

1 Introduction

Digital Rights Management (DRM) enables secure binding of digital content (such as software, music, video, e-books or email) to a *contract*. The contract is a program, which is executed each time the content is released to a user application. The contract grants the user the right to access the content and it enforces consequences to granting the right. Examples of contracts include "grant read access to user X and generate an audit record," "grant read and write access to user X, if the contract executes on a platform Y and the user has paid a fee," "grant execute access to user X if the content has not been accessed more then n times or the user paid a fee," or "grant read access to the user X if she holds a valid subscription certificate".

DRM systems are typically distributed, with access to content granted to applications executing on clients and the content delivered from servers. Both DRM clients and servers may need access to persistent data, which includes:

- The content itself.
- Certificates used for authentication and authorization in the DRM system.
- Account balances or usage counters.
- Start dates used by subscription contracts.

T. Sander (Ed.): DRM 2001, LNCS 2320, pp. 176–191, 2002.

– Auxiliary data used to support efficient or disconnected operation of clients (such as content decryption keys).

Independent of their location, persistent data must be protected against both accidental and malicious corruption. For example, in a video-on-demand application, the user may be motivated to reset a view counter to zero to obtain the movie for free or to extract a decryption key from an application in order to remove the copy-protection from a movie.

In this paper, we survey possible solutions for managing persistent data in DRM systems and discuss their tradeoffs. In particular, we concentrate on mechanisms for protecting data from malicious corruption on the client, which may be hostile.

The paper proceeds as follows. Section 2 describes the system security model that we assume throughout the paper. Section 3 lists the persistent state management requirements of DRM systems. Section 4 surveys mechanisms for managing persistent state, and the requirements from Section 3 that each satisfies. Finally, in Section 5 we provide a retrospective on our own efforts.

2   System Model

A DRM system typically consists of client and server components, with varying levels of security and available resources. Servers generally perform the bulk of the DRM functionality, which includes serving the content, clearing financial transactions and executing (parts of) contracts. They typically run on mainframes, workstations or high-end PC's and have high-throughput connectivity. They are generally located in physically secure environments and, therefore, they can be trusted to perform the operations for which they have been certified.

Clients may execute (parts of) contracts and release content to applications. Client devices vary greatly and may include desktop PC's, set-top boxes, game consoles, portable MP3 players, PDA's, mobile phones, smartcards or secure co-processors. Compared to servers, such devices frequently have limited computing and communication resources. For example, a typical client device may contain a 74 MHz ARM7 chip, a few tens of kilobytes of on-chip SRAM and tens of megabytes of flash RAM, EEPROM or battery-backed DRAM for stable storage. Its connectivity may be intermittent and have a low throughput (e.g., 14.4 kb/s using a wireless connection).

Unlike servers, clients are completely under the control of the user, who may have an incentive to compromise the DRM system and obtain content for free. While it is difficult to secure the client environment, it is possible to provide an acceptable level of security. By acceptable, we mean that the gain resulting from breaking into a DRM system should be less than the cost of the effort required to break the system. A system that is unbreakable would be ideal – however, it is neither practical nor necessary. Commercial banks, for example, must protect highly valuable assets and, therefore, employ very sophisticated security mechanisms (such as surveillence systems, vaults, guards, etc.). Individuals, on the other, hand generally have much less value to protect in their homes and, therefore, rely on much simpler security systems (such as door locks, burglar alarms, etc.). The same range should exist for digital content. For low-valued content, simple software security mechanisms may be sufficient, whereas with highly valuable content, it may be necessary to apply additional hardware security mechanisms, such as manufacturing devices on a single die, using tamper-resistant or tamper-detecting packaging, automatic memory-zeroization when tampering has been detected, power-analysis resistant crypto implementation and bus encryption [19,5,23,18,6,22].

Some devices are also more secure than others by virtue of their intended functions. General purpose PCs are among the least secure devices, because the are intended to execute arbitrary user-loaded programs and hardware peripherals can be easily removed, swapped, examined, etc. On the other hand, devices such as set-top boxes, MP3 players and mobile phones do not (yet) load user-provided code and can only be compromised by tampering with hardware, which, in general is harder to reproduce on a massive scale than software attacks.

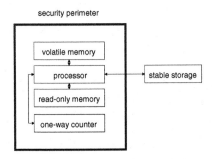

Fig. 1. Client system model

We assume that the hardware architecture of the client comprises a *processor, volatile memory, read-only memory,* a *one-way counter* and *stable storage* as shown in Figure 1. We assume that the processor is secure, i.e., an attacker cannot modify the semantics of its operations. We assume that the volatile memory is secure, i.e., the attacker cannot read or write its content. The secure volatile memory can be implemented using on-chip SRAM. Although it is possible to secure the volatile memory using mechanisms similar to those used for protection of the stable storage [ ], it would result in excessive overhead on existing processor architectures. The read-only memory, which is persistent and cannot be read by an attacker, contains the code of the DRM client and a secret (e.g., 128 bit string). The read-only memory can be implemented using on-chip EEPROM or ROM. If the client platform allows loading of user code, access to the volatile and read-only memories should be limited to trusted code. The one-way counter is a counter that cannot be decremented and whose value persists. However, we assume the attacker can increment the counter. We also assume that the counter is sufficiently long that its wraparound is unlikely (e.g., 64 bits). The one-way counter can be implemented using either a special-purpose microcontroller[21] or on-chip EEPROM[1].

We assume that the large stable storage is insecure, i.e., the attacker can arbitrarily read and update the values stored in it. Unlike the volatile memory or read-only memory, several factors make it difficult to physically secure the stable storage:

— Many technologies used for manufacturing bulk stable storage are hard to integrate on the same die as the processor.
— If the storage is separate, it is possible to power off the device, remove the stable storage and analyze it offline.
— Given its size, it may take a long time to erase the entire stable storage in the short time between detecting tampering and the attacker disabling the zeroization circuitry.

We assume that the stable storage is read and written in units of variable-sized *records*. If the underlying hardware is organized into fixed size pages, an extra software layer (such as a file system) is required to perform the translation. The stable storage can be implemented using a hard drive, a flash RAM, EEPROM or battery-backed RAM.

3   Persistent State Management Requirements

DRM systems place several requirements on the management of persistent state, many of which are similar to many database systems, but some are unique to DRM systems.

3.1   Fault Tolerance

Like database systems, DRM systems often manage data that has monetary value. Consequently, it is important to protect the data against accidental corruption, which may be a result of a software bug or a hardware failure. The methods for implementing fault tolerant database systems are well understood and include the use of error detecting or correcting codes, data replication, backups and *transactions*. A transaction is a program execution that is guaranteed by the database system to have the properties of *atomicity, isolation* and *durability* [8]. Atomicity provides recovery from fail-stop faults by guaranteeing all-or-nothing semantics for database updates; i.e., the database cannot reflect the effects of a partial execution of a transaction that was interrupted by a fault. Isolation guarantees that a transaction is isolated from concurrent updates of other transactions. The database system creates the illusion for each transaction that it is executing alone in the system. Durability guarantees the persistence

---

[1] Since the counter value in EEPROM can be decremented, the EEPROM must be protected from untrusted writes on platforms that load user code.

of updates once a transaction has successfully terminated. If transactions are correct serial programs (i.e., they transform the database from one consistent state to another), atomicity guarantees consistency of the database in presence of hardware or software fail-stop faults.

3.2   Security

Client DRM systems typically reside in hostile environments. Users may have an incentive to tamper with persistent state to circumvent the DRM system. Therefore, unlike database systems, DRM systems must provide protection against malicious data corruption. Some persistent state used in DRM systems (such as encryption keys) also needs to be protected against unauthorized reading. We formalize these requirements in two properties:

- *Secrecy.* Persistent state can only be read through the interface of the DRM system.
- *Tamper-detection.* The DRM system raises an exception if it reads a data value that is different from the one it most recently wrote[2].

DRM systems typically cannot guarantee tamper-resistance (i.e., a guarantee that each data value read by the system is the value most recently written by the system) because the client platform is often under a complete control of the user. For example, it may be difficult to prevent the user from swapping a hard drive on her PC.

It is fairly straightforward to provide data secrecy by encrypting the data with a secret key stored in the read-only memory. Some tamper-detection could be provided by attaching a Message Authentication Code (MAC) to each data record based on a secret key. However, this mechanism does not detect the *replay attack*, where a user takes a snapshot of the current state on stable storage, performs one or more transactions and, finally, restores the snapshot, removing all record of any transactions since the snapshot. The attack is simple, because the user does not need to understand the structure of the data or the algorithms used for its protection. Unfortunately, the replay attack is also one of the most difficult to prevent.

3.3   Performance

Client DRM systems must deliver performance that is acceptable to the user. Typically, this means that the entire DRM transaction should not take more than one second. If the persistent state is resident on the client, it is typically not difficult to satisfy such a requirement and the DRM system does not need to be optimized for performance.

If, on the other hand, the persistent state resides on the server, the network latency may often exceed the delay acceptable to most users (e.g., on wireless networks or on the Internet). In such cases the design of the DRM system should

---

[2] By which, we mean the most recently *committed* value.

aim to perform network communication asynchronously whenever possible. For example, the DRM system may optimistically grant a user access to content and asynchronously execute the contract on the server. If the contract execution denies access to the content, the DRM system may generate an audit trail so that it can detect abuse.

3.4   Resource Consumption

Client DRM systems typically run on devices with limited resources, such as portable MP3 players, mobile phones, PDA's, smartcards or secure co-processors. Therefore, it is important that client DRM systems minimize the consumption of critical resources. Memory and power are typically among the most critical resources on most platforms: smartcards and secure co-processors frequently have less than 10 KB of RAM and most portable devices have a battery life of a few hours. Memory consumption can be reduced by shrinking the code footprint (which can be achieved by a combination of code modularity, elimination of unnecessary features and use of simple algorithms) and minimizing buffering of data in memory. Power consumption can be reduced by avoiding unnecessary I/O and computation. Frequently, the two requirements conflict and the design must aim at achieving an acceptable tradeoff. For example, reducing memory consumption by buffering less data leads to higher power consumption due to increased I/O.

3.5   Scalability

Server DRM systems must be scalable because they may support large numbers of users. Client DRM systems, on the other hand, would typically support only one or a few users. Consequently, their design can be simplified by providing little or no concurrency control. The client persistent state is also likely to be small (i.e., less than 1 MB). Consequently, the storage organization of client DRM systems does not need to scale up and its design can rely heavily on in-memory caching (e.g., by implementing no-steal buffer management or by implementing non-clustered storage organization). Such design simplifications often lead to a smaller code footprint and thus reduced main memory usage.

4   Mechanisms for Managing Persistent State

Architectures of DRM systems can vary from entirely server-based to largely client-based. At the server-based end of the spectrum are universal data repositories (often called *locker services*) that store all persistent state required for execution of contracts, such as content subscriptions, account balances or usage counters. When a client wishes to consume content, it must first contact the locker service in order to execute the contract and obtain access to the content. The primary benefit of the locker service is that it allows ubiquitous access to the persistent state for clients connected to the network. Additionally, it is simpler to ensure secrecy and tamper-detection for the persistent state because servers can be physically secured. Even the threat of accidental corruption is reduced because servers are generally more reliable than client devices and are more likely to keep frequent backups of the persistent state and use transactions to update the state.

However, there are also several drawbacks to executing contracts in the locker service. First, the performance penalty of contacting a server each time content is consumed is often unacceptable. For example, a user may have to wait a second or more after pressing the play button before the DRM system obtains an access right from the locker service to play the song. The performance penalty may be alleviated by caching some of the persistent state on the client or by executing the contracts asynchronously.

The second, and more fundamental, drawback of the locker service is that it does not support offline content consumption. A client must have an active network connection to the locker service at the time of content purchase. Offline transactions generally require persistent state stored on the client. For example, in a video distribution application, a user may receive movies asynchronously (e.g., via satellite or radio broadcast) and be able to watch them without having to connect to a server to obtain an access right each time. Audit records for the number of movies viewed are stored on the client device and can be periodically sent to the server. In the extreme case, a client may be able to perform transactions without ever having to connect to a server. For example, a user may receive a promotional DVD in the mail that she is permitted to preview a fixed number of times (say twice). The client DRM software persistently stores the preview counter to determine when the DVD expires.

In the rest of this section we survey several mechanisms for managing persistent state in a hostile environment.

4.1   Secure Memories

Blum, et al., study the problem of protecting RAM against tampering given a small amount of secure memory. They consider both an off-line detector, which detects tampering using a trace of all accesses (including values read or written, locations accessed and times of access) and an on-line detector, which detects tampering immediately after an operation has been executed [ ]. The on-line detector is based on the Merkle tree [ ], which is schematically shown in Figure 2. The Merkle tree serves as a basis for protecting the persistent state in most of the systems we survey in this section.

Each node in the Merkle tree contains one-way hashes of its children. The leaves of the tree contain hashes of the memory locations. The hash of the root of the tree is stored in the secure memory. Each time a memory location is updated, all hash values on the path from the leaf corresponding to the updated memory location to the root are updated. Each time a memory location is read, the path must be verified by recomputing the hash values.

Although our system model assumes that the volatile memory resides inside of the security perimeter, there exist mechanisms for protecting program

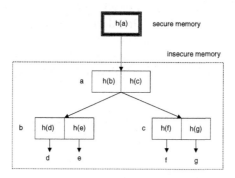

Fig. 2. Merkle tree

instructions and data in an insecure volatile memory [ ]. However, the design
assumes that the processor support special instructions that are not supported
by most existing processors. Secrecy of the data written to the volatile memory
is guaranteed by encryption with a symmetric key stored within the security
perimeter. Tampering with the data is detected by attaching a MAC to every
memory location. However, the MAC cannot detect replay of old values. The
time and space overhead is most likely prohibitive on most existing processors
(each memory reference results in one pass through a symmetric cipher and a
MAC computation, and a 16 byte MAC is added to every cache line). Therefore, we assume in our model that the volatile memory is inside of the security
perimeter.

Even when the volatile memory lies within the security perimeter, it may be
still paged to insecure stable storage by the virtual memory subsystem. Provos
describes a mechanisms for securely paging to insecure stable storage by encrypting all pages swapped out to the stable storage [ ]. The encryption key, which
is stored in pinned volatile memory, is randomly generated by the virtual memory subsystem and destroyed once all references to the page are removed (i.e.,
all processes using that page terminate). A solution that also detects tampering
would be to swap pages out to any of the secure file systems described below.

4.2 Secure Audit Logs

One mechanism for protecting persistent state on the client is to log user transactions in a local secured log. Schneier and Kelsey [ ] describes how to implement
secure audit logs on host machines to aid in intrusion detection. This could be
adapted to provide secure persistent storage on a client. The goal of this work
is to secure a log that could aid in detecting that a host has been compromised.
Once the host has been compromised, it is under the control of the attacker, who
has full control over the host. However, in the process of attacking a machine, the
attacker is likely to trigger events that would suggest intrusion (e.g., becoming
a super user). If such events can be securely logged, the log can be a powerful
aid in detecting intrusions.

The secure logs use encryption to provide data secrecy and a linear chain of hash links, which is a linear form of the Merkle tree, to every element in the log to provide tamper detection. The hash of the end of the log, which protects the entire log through hash links, is periodically sent to a remote server for tamper detection. This mechanism could be adapted to provide secure persistent storage locally by storing the hash of the end of the log and the encryption key in local secure storage.

Bellare and Yee [ ] propose a different mechanism for securing audit logs. In this scheme, the key used to compute the MAC over audit entries is periodically changed such that an attacker cannot modify historical entries, even if the current key is compromised. Periodically, a new key is computed by applying a one-way hash to the old key and the old key is erased. Sequence numbers in the log are used to prevent the replay attack. The mechanism does not detect truncation of the log (for example deleting the most recent transactions). However, as described above, the most recent sequence number could be periodically sent to a remote server to limit the amount of truncation that could go undetected.

Secure logs may be sufficient for applications that store a small amount of append-only persistent state. For example, client devices with intermittent network access can store audit records locally in a secure log and send them to a DRM server when the device connects to the network. However, this approach would be inedficient for applications that require random read and write access to persistent data because entries in the log can be verified only in time linear in the size of the log.

4.3   Secure File Systems

Many contracts require random read and write access to persistent data. For example, they may need to efficiently locate a counter, read its value and increment it. In the case where random read and write access to persistent data is required on the client, a secure file system may be used.

Secure file systems generally fall into two categories: those that provide secrecy and those that provide tamper-detection.

Encrypted File Systems Several file systems have been developed that provide secrecy by encrypting file system data and meta-data [, ,]. Encrypting persistent data is fairly straightforward in DRM systems and most of the work on encrypted file systems involves integration with legacy network file systems (such as NFS) and user authentication, which are not relevant for local file systems.

Tamper Detection File systems that provide tamper-detection are more relevant to the design of DRM systems. Fu et. al. developed SFS-RO to allow a large number of users to access public read-only files, which may be replicated on untrusted servers, and verify their authenticity [ ]. SFS-RO uses a tree of hashes to verify the contents of the file system. In an SFS-RO file system, each inode is referred to by a handle, which is a cryptographic hash of its contents.

Groups of handles are hashed recursively to form a tree of hashes. The root inode, which through the hash links of its children can be used to verify the entire file system, is signed with the private key of the file system. Any client that has the public key of the file system can then verify the file system's authenticity by first verifying the root inode and then verifying the path from the root to each file to be read. SFS-RO is not directly usable for DRM systems, because they must be able to update data. However, the signed root inode could be kept in the local storage and updated when the underlying inodes change.

Stein et. al. designed the Protected File System (PFS) to verify file system data and meta-data blocks without requiring any changes to the file system interface or storage organization [20]. It uses cryptographic hashes over all data and meta-data blocks to detect any tampering with file system blocks. The block hashes are written to the same write-ahead log as the meta-data updates. PFS does not provide protection against replay attacks.

SUNDR [11] is a network file system designed to run on untrusted servers. It supports both data encryption and verification using hash trees similar to SFS-RO. TCSF [4] also supports both encryption and verification, but calculates a message digest on each block and cannot detect replay attacks.

The primary benefit of a secure file system is that it exports the familiar file system interface. However, it may not be appropriate for DRM systems that require efficient access to named records. Moreover, the file systems do not support transactional update semantics.

Secure file systems are also not suitable for a number of clients. Clients, such as set-top-boxes, whose operating systems are not exposed to the user, can install a secure file system on a separate partition. However, it is generally unacceptable to require a user of a general-purpose PC to install a separate file system in order to use a DRM system. Furthermore, the size of a file system implementation makes it inappropriate for use in small devices.

4.4   Secure Database Systems

Although secure file systems detect data corruption (which may be accidental or malicious), they use backups as the only mechanism for recovering user data after data corruption has been detected. Since backup creation is a relatively heavy-weight operation, it is typically performed infrequently and, therefore, a large number of updates can be lost during a backup restore.

Secure database systems such as the Trusted Database (TDB) [10,25] and GnatDb [24] combine the mechanisms for implementing secrecy and tamper-detection described in Section 4.3 with fine-grained recovery based on transactions. The database system recovers a consistent database state after a fail-stop fault by rolling back all partial updates. The design of both database systems demonstrates that similar storage mechanisms can be employed to implement both transactions and security (secrecy and tamper-detection). TDB and GnatDb are both based on log-structured storage organization[15], which implements data updates by appending new versions of the data to the end of a log. The relocation of the data requires a *location map* that maps each data item to its current location in the log. Like SFS-RO, the location map can be hierarchically organized and contain hash values in the pointers to child nodes. Transactional atomicity is reduced to atomic updates of the location map (or of a pointer to its root).

The main differences in the design of TDB and GnatDb stem from the platforms they target. TDB is geared toward devices similar to the modern PC (such as set-top boxes or game consoles), while GnatDb is geared toward devices with very limited resources (such as secure co-processors, smartcards, portable music players and mobile phones).

TDB TDB's architecture is modular so that it is possible to configure the system based on the resources available on a given platform. The lowest layer, the *Chunk Store* implements atomic updates to untyped strings of bytes called *chunks*. The *Object Store* implements transactional access (including isolation of transactions) to typed C++ objects on top of the Chunk Store. The top layer, the *Collection Store*, implements iterator-based access to collections of objects. TDB also provides a *Backup Store* that creates and restores backups of the database.

The Chunk Store implements all storage management and guarantees secrecy and tamper-detection. The storage organization of TDB is shown in Figure 3. It maintains a location map, which is organized for scalability as a tree of chunks. Each node in the tree contains an array of secure pointers, each of which consists of the child location in stable storage and a one-way hash of the child's content. The leaves point to the user data chunks. To prevent snooping, all chunks are encrypted with a secret key stored in the read-only memory. The user chunks and the nodes of the tree are protected against tampering, including replay attacks, similar to the inodes of SFS-RO.

Unlike SFS-RO, TDB stores a signed secure pointer to the root of the tree at the tail of the log in a *commit chunk*. The commit chunk is signed with the secret key stored in the read-only memory. The signature prevents forging of the commit chunks. Its replay is prevented by signing the current value of the one-way counter along with the secure pointer. Writing the commit chunk to the stable storage constitutes a commit point of the transaction (i.e., any updates up to this point would be rolled back at recovery).

Since chunk updates are always written to the end of the log, the location of a chunk changes every time it is updated. Therefore, the entire path from the node pointing to the updated chunk to the root of the location map must be updated in the stable storage along with the chunk. TDB reduces the overhead by updating the path (except for the root pointer) only in the volatile memory. The volatile copies are synchronized with the stable storage during a *checkpoint*. At recovery, the location map nodes are brought up-to-date by redoing all updates to user chunks since the last checkpoint. The unchekpointed part of the log (which contains user data chunks and signed pointers to the location map root) is protected against tampering using a chain of hash values anchored in the commit chunk similar to the secure log described in Section 4.2. Because data

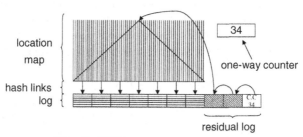

Fig. 3. TDB storage organization

chunks are always relocated when they are modified, a *log cleaner* is used to garbage collect obsolete chunk versions.

The Chunk Store divides the database into *partitions*, each of which consists of both user chunks and meta chunks. Partitions may be configured to use separate cryptographic keys and algorithms for encryption and hashing (or to not encrypt or hash). The meta chunks describing a partition (including the secret key) are stored in a system partition, which is protected using the secret key in the read-only memory. Partitions can be dynamically created and copied using copy-on-write, which serves as a basis for fast backups. The backups can be either full or incremental. Their secrecy is guaranteed by encryption with the partition secret key. Tampering is detected using a signature with the partition secret key (the protection also includes verifying that incremental backups are restored in a well-formed sequence). A backup restore must be authorized by a trusted module external to TDB to ensure that the backup is not too old and the number of requests for backup restores is reasonable (because a backup restore is a controlled form of the replay attack).

Despite the security features TDB provides over other embedded database systems, its performance is quite good. TDB outperforms a popular embedded database system, the BerkeleyDB, on the TPC-B benchmark on average by a factor of 1.8 [25]. The code footprint of the ChunkStore on the x86 is 142 KB, the Backup Store 22 KB and the rest of the modules 86 KB.

GnatDb GnatDb's architecture consists of two layers: the *Secure Device* and the *Store*. The Secure Device implements page-oriented access to a virtual device that provides secrecy and tamper-detection. The Store implements a proper subset of the Chunk Store interface of TDB (without support for partitions), which allows atomic updates of chunk sets.

Unlike TDB, which uses a hierarchical location map, GnatDb organizes its location map as an array (indexed by chunk id), which is written as a single unit (i.e., the entire map forms a single chunk). Although this organization is not scalable, its performance is satisfactory for the small databases that GnatDb is expected to manage and, at the same time, significantly simplifies the implementation, which results in a code footprint reduction. The storage for GnatDB is statically divided into two logs, one for the location map and the other for pages holding user data chunks (the *data log*). Unlike TDB, GnatDb writes both logs round-robin, which simplifies the implementation of the Store at the cost of performance (it would be possible to reduce the volume of cleaning by selecting for cleaning pages that contain mostly "dead" chunks).

The Secure Device provides secrecy by encrypting all pages with a secret key stored in the read-only memory. It detects tampering by appending a MAC to each page, computed over the page contents and location using a key stored in the read-only memory[3]. Unlike other storage systems, GnatDb does not rely on building a Merkle tree to thwart the replay attack. Instead, it relies on the regular pattern of writes to both logs. The Secure Device includes a version number in each page, which contains the value of the one-way counter. The one-way counter is incremented each time a page is written to the data log. Since the data log is written round-robin, the version number of any page can be easily computed given the version number of log tail. The version numbers of all pages holding the most recently written location map chunk are identical and match the version number of the log tail, which in turn must match the current value of the one-way counter. The version number assignment is shown in Figure 4. Therefore, knowing the current value of the one-way counter and the current location of log tail, its is possible to verify the correctness of the version number of any page.

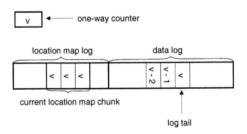

Fig. 4. GnatDb storage organization

GnatDb's design trades off performance for memory consumption. The code footprint of GnatDb is 7.1 KB on the x86 and its total memory consumption (including the space allocated for the stack and the heap) is below 11 KB. Its performance on a typical small device platform using flash-RAM for stable storage remains acceptable (less than 0.6 s) for database utilizations below 50% on a synthetic workload that models a typical DRM transaction [ ].

---

[3] If the read-only memory has a limited size, it is possible to securely derive both the encryption key and the MAC key from a single secret stored in the read-only memory.

5 A Retrospective on DRM Database System Design

In this section, we summarize the experience we gained by designing and implementing TDB and GnatDb.

The management of persistent state on clients is much more complex and less secure than on the server. Therefore, the designers of DRM systems should carefully consider whether the contracts supported by the system indeed require persistent state and, if so, whether it can be stored on the server. For example, subscription contracts do not require updatable persistent state on the client and DRM systems with client that have fast and reliable connectivity to the server generally do not require storage of persistent state on the client.

We found that secure file systems such as SFS-RO or PFS are not suitable for persistent storage in DRM systems. In particular, typical DRM systems require access to named records and transactional semantics for updates. However, if the footprint of the DRM client is not an important constraint and its installation can require creation of a new file system, it is possible to run an embedded database system, such as BerkeleyDB [ ], on top of a secure file system.

Ideally, we wanted to be able to use a database system that provided both secrecy and tamper detection, but were unaware of any such systems. Therefore, we implemented TDB to provide these features as well as typical database system functionality. We later found that DRM systems often ran on small devices and with very limited resources, which precluded the use of TDB. GnatDB, was the result of scaling down TDB to provide only the functionality and scalability required on small devices, while still providing secrecy and tamper-detection.

In designing TDB and GnatDB, we found that log-structured storage organization has several benefits for design of secure database systems. First, it nicely integrates with implementation of tamper-detection mechanisms. Second, it greatly simplifies implementation of atomic updates. Third, it allows an efficient creation of copy-on-write snapshots, which serve as a basis for fast backups. Fourth, by concentrating all writes in a few blocks or pages on the stable storage, it reduces the overall I/O costs on some platforms (e.g., the stable storage based on flash RAM, where the cost of block erase, required to precede each write, dominates all I/O). Fifth, it makes traffic analysis harder because hot records are never overwritten in place. At the same time, the loss of clustering of semantically related data is not significant for DRM databases, which tend to be small and thus frequently cacheable in volatile memory.

We also found that the cryptographic operations represent a relatively small overhead (less than 10%) on modern PC's or similar platforms [ ]. On the other hand, on embedded platforms with slower CPUs (such as an ARM-based processor) and faster I/O (flash RAM or EEPROM) the cryptographic operations dominate the overall costs (more than 70% of the total overhead) [ ]. Consequently, the efficiency of tamper-detection and secrecy implementations is as important as the efficiency of the stable storage management.

References

1. Mihir Bellare and Bennet Yee. Forward integrity for secure audit logs. Technical report, Computer Science and Engineering Department, University of California at San Diego, November 1997. 184
2. M. Blaze. A cryptographic file system for unix. In *In Proceedings of the First ACM Conference on Computer and Communication Security*, November 1993. Fairfax, VA. 184
3. M. Blum, W. Evans, P. Gemmel, S. Kannan, and M. Naor. Checking the correctness of memories. In *In Proceedings of the IEEE Conference on Foundations of Computer Science*, 1991. San Juan, Puerto Rico. 182
4. G. Cattaneo, L. Catuogno, A. Del Sorbo, and P. Persiano. The design and implementation of a transparent cryptographic file system for unix. In *Proceedings of the FREENIX Track: USENIX Annual Technical Conference*, June 2001. Boston, MA. 185
5. S. Chari, C. Jutla, J. Rao, and P. Rohatgi. Towards sound approaches to counteract power-analysis attacks. In *In Proceedings of the 19th Annual International Cryptology Conference*, 1999. Santa Barbara, CA. 178
6. Dallas Semiconductor. *DS5002FP Secure Microprocessor Chip*, July 2001. 178
7. K. Fu, F. Kaashoek, and D. Mazieres. Fast and secure distributed read-only file system. In *Proceedings of the 4th Symposium on Operating Systems Design and Implementation*, 2000. San Diego, CA. 184
8. J. Gray and A. Reuter. *Transaction Processing: Concepts and Techniques*. Morgan Kaufmann, 1993. 179
9. D. Lie, C. Thekkath, M. Mitchell, P. Lincoln, D. Boneh, J. Mitchell, and M. Horowitz. Architectural support for copy and tamper resistant software. In *In Proceedings of the 9th International Conference on Architectural Support for Programming Languages and Operating Systems*, 2000. Cambridge, MA. 178, 183
10. U. Maheshwari, R. Vingralek, and W. Shapiro. How to build a trusted database system on untrusted storage. In *Proceedings of the 4th Symposium on Operating Systems Design and Implementation*, 2000. San Diego, CA. 185, 189
11. D. Mazieres and D. Shasha. Don't trust your file server. In *In Proceedings of the 8th Workshop on Hot Topics in Operating Systems*, May 2001. Schloss Elmau, Germany. 185
12. R. Merkle. Protocols for public key cryptosystems. In *Proceedings of the IEEE Symposium on Security and Privacy*, 1980. Oakland, CA. 182
13. N. Provos. Encrypting virtual memory. In *Proceedings of the 9th USENIX Security Symposium*, August 2000. Denver, CO. 183
14. P. Reiher, T. Page, S. Crocker, J. Cook, and G. Popek. Truffles—a secure service for widespread file sharing. In *In Proceedings of the The Privacy and Security Research Group Workshop on Network and Distributed System Security*, February 1993. 184
15. M. Rosenblum and J. Ousterhout. The design and implementation of a log-structured file system. In *Proceedings of the 13th ACM Symposium on Operating Systems Principles*, 1991. Pacific Grove, CA. 185
16. B. Schneier and J. Kelsey. Cryptographic support for secure logs on untrusted machines. In *In Proceedings of the USENIX Security Symposium*, 1998. San Antonio, TX. 183
17. M. Seltzer and M. Olson. Challenges in embedded database system administration. In *Proceeding of the Embedded System Workshop*, 1999. Cambridge, MA (software available at www.sleepycat.com). 189

18. Dallas Semiconductor. Java-powered cryptographic iButton. www.ibutton.comibuttonsjava.html, July 2001. 178

19. S. Smith, E. Palmer, and S. Weingart. Using a high-performance, programmable secure coprocessor. In *Proceedings of the International Conference on Financial Cryptography*, 1998. Anguilla, British West Indies. 178

20. C. Stein, J. Howard, and M. Seltzer. Unifying file system protection. In *Proceedings of the USENIX Annual Technical Conference*, 2001. Boston, MA. 185

21. Infineon Technologies. Eurochip II - SLE 5536. available at `www.infineon.com/cgi/ecrm.dll/ecrm/scripts/prod_ov.jsp?oid=14702&cat_oid=-8233`, 2000. 179

22. InterTrust Technologies. Rightschip. available at `www.intertrust.com/main/products/rightschip-fs.html`, July 2001. 178

23. J. Tual. MASSC: A generic architecture for multiapplication smart cards. *IEEE Micro*, 19, 1999. 178

24. R. Vingralek. GnatDb: A small footprint, secure database system. Technical Report STAR-TR-01-05, InterTrust Technologies, 2001. available at `www.star-lab.com/tr/star-tr-01-05.html`. 185, 188, 189

25. R. Vingralek, U. Maheshwari, and W. Shapiro. TDB: A database system for digital rights management. Technical Report STAR-TR-01-01, InterTrust Technologies, 2001. available at `www.star-lab.com/tr/star-tr-01-01.html`. 185, 187

26. E. Zadok, I. Babulescu, and A. Shender. Cryptfs: A stackable vnode level encryption file system. Technical Report CUCS-021-98, Computer Science Department, Columbia University, June 1998. 184

A Cryptanalysis of the
High-Bandwidth Digital Content
Protection System

Scott Crosby[1], Ian Goldberg[2], Robert Johnson[3],
Dawn Song[3], and David Wagner[3]

[1] Carnegie-Mellon University
[2] Zero Knowledge Systems
[3] University of California at Berkeley

Abstract. We describe a weakness in the High Bandwidth Digital Content Protection (HDCP) scheme which may lead to practical attacks. HDCP is a proposed identity-based cryptosystem for use over the Digital Visual Interface bus, a consumer video bus used to connect personal computers and digital display devices. Public/private key pairs are assigned to devices by a trusted authority, which possesses a master secret. If an attacker can recover 40 public/private key pairs that span the module of public keys, then the authority's master secret can be recovered in a few seconds. With the master secret, an attacker can eavesdrop on communications between any two devices and can spoof any device, both in real time. Additionally, the attacker can produce new key pairs not on any key revocation list. Thus the attacker can completely usurp the trusted authority's power. Furthermore, the protocol is still insecure even if all devices' keys are signed by the central authority.

1 Introduction

The High-bandwidth Digital Content Protection (HDCP) scheme is a cryptographic extension to the Digital Visual Interface (DVI) designed to prevent the copying of video data transmitted over the DVI bus. DVI is already commonly used between personal computers and display devices such as LCD monitors. If the HDCP enhanced DVI standard is also adopted by monitor and television manufacturers, then it could serve as the last leg of a secure channel for the online distribution of television, movies, and other video data. Online content distributors would like to build this channel to prevent perfect digital copies by never exposing the digital video signal as plaintext in the receiver's computer.

Because DVI devices from many different manufacturers need to interoperate and perform key exchange with no user intervention, the HDCP authors chose to use an identity-based cryptosystem. It appears that the authors wanted the implementation of the scheme to be extremely low cost, and so avoided any of the conventional public-key schemes in the literature [1,2,3,4,5]. In personal communication with the HDCP authors, we learned that they designed HDCP to be

T. Sander (Ed.): DRM 2001, LNCS 2320, pp. 192–200, 2002.

implementable in fewer than 10,000 gates[ ]. This stringent design requirement led the HDCP authors to develop custom algorithms which are insecure.

In the HDCP scheme, device manufacturers purchase HDCP licenses from a trusted authority. A license includes, for each device A, a public vector v_A, called the Key Selection Vector (KSV), and a private vector, u_A. When devices A and B wish to communicate, they exchange v_A and v_B. Device A computes the dot product $u_A \cdot v_B$ and B computes $u_B \cdot v_A$, and they use this as their shared secret for the rest of their interactions. The trusted authority uses some secret information to choose v_A, v_B, u_A, and u_B so that the above computations will produce the same answer. This protocol is used in both the Upstream and Downstream versions of HDCP. The Upstream version of HDCP is designed for the communication link between software running on a personal computer, such as a user friendly video playback utility, and the HDCP devices attached to that computer. The Downstream protocol is used between HDCP devices. Since the cryptographically relevant portions of these protocols are identical, our attack applies to both.

Our purpose in presenting these results is not to enable illegal copying. Rather, we hope to advance the cryptographic science, to help systems designers build more secure systems in the future, and to help users assess what level of security they can reasonably expect from these technologies.

We observe that attackers can exploit a well-known cryptographic design mistake: the shared secret generation is entirely linear. The attack only needs 40 public/private key pairs such the public key pairs span $M \subset (\mathbb{Z}/2^{56}\mathbb{Z})^{40}$, the module generated by all public keys. Since HDCP devices divulge their public keys freely, one can easily test whether a set of 40 devices have public keys spanning M before expending the effort to extract their private keys. With these keys, the authority's secret can be recovered in only a few seconds on any desktop computer.

The consequence of these flaws is that, after recovering the private keys of 40 devices, one can attack every other interoperable HDCP device in existence: an attacker can decrypt eavesdropped communications, spoof the identity of other devices, and even forge new device keys as though he were the trusted center. Note that this allows an attacker to bypass any revocation list or "blacklisting": such mechanisms are rendered completely ineffective by these flaws in HDCP. We also describe several further attacks on the HDCP protocol (see Section 6). Therefore we recommend that the current HDCP cryptosystem should be abandoned and replaced with standard cryptographic primitives.

The HDCP cryptosystem is also unusual in that it can be broken without fully understanding its operation. The HDCP specification does not describe the key generation process used by the center but, based solely on the properties of generated keys, we can characterize all possible key generation strategies and show that they are all insecure. In other words, we can prove, given just the interface, that every possible implementation that follows this interface is insecure.

Table 1. The HDCP Authentication Protocol

$$A \rightarrow B: \quad v_A, n_A$$
$$B: \quad K' = v_A \cdot u_B, \ R' = h(K', n_A)$$
$$B \rightarrow A: \quad v_B, R'$$
$$A: \quad K = v_B \cdot u_A, \ R = h(K, n_A)$$
$$A: \quad \text{Verifies } R = R'$$

2   Related Work

Blom described a scheme very similar to HDCP as an alternative to the emerging public-key schemes of the time[,]. He realized immediately the danger of colluding users, and tried to maximize the number of traitors required to compromise the scheme while minimizing the storage requirements placed on the system's users. We should note that since HDCP is closely related to Blom's protocol, it achieves the same storage lower-bound he presented in his paper. Blom's analysis considered only information-theoretic security; we show that with only a small number of colluding users, the scheme is computationally insecure, as well.

Other researchers have looked at HDCP, too. An author of the present paper informally published similar results[ ]. Irwin independently discovered this attack, and pointed out several other weaknesses in HDCP[ ]. Niels Ferguson has discovered weaknesses in HDCP, but has not published them because of the Digital Millennium Copyright Act[ ].

3   The HDCP Authentication Protocol

The HDCP protocol is described completely in [ ]. We present an abstracted version that captures the cryptographically relevant portions of both the Upstream and Downstream versions of HDCP. A trusted authority assigns to each device, A, a public vector $v_A \in (\mathbb{Z}/2^{56}\mathbb{Z})^{40}$, called the Key Selection Vector (KSV), and a private vector, $u_A \in (\mathbb{Z}/2^{56}\mathbb{Z})^{40}$. The vector v_A consists of 20 zeros and 20 ones. The vector u_A must be kept in tamper-proof hardware or, in the case of a software implementation, obscured by code obfuscation techniques. When devices A and B wish to communicate, they exchange v_A and v_B. A computes $K = u_A \cdot v_B$ and B computes $K' = u_B \cdot v_A$. The trusted authority has used some secret information to choose v_A, v_B, u_A, and u_B so that $K = K'$.

In HDCP, one device is the transmitter and one is the receiver. To verify that the key agreement process has been successful, the transmitter A also sends a nonce n_A, and the receiver replies with the 16-bit value R' computed by $R' = h(K', n_A)$. The transmitter performs the analogous computation and verifies that the results are the same. The non-invertible function h is completely described in the specification, but the details of its operation are not important here. We assume that all DVI transmitters can interoperate with all DVI receivers, an assumption that seems to be implied by the specification.

HDCP also supports revocation of certain KSVs. Transmitters are required to check that their peer's KSV is not on the current revocation list. According to the HDCP license, KSVs can be placed on the KRL if the corresponding private key has been leaked, or if requested by the National Security Agency.

Table 2. Summary of HDCP Protocol Variables

Name	Size	Comment
v_A, v_B	40 bits	Must have Hamming weight 20
u_A, u_B	Vector of 40 56-bit numbers	
n_A	64 bits	
K, K'	56 bits	$K = v_B \cdot u_A, K' = v_A \cdot u_B$
R, R'	16 bits	$R = h(K, n_A), R' = h(K', n_A)$

4 Linear Algebra over $\mathbb{Z}/2^{56}\mathbb{Z}$

Computations in HDCP are done in the ring $\mathbb{Z}/2^{56}\mathbb{Z}$. Since $\mathbb{Z}/2^{56}\mathbb{Z}$ is not a field, not all the basic facts from linear algebra hold in this setting. Nonetheless, much of our intuition carries over with not too many changes. In this section we set down the few results we need. These results are not new, but some of them are a bit obscure, so we include them here. Let $R = \mathbb{Z}/p^n\mathbb{Z}$, where p is prime. The following fact is used without proof.

Fact 1. *The standard determinant function, det, is multiplicative, and a matrix T is invertible if and only if $\det T$ is a unit in R. Since $R = \mathbb{Z}/p^n\mathbb{Z}$, this implies T is invertible if and only if $\gcd(\det T, p^n) = 1$.*

R has exactly one chain of ideals, $(0) = (p^n) \subset (p^{n-1}) \subset \ldots \subset (p^1) \subset (p^0) = R$. This makes Gaussian elimination work almost as well as over a field.

Proposition 1. *Any $m \times n$ matrix A over R can be transformed, via invertible row operations, into an upper triangular matrix such that if the leading nonzero term of row i is in column j, then the leading nonzero term of row $i + 1$ is in column $j + 1$ or later. Furthermore, the leading terms will all be powers of p.*

Proof. The Gaussian elimination algorithm need only be modified slightly.

$$
A = \begin{bmatrix}
a_{1,c_1} & & & & & & & \\
0 & \ddots & & & & & & \\
& & a_{k,c_k} & & & & & \\
& & 0 & a_{k+1,c_{k+1}} & * & \cdots & & * \\
& & & * & & \ddots & & \\
\vdots & & \vdots & \vdots & & \ddots & & \\
0 & & 0 & * & & \cdots & & *
\end{bmatrix}
$$

Let c_1 be the first non-zero column. Let r_1 be a row such that, for all r, $(a_{r,c_1}) \subseteq (a_{r_1,c_1})$. By dividing row r_1 by a unit, we can transform a_{r_1,c_1} into p^{e_1} for some e_1. We then interchange row r_1 with row 1. We can now use row 1 to cancel all the other non-zero terms below a_{1,c_1}, since the column c_1 entries of all the other rows now lie in (a_{1,c_1}). We now repeat with column c_2, the first column with a non-zero entry in rows $2, \ldots, m$, and so on. If, after swapping, entry $a_{k,c_k} = 1$, then we may optionally use row k to cancel the non-zero terms above a_{k,c_k}. It is a standard fact that the row operations used here are invertible.

Define $\sigma : (\mathbb{Z}/2^{56}\mathbb{Z})^{40} \to \mathbb{Z}/2^{56}\mathbb{Z}$ by $\sigma(v_1, \ldots, v_{40}) = \sum_{i=1}^{40} v_i$. Then, since KSVs have Hamming weight 20, for any KSV v, $\sigma(v) = 20$. Since σ is linear, σ applied to any linear combination of KSVs will be in the ideal $(4) \subset \mathbb{Z}/2^{56}\mathbb{Z}$. Since not all vectors α in $(\mathbb{Z}/2^{56}\mathbb{Z})^{40}$ have $\sigma(\alpha) \in (4)$, no set of KSVs will ever span $(\mathbb{Z}/2^{56}\mathbb{Z})^{40}$. Let M be the module spanned by all possible KSVs. The following proposition tells us when a set of KSVs spans M.

Proposition 2. *A set of KSVs $v_1, \ldots, v_{40}$ spans M if and only if the matrix V whose rows are $v_1, \ldots, v_{40}$ has $\gcd(\det V, 2^{56}) = 4$.*

Proof. Let $V' = [v'_{ij}]$ be the result of applying the above Gaussian elimination algorithm to V. Since the Gaussian elimination is invertible, there exists a matrix U, with $\gcd(\det U, 2^{56}) = 1$, such that $V' = UV$. Thus $\det U^{-1} \det V' = \det V$. Since $\det U^{-1}$ is coprime to 2^{56}, we must have $\gcd(\det V', 2^{56}) = \gcd(\det V, 2^{56}) = 4$. Since V' is upper triangular, $\det V' = \prod_{i=1}^{40} v'_{ii}$. But v'_{ii} is a power of 2 for each i, so $\det V' = \prod_{i=1}^{40} v'_{ii} = 4$. Since the only nonzero entry in row 40 is $v'_{40,40}$, we must have $v'_{40,40}$ a multiple of 4 by σ considerations. Since $\det V' = 4$, V' has the following form.

$$V' = \begin{bmatrix} 1 & 0 & 0 & * \\ 0 & \ddots & 0 & * \\ 0 & 0 & 1 & * \\ 0 & 0 & 0 & 4 \end{bmatrix}$$

Let v'_i be the ith row of this matrix. If $w = (w_1, \ldots, w_{40})$ is a KSV, then put $w' = w - \sum_{i=1}^{39} w_i v'_i = (0, \ldots, 0, w'_{40})$. As we observed above, $\sigma(w') = w'_{40}$, lies in $(4) \subset \mathbb{Z}/2^{56}\mathbb{Z}$. So there exists a c such that $w'_{40} = 4c$. Hence $w = \sum_{i=1}^{39} w_i v'_i + cv'_{40}$. Note that this does not prove the existence of a KSV matrix V with $\gcd(\det V, 2^{56}) = 4$, but such matrices can easily be found experimentally. Thus the rows of the matrix V' above do lie in M.

If, on the other hand, $v_1, \ldots, v_{40}$ span M, then there exists a matrix U such that $V' = UV$. Thus, by the multiplicativity of det, $\gcd(\det V, 2^{56})$ is at most 4. By a σ argument similar to the above, $\gcd(\det V, 2^{56})$ is at least 4. Thus $\gcd(\det V, 2^{56}) = 4$.

It will also be useful to know the probability that $40 + m$ KSVs contain a set of 40 KSVs that span M. The following table was created by generating 10000 sets of $40 + m$ random KSVs and testing whether the set contained a spanning subset of 40 KSVs.

Number of KSVs	40	42	44	46	48	50
Prob. of Spanning M	.295	.773	.940	.982	.997	.999

5   The Authority's Secret

We now prove that the authority's secret information can be recovered by an attacker. The main insight is that the secret can be captured in a 40×40 matrix, and hence techniques from linear algebra suffice to recover it. Before we proceed, we must note that the center may choose to issue only KSVs from a submodule, N, of M, the module spanned by all KSVs.

Observation 1. *Let v be a KSV, and suppose u_1 and u_2 are both valid private keys for v. Then $u_1 - u_2 \in N^\perp$.*

Proof. Let (v', u') be any other valid key pair. Since $v' \cdot u_1 = v \cdot u' = v' \cdot u_2$, we have $v' \cdot (u_1 - u_2) = 0$ for all $v' \in N$.

The content of this observation is that, if two different key vectors, u_A and u'_A, form valid key pairs with the same KSV, then $K = K' = u_A \cdot v_B = u'_A \cdot v_B$ for all devices B. Hence u_A and u'_A are functionally indistinguishable.

Corollary 1. *The map $T : M \to (\mathbb{Z}/2^{56}\mathbb{Z})^{40}$, mapping public keys to private keys, is well defined   mod $N^\perp$.*

We can now prove that the map S has a particularly nice form.

Observation 2. *T can be represented by a 40×40 matrix, S.*

Proof. To show that a map can be represented by a matrix, we only need to show that it is linear. So let $v = cv_1 + v_2$. Then $(cT(v_1) + T(v_2)) \cdot v' = cT(v_1) \cdot v' + T(v_2) \cdot v' = cT(v') \cdot v_1 + T(v') \cdot v_2 = T(v') \cdot v = T(v) \cdot v'$, for arbitrary $v' \in N$. Thus $T(v) = cT(v_1) + T(v_2)$ mod $N^\perp$.

Recovering S is now straightforward. First collect a set of key pairs $(v_i, u_i)_{i=1}^n$ such that the v_i span N. Then use any standard technique to solve the systems of equations $U = SV$. For example, the Gaussian elimination algorithm of Section 4 can be applied here. This allows an attacker to recover all of the trusted center's secret, no matter how the center picks keys.

6   Forging Key Pairs

Let G be a matrix recovered as in Section 5. Then G and S agree on the submodule spanned by the recovered vectors $v_1, \ldots, v_n$, and quite probably disagree everywhere else. If $v_1, \ldots, v_n$ span M, then G is equivalent to S. In other words,

$Gv = Sv$ for all valid KSVs v. Thus, to forge a new key pair, one can simply pick a random KSV, v, and compute the corresponding private key $u = Gv$.

The authority may try to prevent the total recovery of S by only assigning to devices key pairs with KSVs in a submodule of $N \subset M$. If $\langle v_1, \ldots, v_n \rangle = N \neq M$, then attackers using linear algebra can only forge key pairs (v, u) where $v \in N$. Finding new KSVs in the span of the recovered KSVs may be difficult.[1] This could be a problem if the attacker wishes to build a device that interoperates with other HDCP devices and if the authority has placed all recovered KSVs on the key revocation list.

However, the HDCP protocol does not require devices to check that their peer's key is not the same as their own, and so a "parroting" attack is possible. To build an interoperable receiver, we can simply embed the matrix G in the device, and program it to reply to all authentication challenges with the KSV it just received from the transmitter. It can compute the corresponding private key on the fly and proceed with the authentication protocol. We note that an attacker could use essentially the same trick to build an interoperable transmitter, but the transmitter will have to perform two authentications. The first time, it will send a random KSV and collect the KSV of its peer. The transmitter will then abort the authentication and restart it using the KSV it just learned from the receiver. This attack only works if the authority uses the same mapping, T, for both transmitters and receivers. For reasons of clarity, we have made this assumption in our presentation of HDCP and our other attacks. The other claims in this paper hold in the more general setting, but the parroting attack does not.

One might be tempted to correct the defects in HDCP by signing the KSVs with a private key known only to the central authority. Then, when two devices execute the authentication protocol, they exchange the certificates containing their KSVs, verify each others' certificates using the authority's public key, and proceed as before. This change accomplishes very little. Eavesdropping would still be possible since the certificates, and hence the KSVs, of each device would be available to the eavesdropper who could then compute the corresponding private keys needed to decrypt the traffic. Devices would still be clonable by embedding the victim's certificate and private key in the clone. The paroting attack above is still available, too. The only thing certificates prevent is forging new keys. The Digital Transmission Content Protection (DTCP) standard includes a Restricted Authentication protocol that may be just such a certificate-enhanced variant of HDCP [ ]. The information needed to fully evaluate the security of DTCP is not publicly available, but what little is public gives reason to be sharply concerned that DTCP's restricted authentication protocol may be susceptible to similar attacks.

---

[1] It's not hard to reduce the subset-sum problem to the problem of finding a new KSV in the span of some other KSVs. However, since the dimension is only 40, an attacker could brute-force this problem if necessary.

7   Conclusion

These attacks are very powerful and very flexible. To recover the center's master secret, an attacker needs 40 key pairs, and we point out a variety of ways to get them. An attacker can reverse engineer 40 different HDCP video software utilities, he can break open 40 devices and extract the keys via reverse engineering, or he can simply license the keys from the trusted center. According to the HDCP License Agreement, device manufacturers can buy 10000 key pairs for $16000. Given these 40 spanning keys, the master secret can be recovered in seconds. So in essence, the trusted authority sells a large portion of its master secret to every HDCP licensee. With the master secret in hand, one can eavesdrop on all device communications, spoof any device, and clone any device, all in real time. One can produce a device that, by parroting back the KSVs of its peers, cannot be disabled by any blacklist. With a reasonable amount of computation, an attacker can also produce new device keys not on any key revocation list. For these reasons, we recommend that HDCP be abandoned in favor of conventional cryptographic schemes.

The HDCP design requirements called for an implementation in less than 10,000 gates. The fact that the designers chose a custom cryptosystem instead of off-the-shelf algorithms shows that there is work to be done in the area of efficient, secure hardware design. A brief search for the state-of-the art turned up an RSA implementation in 18,000 gates[ ] [2], and the KASUMI cryptosystem, which can be implemented in 3,000 gates[ ]. [3] Coupling these with a generous 9,000 gates of HDCP state machine would give a secure authentication and encryption subsystem in under 30,000 gates, but building a secure system in 10,000 gates is still a challenge.

Acknowledgements

We would like to gratefully acknowledge Intel and Digital Content Protection, LLC for helpful comments on this paper and for pointing us to Blom's work on key distribution systems. We thank Adrian Perrig for suggesting identity-based cryptosystems as a secure alternatve to HDCP.

References

1. A. Shamir. Identity-based cyrptosystems and signature schemes. In *Crypto'84*, 1984. 192
2. Y. Desmedt and J. Quisquater. Public-key systems based on the difficulty of tampering. In *Crypto'86*, 1986. 192

---

[2] The cited RSA design supports up to 2048-bit keys. We imagine the gate count could be cut substantially without compromising security by using only 768-bit keys.

[3] We have not evaluated KASUMI's ability to achieve the data rates required for uncompressed video.

3. H. Tanaka. A realization scheme for the identity-based cryptosystem. In *Crypto'87*, 1987. 192

4. S. Tsuji and T. Itoh. An ID-based cryptosystem based on the discrete logarithm problem. In *IEEE Journal of Selected Areas in Communication*, volume 7, 1989. 192

5. Dan Boneh and Matthew Franklin. Identity-based encryption from the Weil pairing. In *CRYPTO'2001*, 2001. 192

6. David Barth. Personal communication. September 2001. 193

7. Rolf Blom. An optimal class of symmetric key generation systems. In T. Beth, N. Cot, and I. Ingemarsson, editors, *Proc. EUROCRYPT 84*, pages 335–338. Springer-Verlag, 1985. 194

8. Rolf Blom. Non-public key distribution. In R. L. Rivest, A. Sherman, and D. Chaum, editors, *Proc. CRYPTO 82*, pages 231–236, New York, 1983. Plenum Press. 194

9. Scott Crosby. Apparent HDCP authentication protocol weaknesses. http://cryptome.org/hdcp-weakness.htm, May 2001. 194

10. Keith Irwin. Four simple cryptographic attacks on HDCP. http://www.angelfire.com/realm/keithirwin/HDCPAttacks.html, July 2001. 194

11. Niels Ferguson. Censorship in action: Silenced by the DMCA. http://www.macfergus.com/niels/dmca/index.html, August 2001. 194

12. Intel Corporation. *High-Bandwidth Digital Content Protection System*, 1.00 edition, February 2000. 194

13. Hitachi, Ltd. and Intel Corporation and Matsushita Electronic Industrial Co., Ltd. and Sony Corporation and Toshiba Corporation. *Digital Transmission Content Protection System, Volume 1*, July 2001. 198

14. Semiconductor Design Solutions. RSA2048A RSA coprocessor data sheet. http://www.sidsa.com/datasheets/RSA/ds_rsa2048a_short.html. 199

15. 3GPP Security Algorithms Group of Experts. 3GPP KASUMI evaluation report. Technical report, 3rd Generation Partnership Project, Oct 2000. 199

Implications of Digital Rights Management for Online Music – A Business Perspective

Willms Buhse

Dept. of General and Industrial Management, Technical University of Munich
Germany

Abstract This paper will examine and categorize potential business model scenarios for online music. The virtualization of music leads to market uncertainties. On the supply side, the offering party might not be able to sufficiently privatize online music by using digital rights management technologies. On the demand side, with a changing cost structure for digital goods, consumers might not be willing to pay directly for digital goods so that revenues would have to be collected indirectly by public or private entities. As a result, business models for online music can be categorized into four scenarios. In the first scenario, online music is used to promote the traditional offline business while in the second scenario, consumers are willing to pay for additional services to access online music. The third scenario is significantly different from the first two scenarios as music providers are expected to be able to protect their content by using digital rights management technology. In the fourth scenario peer-to-peer technologies allow consumers to use a mechanism called super distribution with which they can share and recommend songs. The paper concludes with a recommendation to music companies regarding privacy and strategic positioning.

1 The Need for Digital Rights Management in the Evolving Online Music Industry

This paper will examine and categorize potential business model scenarios for online music. In this article, online music is defined as commercially available digital music that is distributed over networks like the Internet. Thereby music has become the ideal case study for digital commerce with its unique availability in digital form on billions of CDs.

Regarding privacy, monitoring usage behavior of music consumers can potentially create a vast amount of usage data. Playlists made of songs with about three min title length can generate comprehensive sets of data over time, provided 4 hours of daily music consumption, usage data from 80 songs might be collected on a daily basis almost automatically.

T. Sander (Ed.): DRM 2001, LNCS 2320, pp. 201-212, 2002.
© Springer-Verlag Berlin Heidelberg 2002

From the beginning online distribution became an underground phenomenon.[1] The music industry, though small in its market size, has become a prominent case study for new technology concepts, introduced by companies like Napster for peer-to-peer file sharing, RealNetworks for streaming media, InterTrust for digital rights management and others. Forecasts from analysts regarding the market size for online-music, vary significantly between 7.8b US $ (Forrester), 2.6b US $ (Jupiter) and 1.9b US $ (Market Tracking International).[2]

Though much literature can be found prognosticating a significant change in the competitive environment of the music industry, little research exists on the combination of revenue models and property rights in the field of online music.[3] The starting point for this analysis is the assumption that the basic principle of the electronic market as an efficient allocation mechanism works. But uncertainties on both the supply and demand side of the electronic market are leading to insufficiencies. In the following, two significant consequences regarding the business models caused by the virtualization of music are analyzed: first the cost structure for the delivery is structured differently and thereby revenues might be affected. Second the protection of copyrights has become more difficult in today's networks. Combining these two uncertainties into a scenario matrix, case studies will be given for each of the resulting four categories. Concluding remarks are made about possible positioning of companies in the music industry.

2   The Demand-Side Perspective: Influences on Cost Structure and Revenue Models

According to Forsa, the majority of the Internet users (69 percent) in Germany are not willing to pay for information or entertainment on the net.[4] One reason that may limit the willingness to pay for online-music may lie in the loss of a physical representation of the artist's work, which has become a collectible good with comprehensive artwork associated with it.[5]

Information goods are characterized by having high fixed costs, or first-copy costs, but very low incremental costs.[6] In the case of the music industry, the production of the master-copy accumulates a high amount of costs, while the production of additional copies can be estimated as marginal costs.[7] A study conducted in England, Germany, Italy and France by Doglio/Richeri found that in the music industry, the first-copy cost amounts to an average of 21.1 percent, followed by manufacturing costs of 8.5 percent. The highest per-unit cost is attributable to marketing and sales with 49.9 percent, with the remaining 20.5 percent allocated to label costs and

---

[1]   Pettauer, Richard (2000)
[2]   Becker, A.; Ziegler, M. (2000) p. 14
[3]   Zerdick, A. et al. (1999) p. 53
[4]   Forsa-Study conducted from October, 26th – 29th, 2000 with 1005 internet users in Germany
[5]   In fact, a trend similar to the times of the LP, when printing costs for booklets increased in contrast to the production cost of the CD itself
[6]   Skiera, B. (1999), p. 97
[7]   Kelly (1998), p. 54

margin.[8] Cost elements, which might be affected are not only limited to manufacturing costs, but retail obsolesce, returns, physical distribution and transport. On the other hand, costs for technology, bandwidth and customer service have to be factored in. Consequently, the benefits of digital distribution do not significantly change the per-unit cost at current volumes. It does however offer the possibility to distribute in much larger quantities than in the physical world.

As a result, the Internet seems to have a significant impact on the music industry's revenue model and thereby on the competitive environment. In the literature, revenues are divided into two main categories: *direct revenues, which* result from the consumer, and *indirect revenues*, which are refinanced through associated products via public or private entities.[9] While in the literature a separation between different revenue streams seems possible, in the business environment, a wide spectrum of combinations can be found just like a newspaper might have revenue streams from advertising, subscription and single transactions. Additionally, in the television market, which closely resembles the music industry, the revenues tend to grow towards direct revenues. Ten years ago, direct and indirect revenues were split equal, while today, direct revenues mainly from subscriptions increased to 58 percent, compared to 42 percent for advertising based indirect revenues.[10] The possible reason for this is consumer preferences regarding the allocation of their limited time.[11] Also, indirect revenues are merely based on costumer information and data mining e.g. for personalized advertising. Nevertheless, at this time security concerns regarding registration and credit card payments seem to be higher than privacy concerns. Over time though, rising privacy concerns on an individual basis might start to influence buying behavior. This phenomenon then would lead to an additional increase in direct revenues as consumers become willing to pay an add-on for privacy.

3   The Supply-Side Perspective: Differentiation between Public and Private Goods through Digital Rights Management

The theory of public goods holds that goods have different characteristics whether or not there is rivalry or non-rivalry in using them. *Public goods* are *non-excludable* and *non-rivalrous* in consumption while private goods are sold to those who can afford to pay the market price.

In the music market, broadcasting as a public good is used to promote songs while CDs function as a container for music sold as private goods.[12] *Copyrights* are a means of establishing the boundaries between who is allowed to use a particular good and under which conditions, and who is not allowed to use it. Developments in technology seem to take away the grounds for these boundaries. Burke has shown how technological developments in the past gave rise to changes in copyright.[13] At the same time, piracy has always had a significant share in the music market. In 1999,

---

[8]   Doglio, D.; Richeri, G. (1996), p. 33ff.
[9]   Zerdick, A. et al.(1999), p. 25f.
[10] Veronis Suhler & Associate (1998), p. 39
[11] Berman, S., McCelellan, B. et al (2000) p. 27
[12] Tschmuck, P. (2000)
[13] Burke, A.E. (1996) p. 51

according to IFPI about 1.9b units of illegal copies were found with a value of 4,1b US $ leading to a hypothetical market share of 36 percent.[14] On the Internet, piracy has become an even larger mass phenomenon due to the availability of perfect digital copies. With non-excludable online-music, end consumers become *free riders*, which are not willing to pay the market price for music as long as others might be accessing the music for free.[15]

Traditionally, the distribution of music is dominated by an oligopoly of five major labels. For these music labels, the economic value lies in their artist contracts and in the exclusive distribution for recordings, which enables promotional distribution channels like free TV or radio.[16] Statistically, infrequent consumption of music albums as private goods accounts for about one hour, with revenues of 68 US $ per music listener per year. On the other hand, public broadcast amounts to frequent but superficial consumption of 3 hours a day. This results in 58 US $ in advertising revenues for the broadcast stations per year, from which music labels receive a much smaller percentage than from the album sales.[17] As a result, the music industry shows high interest in privatizing the music in order to generate higher revenues not only from traditional products but also from the online market. Increasing online piracy challenges the privatization of online music; therefore the music industry has started a number of legal, marketing, educational, and technology initiatives.

Law suits from the RIAA against MP3.com, Scour and Napster and others in the U.S. demonstrate the music industry's efforts to minimize copyright infringement. Though the industry might reach successes in certain countries, concepts like "Offshore-Web-Hosting" from companies like HavenCo.Com or Offshore.com.ai and de-central file sharing systems like Gnutella and FreeNet might well continue to operate despite law suits and even drive consumers to "underground" systems.[18]

From a technology point of view, the music industry started the Secure Digital Music Initiative (SDMI) to develop specifications jointly with technology companies like Microsoft, IBM, InterTrust and many others. Many doubt that the music industry can successfully introduce security mechanisms that are either unbreakable or at least can raise the barrier for piracy without creating unproportional high costs.[19] Many examples in other media industries like currently the DVD-protection scheme have shown failures of secure protection mechanisms.[20] Additionally, on the Internet only a single copy (even by re-digitizing from analog versions) made available is sufficient to be globally distributed in a short period of time leading to a total loss of control by the owner. But it is quite possible that the biggest challenge the music industry is facing is not hackers but instead infrastructure. Today's infrastructure with 200m multimedia PCs, 1b CD- audio-devices and 17b unprotected audio CDs with 150.000 different titles will be very difficult to replace.[21]

---

[14] IFPI (2000) p.2
[15] Heinrich, J. (1994), p.26
[16] Thurow, N. (1994), p. 81f.
[17] Bertelsmann internal research
[18] Schreirer, E. (2000), p. 9
[19] Albers, S.; Clement, M.; Skiera, B. (1999), p. 83
[20] DeCSS
[21] Gurley, W. (2000), p. 268f.

4   Four Business Model Scenarios

The goal of using scenarios is to categorize various business models according to several case studies involving new distribution mechanisms like file sharing, digital rights management and super distribution. As in the previous chapters described, the virtualization of music has two significant consequences regarding the business models: first the cost structure for the delivery is structured differently and thereby revenues might be affected. Second the protection of copyrights has become more difficult in today's networks.

Table 1. Scenario matrix for online music

	Public Good	Private Good
Indirect Revenues	Open-Source-Filesharing	Subscription Systems
Direct Revenues	Music Service Provider	Superdistribution

Four scenarios can be deduced by combining these two uncertainties into a matrix, which represents both, supply and demand. In this article, for each of the scenarios, one case study is described and possible revenue models are given.

4.1   Assumptions

These four business model scenarios are subject to the following assumptions:

- in the mid- to long-term, no business models will be viable which infringe on copyright laws. However, there might be systems without commercial interest that face no legal consequences for enabling illegal copies. Open-source-file sharing systems belong to this category.
- revenue models are based on rational entrepreneurial decisions, excluding artistic, voluntary or otherwise motivated scenarios.
- most importantly, these scenarios anticipate a slow migration towards online technologies. Meaning, traditional media companies maintain distribution control over physical storage media like CD and DVD. The hypothesis from Zerdick et al. states that electronic markets do not lead to an immediate substitution of the existent value chain. Nevertheless it is leading to a constant erosion of traditional value chains and the orientation towards the demand side.[22]

4.2   First Scenario: Open Source File Sharing Systems

Within less than two years, Napster became the largest music library ever with about 1b titles, without economic incentive, marketing activities, and even more important without involvement of the music industry.[23] At a very high level, file sharing systems

---

[22]   Zerdick, A. et al. (1999) p. 177

[23]   Becker, A.; Ziegler, M. (2000) p. 14

or peer-to-peer-networks (P2P) aggregate and distribute information. With either central or de-central listings, files be can searched for, transferred and stored locally. The main challenge for content owners is its mass phenomenon. Since its launch, Napster attracted almost 70 Million users who knowingly violate copyright laws.

While Napster through its partnership with Bertelsmann plans membership fees and the compensation of content owners, other open-source-file-sharing systems are developed without any commercial purpose. Their purpose is to freely distribute information beyond any control. Examples are Gnutella developed by Gene Kan and FreeNet designed by Ian Clarke. Both are designed to run de-centralized, which makes it almost impossible to control or shut down their operations. As a result, besides music files, other illegal content like children pornography and terrorist instructions can be found. The main challenge of these systems is that they only can scale with resources like content, bandwidth and storage from their users. As their content can be viewed as public goods, these systems attract *free riders* not willing to give any contribution in return. During a study of the Gnutella Network, it was found, that 70 percent of the users don't give any contribution to the system, and that half of the searches were answered by just one percent of the participants.[24] Apart from significant loss of system performance with longer search and download times, it adds vulnerability to the system as it might collapse with the shut down of few peers. On the other hand, there are concepts like seti@home with users voluntarily contributing resources in exchange for prestige and reputation. As a result, file-sharing systems seem to be able to overcome today's challenges and will play an important role in the distribution of online music.

How can the music industry embrace such systems to generate revenues? Revenues can be generated indirectly from online music in return for the value of consumers' attention.[25] This can be used to promote either the physical album or the artist in order to reach more popularity and thereby earn higher merchandising and advertising revenue. As a result, with online music being a public good, the combination of online and offline business by integrating online-music and traditional marketing and distribution seems a profitable business model.[26] Despite legal battles from RIAA arguing that illegal copies cannibalize album sales, market studies are inconclusive at this point. Jupiter identified Napster usage as one of the most important factors for increased music purchases.[27] On the other hand, VNU found album sales decreasing in record stores close to universities, where file sharing supposingly reaches high usage among students.[28] Creed offered their hit song in 1999 from 100 web sites for free downloads, and in the process stimulated their album sales. Coincidentally their album "Human Clay" reached the top of the billboard charts.[29] A recent example is the partnership between the online retailer CDNow and Napster, where the file sharing system receives a commission of about 15 percent for every album sale.

---

[24] Adar, E.; Huberman, B. (2000)

[25] Seidel, N. (1993), p. 87

[26] Tomczak et al (2000) p. 234; Zerdick et al. 1999, p. 187

[27] Sinnreich et al. (2000), p. 1

[28] VNU Entertainment Marketing Solutions (2000), p. 2f.

[29] Committee on Intellectual Property Rights and the Emerging Information Infrastructure (2000), p. 80f

Nevertheless, substitution of traditional media like CDs and DVD-Audio might increase as soon as a comparable infrastructure for online music exists. Physical goods have always served as "containers" for services. For example, a CD has no intrinsic value, only the value of delivering music. In the age of downloadable music, though, the CD loses its value as a container for music.[30]

4.3   Second Scenario: Music Service Provider

Provided online music is a public good, collecting direct payments seems almost impossible unless, the value lies primarily in the functionality and services, rather than in the content itself.[31] In this scenario, instead of copy protection, service-oriented new business models are developed that prevent the motive to copy. Besides content, these services offer convenience, reliability and fast access to music almost anywhere and at anytime and are referred to as the *celestial jukebox*. This services sector is expected to grow from 2.5m today to 12.3m in 2003 in the U.S.[32] Ultimately, those companies would have to combine content, community, application services, context and search functionality. Personalization plays a crucial role in attracting consumers and providing lock-in.[33] In the networked economy, these versions and even individual products and services are achievable due to smaller transaction and production/service costs.[34] Using a feedback loop mechanism for online-music, personal playlists can be generated, recommended, updated and shared among other users. Large description databases like Moodlogic analyze relationships among titles and artists according to rhythm, instruments, contextual information and even mood.

It might be easy to maintain a piracy site with some illegal copies, but to provide access, payment mechanisms and customer service to many thousand people simultaneously is a more complex task. Which companies might position themselves in the role of music service providers? First, relationships, such as those established by radio or television stations, emphasize repeat visits. They have already proven their ability for selection and aggregation of music.[35] Second, those with existing billing and services relationships like ISPs and Telcos, e.g. AOL TW. Third, there are companies with a link to end devices, like hardware-, OS-software-, and CE-device-manufacturers, though they might as well bet on copy protection technologies, as they are able to choose and set standards. Nevertheless, under current copyright law, most companies might have to negotiate licenses either directly with the music labels, their syndication partners or through royalty collecting entities, in order to be able to offer these services.

4.4   Third Scenario: Digital Rights Management-Based Subscription Models

Protection technologies play an important role in determining whether a media product is a public or a private good. In scenarios three and four, online music is

---

[30]   Rifkin, J (2000)

[31]   Deutsche Bank (2000) p. 14

[32]   Black, L. (2000)

[33]   Heinrich, J. (1999) p.32

[34]   Piller, F. (1998) p. 16

[35]   Hull, G.; Greco, A.; Martin, S. (2000), p. 129

considered a private good, as content owners are able to restrict access to the content and thereby introduce the possibility to exclude free riders and charge for their online music. To securely protect online music, all major labels incorporate *digital rights management* technologies, which basically fall into four categories: first the *access* is controlled with authentication and/or encryption mechanisms. Second, the *usage* is controlled according to rules that are set by the distributor of the music. This determines how the user can interface with the information, e.g., listen-only rights, where the user is unable to save or distribute the music. Third a *tracking* mechanism allows the information provider to track subsequent use with watermarking and digital footprints. Fourth and last, *payment* systems enable the information provider to generate revenue for the rights granted to the user. As a result of inefficient micro payment systems, subscription models are viewed as a method to overcome high transaction costs.[36]

For subscription models watermarking can provide important contributions to the field of intellectual property protection within a more extensive security framework for identification and proof of ownership, which is comparable to IRSC-Codes used by the GEMA for recognition of CD-Audios.[37] By embedding a watermark into the compressed audio signal during delivery, the customers are aware that a watermark may identify them.[38] Hence, they can be made responsible if the signal is found outside the legal domain by a trigger technology, even in a decompressed and analog representation.[39] In contrast to encryption technologies, watermarks could be used with today's infrastructure for CD-Audio as well as MP3-devices. Subscriptions bundle a large number of information goods for a fixed price. In a variety of circumstances, a multi-product monopolist can extract substantially higher profits by offering one or more bundles of information goods than by offering the same goods separately.[40] At the same time, bundling can be used to introduce new artists and titles as a strategy to overcome the information paradox, which states that the value of an information can't be determined a *priori* of consumption.

In this scenario, for the first time in their history, music labels have the opportunity to create a continuous relationship with the end consumer. This relationship offers a foundation on which music labels can generate revenues. The subscription model may represent a mix between indirect and direct revenues with the option of consumption combined with transparent pricing.[41] Forrester expects additional revenues from subscriptions of 3.3b US $.[42] A premium membership might offer a flatrate, eventually combined with services from the second scenario, while an advertising-based membership might limit access in quantity, time or actuality.

---

[36] Picot, A.; Reichwald, R.; Wigand, R. (2001) p. 372

[37] Goldhammer, K.; Zerdick, A. (1999), p. 96

[38] Tang, Puay (1998) p. 24

[39] Specifications for such an infrastructure is currently designed by the Secure Digital Music Initiative. www.sdmi.org SDMI, Document Nr. pdwg99070802, „SDMI Portable Device Specification Part 1, Version 1.0", p. 21

[40] Bakos, Brynjolffson (1999), p. 2f

[41] Zerdick, A. et al.(1999), p. 26; Sinnreich, A. (2000), p. 12.

[42] Schreirer, E. (2000), p. 12

4.5   Fourth Scenario: Super-Distribution

In 1990, a visionary architecture was developed for the distribution of digital goods. The Japanese Ryoichi Mori coined the term *Superdistribution* for this new concept of licensing information.[43] The fundamental idea is to allow free distribution of digital content, while controlling access to usage and changes with the content owner defining the terms. According to his prototype, called Software Service System (SSS), which was implemented as a peer-to-peer-architecture, the following components must be available:[44]

- a persistent *cryptographic wrapper* must stay in place when the digital property is used, copied, redistributed, etc.
- a *digital rights management system* with a trusted tool that tracks the deals and the usage associated with the access to the digital property
- *payment information* have to be exchanges securely among the parties

After securely encrypting the music with a key, the package can be digitally delivered to the consumers end device.[45] There, the locally installed trusted tool gains access to the digital content with an unlock key which leaves the file locally encrypted and streams the digital content into the memory for "on the fly" decryption. The user, who has agreed to the terms and conditions of use, has now the license to access the content. His usage is recorded and the transaction is reported to a clearinghouse to initiate payments and backup system information. Using the superdistribution concept, consumers can recommend and share files among each other via email, FTP, physical media and even file sharing networks. Still the copyright is being protected and the content owner maintains control and determines payment collection.

Under the third scenario, bundling was mentioned as being attractive for content companies to extract higher profits. In the music industry, this has always been the case with album sales, where only one or two hits from an entire album initiate the purchase. Digital products possess optimal de-bundling capability, which in return can be re-bundled again for custom-mixes.[46] With digital downloads and superdistribution, consumers might start "cherry picking" their hits and thereby endanger the traditional revenue model of album sales. In this scenario, using digital rights management and superdistribution, major labels maintain control over the distribution of music - they might even be able to enforce their copyrights more than in the traditional world.

5   Conclusions Regarding Positioning and Privacy

In this paper scenarios for online business models that depend on uncertainties on the supply and demand side of the music industry were examined. It was argued that on

[43]   Mori, R. (1990); Cox, Brad (1996); Morin, Jean-Henry (1999) p. 22. It seems as if in parallel Brad Cox has developed a similar system, that is documented in 1994 with his system, CopyFree Software
[44]   Morin, Jean-Henry (1999) p. 21
[45]   Tang, Puay (1998) p. 23
[46]   Albers; Clement; Peters (1998) p. 275; Kulle, Jürgen (1998) p. 80

the one hand, online music could either be a public or a private good, due to insufficiencies in absolute content protection using digital rights management technologies. On the other hand, the willingness for consumers to pay for digital goods might determine the nature for direct or indirect revenue streams. As a result, consistent business models in all four scenarios were developed. The scenarios have shown that there is a spectrum of potential revenue streams for online music both as public and private goods. Therefore, the main distinction between the scenarios depends on the supply side, where copyright for online music can either be protected by technical means or not. At the same time, decisions regarding the usage of consumer data and privacy policies are made.

Although online music distribution has been in place for some time, it is too early to determine which scenarios will evolve. Nevertheless, it is quite possible for all these scenarios to exist in parallel under certain market conditions. In this case, it is assumed that all four scenarios can come into affect during the life cycle of an online music release. Starting with the secure superdistribution concept (scenario 4) at the time of release, followed by a time lag for subscription based accessibility (scenario 3). Over (short or long) time, the value might decrease and with pirates distributing illegal copies, the release might become widely accessible as a public good. Then services might be offered (scenario 2) and at the same time additional value from the user's attention and usage data for promotion and advertising might be extracted through data mining (scenario 1).

One of the key difficulties in data mining are insufficiently prepared usage data leading to wrong conclusions and decisions. By giving the consumers the option to manage their own usage data, inaccurate, irrelevant or personal data sets can be deleted or corrected. Thereby, the music label's interest in high quality conclusions and the consumer's interest in privacy can be matched. Then, improved usage data can be used to expand services and revenues in all four scenarios.

As a result, the music labels should prepare themselves to claim strategic positions in all four scenarios, otherwise their traditionally dominant role in the music market, and the barrier-to-entry that currently prevents external competition will diminish. Therefore, the optimal strategy is not only to reduce the motives for copy infringement, but at the same time to increase the accessibility for consumers to digital products and services.

References

1. Adar E., Huberman B. (2000) Free Riding on Gnutella, http://www.firstmonday.org/issues/issue5_10/adar/index.html,   viewed   at December 10th, 2000
2. Albers S., Clement M., Peters K. (1998) Marketing mit Interaktiven Medien. Strategien zum Markterfolg, Frankfurt am Main
3. Albers S., Clement M., Skiera B. (1999) Wie sollen die Produkte vertrieben werden? – Distributionspolitik. In: Albers S., Clement M. et al. E-Commerce – Einstieg, Strategie und Umsetzung im Unternehmen. Frankfurt, pp. 79-94
4. Bakos Y., Brynjolffson E. (1999) Bundling information Goods: Pricing, profits and Efficiency, Working Paper

5. Becker, A.; Ziegler, M. (2000) Wanted: A survival plan for the music industry – Napster and the consequences, Diebold Study

6. Benjamin, Robert; Wigand, Rolf (1995) Electronic Markets and Virtual Value Chains on the Information Superhighway. In: Sloan Management Review, winter, pp. 62 - 72.

7. Berman, S., McCelellan, B. et al. (2000) The Future of the Entertainment and Media Industries: 2005, PriceWaterhouseCoopers, New York

8. Black, L. (2000) Understanding Consumer Demand to create business models that work, Webnoize research, SGAE, Madrid, 25. 10. 2000

9. Burke, A.E (1996) How Effective Are International Copyright Conventions in the Music Industry? Journal of Cultural Economics, volume 20, number 1, pp. 51-66

10. Choi, S.Y., D.O. Stahl, and A.B. Whinston (1997) The Economics of Electronic Commerce. Macmillan Technical Publishing

11. Committee on Intellectual Property Rights and the Emerging Information Infrastructure (2000) The Digital Dilemma – Intellectual Property in the Information Age. National Academy Press, Washington

12. Cox, Brad (1996) Superdistribution: Objects as Property on the Electronic Frontier, Addison-Wiley

13. Deutsch Bank (2000) New Media Mechanics - Value of Content Online

14. Doglio, D.; Richeri, G. (1996) The Economics of Publishing: Prospects for Online Distribution, Centro Studi Salvador, Telecom Italia, Venice

15. Evans, P.; Wurster T. (1999) Blown to Bits - How the new economics of information transforms strategy. Harvard Business School Press, Boston, Massachusetts

16. Forsa-Study (2000) viewed at
    http://www.berlinonline.de/wissen/computer/internet/.html/200011/net01105.html

17. Goldhammer, K.; Zerdick, A. (1999) Rundfunk Online – Entwicklung und Perspektiven des Internets für Hörfunk- und Fernsehanbieter, Berlin

18. Gurley, W. (2000) Digital music: The real law is Moore's law, Fortune; New York; Oct 2, 2000;; Volume: 142, Issue: 7 pp. 268f.

19. Heinrich, J. (1994) Medienökonomie, Vol. 1 Opladen Westdt. Verlag

20. Heinrich, J. (1999) Medienökonomie, Vol. 2 Opladen Westdt. Verlag

21. Hull, G.P.; Greco, A.P.; Martin, S. (2000): The Structure of the Radio Industry, in: Greco, A. (2000): The Media and Entertainment Industries. Readings in Mass Communications, Boston, pp. 122-156

22. IFPI (2000) Piracy Report 2000, June 2000

23. Kelly, K. (1998) New Rules for the New Economy. 10 Radical Strategies for a Connected World. Viking Press, New York

24. Kulle, Jürgen (1998) Ökonomie der Musikindustrie: Eine Analyse der körperlichen und unkörperlichen Verwertung von Musik mit Hilfe von Tonträgern und Netzen, Frankfurt a. M.

25. Morin, Jean-Henry (1999) Commercial Electronic Publishing over Open Networks: A Global Approach Based on Mobile objects (Agents). Dissertation University of Geneva

26. Mori, R. (1990) Superdistribution: The Concept and the Architecture. The Transactions of the IEICE E73, No 7.

27. Pettauer, Richard (2000) Die Blitzkarriere von MP3. Micafocus 1: Reales Musikschaffen Für Einen Virtuellen Markt, March 18th 2000, http://www.mica.at/mf_pettau_p.html, viewed at 10.10.2000

28. Picot, A.; Reichwald, R.; Wigand, R. (2001) Die grenzenlose Unternehmung, 4. Ed., Wiesbaden

29. Piller, F. T. (1998) Kundenindividuelle Massenproduktion. Die Wettbewerbs-strategie der Zukunft, München.

30. Rifkin, J. (2000) The Future of Digital Music: Is There an Upside to Downloading? Hearing Statements U.S. Senate Committee on the Judiciary, viewed at http://www.senate.gov/~judiciary/7112000_jg.htm

31. Schreirer, E.(2000) Content out of Control, The Forrester Report, Cambridge, MA

32. SDMI (2000) SDMI Portable Device Specification Part 1, Version 1.0, Document Nr. pdwg99070802, p. 21

33. Seidel, N. (1993) Rundfunkökonomie: Organisation, Finanzierung und Management von Rundfunkunternehmen, Wiesbaden

34. Shapiro, C.; Varian, H.R. (1998) Information Rules. A Strategic Guide to the Network Economy, Boston

35. Sinnreich, A. (2000) Digital Music Subscriptions: Post-Napster Product Formats, Jupiter Studie

36. Skiera, B. (1999) Wie teuer sollen die Produkte sein? – Preispolitik. In: Albers, S.; Clement, M. et al. (Hrsg.) E-Commerce – Einstieg, Strategie und Umsetzung im Unternehmen. Frankfurt, pp. 94-108

37. Tang, Puay (1998) How Electronic Publishers are Protecting against Privacy: Doubts about Technical Systems of Protection The Information Society Vol. 14, n. 1, pp. 19-31

38. Thurow, N. (1994) Die digitale Verwertung von Musik aus der Sicht von Schallplattenproduzenten und ausübenden Künstlern, in: Becker, Jürgen / Dreier, Thomas, Urheberrecht und digitale Technologien, Vortragssammlung der Sitzung des Instituts für Urheber- und Medienrecht, UFITA-Schriftenreihe, Baden-Baden, p. 77

39. Tomczak, T. et al. (2000) Online-Distribution als innovativer Absatzkanal. In:

40. Tschmuck, P. (2000) Internetökonomie und Musikwirtschaft. During: Micafocus 1: Reales Musikschaffen Für Einen Virtuellen Markt, March 18th, 2000, http://www.mica.at/mf_tschmuck_p.html, viewed at 10.10.2000

41. Veronis Suhler & Associate (1998), Communications Forecast

42. VNU Entertainment Marketing Solutions (2000) Measuring the Influence of Music File Sharing, New York

43. Zerdick, A. et al.. (1999) Die Internet-Ökonomie – Strategien für die digitale Wirtschaft. Springer, Berlin, Heidelberg (u.a.)

From Copyright to Information Law – Implications of Digital Rights Management[*]

Stefan Bechtold

Stanford Law School
559 Nathan Abbott Way, Stanford, CA 94305-8610, USA
stef@n-bechtold.com
http://www.jura.uni-tuebingen.de/~s-bes1

Abstract. Digital Rights Management (DRM) promises to enable a secure electronic marketplace where content providers can be remunerated for the use of their digital content. In the last few years, countless
research efforts have been devoted to DRM technologies. However,
DRM systems are not only technological phenomena: they pose complex legal, business, organizational and economic problems. This article
tries to show that from a lawyer's perspective some of the innovativeness and potential of DRM can only be understood when one looks at it
from a multidisciplinary viewpoint. The article gives an overview of the
various ways by which digital content is protected in a DRM system.
The intertwining protection by technology, contracts, technology licenses and anti-circumvention regulations could lead to a new "property right" making copyright protection obsolete. However, there is a
danger of over-protection: questions of fair use and other limitations to
traditional copyright law have to be addressed. If competition is not
able to solve this tension between the interests of content providers and
the interests of users or the society at large – which seems to be doubt-
ful at least – it is the law that has to provide a solution. The legislators
in the U.S. and Europe use different approaches to address this problem. By looking at DRM in this way, several patterns can be observed
which are characteristic of many areas of Internet law.

1 Introduction

Digital Rights Management (DRM) promises to offer a secure framework for distributing digital content (music, video, text, rare data etc.). DRM enables an electronic
marketplace where previously unimaginable business models can be implemented. At
the same time, DRM ensures that content providers – particularly copyright owners –

---

[*] This article is based on an extensive treatise on Digital Rights Management written in German by the author at the University of Tübingen Law School, Germany (1999–2001),
see [1].

T. Sander (Ed.): DRM 2001, LNCS 2320, pp. 213–232, 2002.
© Springer-Verlag Berlin Heidelberg 2002

receive adequate remuneration for the creation of the content that is distributed over the DRM system.

From a technological perspective, DRM poses intricate problems that have led to large research efforts at technology companies, universities and research centers worldwide. However, DRM systems are not only technological phenomena. From an organizational perspective, DRM interoperability and standardization remain open problems to a large extent. From a business perspective, it is intriguing to look at the new business models which DRM systems could enable. From an economic perspective, DRM could challenge – jointly with other technologies surrounding the Internet – some aspects of the standard economic theory taken for granted hitherto. From a sociological perspective, DRM could have an influence on the distribution of information and therefore power in a society. From a legal perspective, DRM creates a whole assemblage of problems ranging from copyright, contract, privacy, patent and antitrust problems to freedom of speech issues.

This article intends to provide an overview of the copyright-related parts of the legal framework in which DRM systems operate. It intends neither to give a comprehensive overview of DRM in general nor to provide an in-depth analysis of all the questions being raised. It is the firm belief of the author that some of the real innovation and potential of DRM can only be understood if one looks at several disciplines engaged in the creation or analysis of DRM systems at the same time. There is a clear lack of interdisciplinary work in the DRM field. Therefore, while this article ultimately has a legal argument, it will describe some technical and economic aspects of DRM and correlate these aspects with the legal discussion of DRM systems. As used in this article, the term "Digital Rights Management" has a broad scope. It not only covers a great number of different technologies by which digital content can be secured. It also covers the protection of digital content offered by various legal instruments as well as business and economic aspects of DRM.

The article proceeds as follows. Sections 2 to 4 give an overview of the various means of protection (both technical and legal) available in a DRM system. Section 5 correlates those means with each other both from a legal and a law and economics perspective. Section 6 asks what role copyright law still plays in a DRM system. Section 7 gives an overview of how the legislators in the U.S. and Europe have responded to some of the challenges to copyright law created by DRM systems. Finally, section 8 puts the results of this article in the broader context of Internet law.

2   Protection by Technology

2.1   Overview

In order to ensure that consumers pay for using digital content and that content providers are adequately remunerated, DRM systems intend to control access to and use of digital content. This can be achieved by implementing various technological protection measures. Encryption techniques are especially important; "digital containers" enable the durable encryption of distributed content. Copy control technologies such as the "Copy Generation Management System" (CGMS) used in DVD players or the

"Serial Copy Management System" (SCMS) used in DAT and Minidisc players control the number of copies of digital content a user is able to make.

In order to facilitate the automated trading of digital content and associated digital rights, DRM systems use metadata to formally describe digital content and related parameters. Thereby, the content provider is able to control automatically in a very fine-grained way when and where which consumer uses a particular content for what purpose. Metadata systems use standards that enable the description of digital content (e.g. DOI, ISBN, ISRC, ISWC and PII), its rights holders (e.g. CAE/IPI) and its accompanying usage terms (so-called "usage rules" defined in "rights management languages" such as XrML or ODRL).[1] Either metadata can be stored in special headers of a digital content format, or they can be embedded directly into the digital content by using digital watermarking techniques.

DRM systems employ different techniques to identify consumers and trace back illegally copied content (e.g. serial numbers, digital fingerprints, traitor tracing). In order to provide a uniformly high level of security, various techniques are used that ensure the integrity and authenticity of digital content, its accompanying metadata and the hardware and software components of a DRM system (e.g. digital signatures, fragile watermarks, challenge-response protocols). Furthermore, security attacks are complicated by tamper-proof hard- and software (e.g. smart cards, code obfuscation). In order to prevent the copying of protected content after it has been transformed into an analog format, special analog protection systems and digital watermarks intend to make such copying more difficult at least.

DRM systems not only provide passive protection mechanisms. They also can employ various means that prevent or respond actively to security breaches. Specialized filters and "audio fingerprinting" or "robust hash" techniques can block access to pirated content. Fair-exchange protocols ensure technically that the consumer receives access to protected content only after having paid the appropriate price. If the DRM system detects a security breach, it can revoke and disable compromised consumer devices.

In order to be successful on the mass-market, DRM technologies have to be integrated into consumer devices in a standardized way. Various working and standardization groups try to coordinate the development process of DRM technology.[2] Today, various media systems available on the market use one or the other DRM technology. DRM components can be found in pay TV systems, DAT and Minidisc players as well as some videocassettes. The DVD system employs various technological protection measures, e.g. the "Content Scramble System" (CSS), the regional code playback control and the aforementioned CGMS. Other important DRM standards include the "Content Protection for Recordable and Prerecorded Media" (CPRM/CPPM), the "Digital Transmission Content Protection" (DTCP, protecting IEEE 1394 bus systems) and the "High-bandwidth Digital Content Protection" (HDCP, protecting digital video outputs). Furthermore, DRM solutions are being integrated into standard audio

---

[1] This is not an exhaustive listing of existing metadata standards, of which there are dozens, if not hundreds. Besides, there are numerous proprietary metadata systems.

[2] Two of the most well-known groups include the "Copy Protection Technical Working Group" (CPTWG) and the "Secure Digital Music Initiative" (SDMI).

and video software players, ebook reading software, operating systems and mobile devices.

In summary, DRM is a general term for a set of intertwining technologies that can be used to establish a secure distribution channel for digital content. The specific elements used vary from DRM system to DRM system. As understood in this article, DRM ranges from simple copy-prevention technologies to comprehensive secure distribution systems.

2.2   Supporting Protection by Anti-circumvention Regulations

Although DRM systems promise to provide a high level of technical security, no commercially viable system will be technically 100% secure. Technological protection measures have been hacked in the past and this will not change in the foreseeable future. In order to increase the overall security of a DRM system, over the last few years special legal regulations have been created that outlaw the circumvention of technological protection measures as well as the manufacturing and distribution of devices which can be used to circumvent such measures ("preparatory activities").

On the international level, such provisions can be found in two treaties adopted in 1996 under the aegis of the World Intellectual Property Organization (WIPO Copyright Treaty and WIPO Performances and Phonograms Treaty). In the U.S., Congress enacted complex anti-circumvention regulations as part of the Digital Millennium Copyright Act of 1998 (17 U.S.C. §§ 1201-1205). Additionally, provisions of the Audio Home Recording Act of 1992 (17 U.S.C. §§ 1001-1010), of communications law (47 U.S.C. § 553 and § 605) and of trade secret law can apply. In the European Union, article 6 of the recently adopted Copyright Directive of 2001 [2] contains a detailed provision outlawing the circumvention of technological protection measures and certain preparatory activities. Furthermore, the European Conditional Access Directive of 1998 [3] protects a wide variety of conditional-access-based services against preparatory activities (e.g. pay TV, but also Internet-based services). Additional prohibitions can be found in the laws of the member states of the European Union (e.g. copyright, criminal, unfair competition, telecommunications, broadcasting and tort law).

Another set of regulations outlaw the manipulation of DRM metadata. Such provisions can be found in the aforementioned WIPO treaties, the U.S. Digital Millennium Copyright Act (17 U.S.C. § 1202) and in article 7 of the European Copyright Directive [2]. Usually, these regulations protect metadata identifying the digital content, its rights holders and its usage rules. In contrast, metadata identifying the individual consumers (e.g. by digital fingerprints or traitor tracing) are not covered by this protection due to privacy concerns.

All these provisions have little to do with traditional copyright law. They are part of an emerging body of information law regulating the access to and use of information.

3   Protection by Contracts

3.1   Overview

In a DRM system, content providers are not protected by technology and anti-circumventions regulations alone. Rather, they can use contracts to oblige consumers to use the protected content only in certain ways. In such a contractually protected DRM system, consumers are required to enter into a contractual agreement either at the time they acquire some DRM-enabled hardware or software device or at the time they want to access an individual content within the DRM system (by entering into so-called "click-wrap contracts").

Such DRM contracts may be used to protect digital content and the DRM system itself. For instance, they may include terms obligating consumers to download the content only to DRM-secured devices, not to burn it onto CD-ROMs or DVD-ROMs, not to copy and paste it and not to print out images or text. They also may define how often, when and where the protected content may be used ("usage rules"). Other terms may protect the security of the DRM system itself. Consumers may be forbidden from reverse engineering system software or from circumventing the technological protection measures used in the system (cf., e.g., [4]).

This contractual protection is only helpful if the contracts are legally enforceable. Similarities to "shrink-wrap licenses" used in the software business could suggest that DRM consumer contracts are invalid. However, at least in the U.S. a tendency within courts and legislators to consider shrink-wrap licenses as valid contracts is observable.[3] Furthermore, the legal problems of shrink-wrap licenses greatly depend on the specific design of the licenses and the accompanying business model (e.g. when and how the contract is concluded and who the parties to the contract are). The validity of consumer contracts in DRM systems raises complex legal problems that are beyond the scope of this article. However, no basic obstacles exist for content providers to contractually protect their content in a DRM system. It is possible to design a DRM system and its business models in a way that such contracts are legally enforceable.

3.2   Supporting Protection by Technology

As described above, DRM consumer contracts contain usage rules defining the ways in which the consumer is authorized to use the content. These usage rules can be expressed as metadata in rights management languages (see above at section 2.1). From a legal perspective, this is a very important feature of DRM systems as compliance to the contractual terms not only can be controlled by law, but also by technology: if the contract and the metadata of a digital content allows a user only to make two copies, any further copy will be prevented by the technological measures of the DRM system. This shows that the contractual protection is supported by a technological protection: Technology makes it harder or even impossible to disobey contractual obligations.

---

[3]   Cornerstones of this development are a decision by the 7th Circuit Court of Appeals (see [5]) and the "Uniform Computer Information Transactions Act" (UCITA), see [6].

3.3   Supporting Protection by Anti-circumvention Regulations

However, this technological protection of DRM contracts is not failsafe. Once in a while, attackers will succeed in altering or deleting usage metadata. Against this attack, the law provides regulations which specifically prohibit the manipulation or deletion of metadata (see above at section 2.2). This shows the intertwining of the means of protection in a DRM system: content providers may protect their content by contracts, which can be protected themselves by various technological protection measures which are in turn legally protected against circumvention.

4   Protection by Technology Licenses

Many DRM technologies are protected by a patent or kept as a trade secret. For instance, the developer of a symmetric DRM encryption system keeps the decryption keys secret due to security reasons.[4] If a computer or consumer electronics manufacturer wants to enable his devices to process content that is protected by this DRM technology, he has to enter into a technology license agreement with the developer of the technology. Thereby, the manufacturer gains knowledge of the decryption keys and of other details of the technology. Licensees of DRM technologies include manufacturers of consumer electronics, computers, storage media and other DRM-enabled devices or components as well as content providers.

DRM technology license agreements can be used to protect the interests of content providers although the content providers typically are not the licensors of the DRM technology. In long lasting negotiations between the content, computer and consumer electronics industry, the content industry has made clear that it would be willing to distribute its content in a digital format only if an adequate level of security could be assured. As no DRM system will be successful on the market without an appropriate amount of content accessible within this system, every technology developer of a DRM solution has vital commercial interests that his technology be implemented in consumer devices in the most secure way. Therefore, DRM developers license their technology only on the condition that the interests of content providers are preserved when the technology is implemented in consumer devices. Thereby, DRM technology licenses indirectly serve the interests of content providers (see also [7, at 15, 27]).

So far, this close connection between DRM technology licenses and copyright protection has not been discussed a great deal among legal scholars. Only the U.S. Federal Communications Commission has looked at a specific DRM technology license in the pay TV sector from this angle (cf. [7]).[5] This article cannot describe any DRM technology license in detail. However, it gives an overview of some common license terms.[6]

---

[4]   If consumer devices need the symmetric key for decryption, it is regularly stored in a tamper-proof environment.

[5]   The FCC examined the validity of the "POD Host Interface License Agreement", a technology license of the OpenCable initiative, [8].

[6]   The technology licenses analyzed for this purpose are publicly available from the respective licensing administrators or other websites. They include: the CSS License Agreement and

It is crucial for commercial success that content is protected at every stage within the DRM system. However, a DRM system is not a monolithic technology, but consists of a large number of different technologies. Therefore, numerous protection measures have to be combined to provide a continuous level of high security. To achieve this goal, technology licenses tie together several DRM technologies by requiring that the licensor of one specific DRM technology also use another DRM technology in his implementation.[7] For instance, the CSS License Agreement requires that the manufacturer of stand-alone DVD players also incorporate the region coding technology into his players. Furthermore, the players are only allowed to transmit analog video data in a format protected by analog copy protection technologies of Macrovision and equipped with CGMS copy control signals. Digital video data may only be transmitted to outputs which are equipped with copy-protection technologies (either DTCP or HDCP, see above section 2.1). Similar provisions can be found in other technology license agreements.

DRM technology licenses also require that DRM-enabled devices obey the usage rules of digital content that are determined by the content provider in metadata. Sometimes, the licenses contain default usage rules (e.g. by determining that content can only be copied once). DRM technology licenses also contain provisions to ensure that consumer device manufacturers implement the DRM technology in a robust way. For this reason, manufacturers are required to use security technologies such as encryption, self-checking and tamper-proof hard-/software in their DRM implementations. Technology licenses require that it be difficult at least to defeat the DRM protection by using professional tools such as logic analyzers, chip disassembly systems or in-circuit emulators. If the licensed DRM technology is defeated nevertheless, the licensee is required to redesign or replace its affected products within clearly defined time frames. Finally, technology licenses prohibit manufacturers of DRM-enabled consumer equipment to produce devices or software that can be used to circumvent the DRM protection.

In summary, DRM technology licenses are used to establish a comprehensive DRM environment that enables secure transmissions from the content provider to each consumer. They contain numerous terms that indirectly serve the copyright and security interests of the content providers.

5   Paradigm Shift in Protection

As this article has shown so far, the protection of digital content in a DRM system is based on various means of protection: (1) protection by technology with supporting protection by anti-circumvention regulations, (2) protection by contracts with supporting protection by technology and anti-circumvention regulations and (3) protection by technology licenses (see figure 1).

CSS Procedural Specifications, the HDCP License Agreement, the POD Host Interface License Agreement, the CPRM/CPPM License Agreement and the DTCP License Agreement.

[7]   In principle, such tying arrangements could raise antitrust concerns. An analysis of this aspect is beyond the scope of this article. However, such an analysis is likely to lead to the result that the license agreements are valid to a large extent.

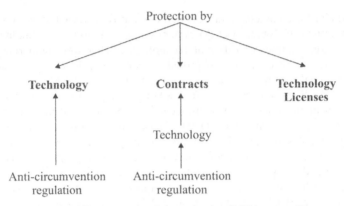

Fig. 1. Different means of protection in a DRM system (1)

In the following section, the implications of these different means of protection will be analyzed from both a legal and a law and economics perspective.

5.1   Legal Perspective

5.1.1   Intertwining Means of Protection

One of the most prominent features of the protection by DRM systems is that the various means of protection do not exist independently of each other. Only when one looks at DRM protection as a whole can one see some of the innovativeness and potential of DRM systems. The following two examples should clarify this proposition:

1. In order to prevent large-scale piracy, content providers have strong interests to hinder consumers from making unlimited copies of digital content. A fully developed DRM system provides numerous ways to realize these interests: encryption and other technologies can be employed to control the uses a consumer can make of a digital content (*protection by technology*). If an attacker is able to circumvent these technologies, he may violate legal circumvention prohibitions (*legal protection of the technological protection*). Furthermore, consumers can be required by contract to make only a specified number of copies (*protection by contracts*). Such usage rules can be expressed in metadata which are the basis for copy-control technologies such as SCMS or CGMS. Thereby, it is ensured technologically that users obey the terms of their usage contracts. Metadata can be embedded in the content by using robust digital watermarks (in each case a *technological protection of the contractual protection*). If an attacker succeeds in altering or deleting the metadata, anti-circumvention provisions may apply again (*legal protection of the technological protection of the contractual protection*). Finally, manufacturers of DRM-enabled hardware and software are obliged by technology licenses to ensure that their products obey the metadata determined by the content providers (*protection by technology licenses*).
2. A DRM system should provide the highest security that is technically possible but still commercially viable. This can be achieved by different means of protec-

tion: from a technical viewpoint, this involves tamper-proof hardware and software as well as technologies to check the inegrity and authenticity of DRM components and to revoke compromised devices (*protection by technology*). If these technologies are circumvented, anti-circumvention provisions may apply (*legal protection of the technological protection*). At the same time, users are forbidden by contract from circumventing the technological measures (*protection by contracts*). Finally, manufacturers of DRM-enabled devices are prohibited by technology license agreements from producing devices or software that can be used to circumvent the technological protection (*protection by technology licenses*).

These and many other examples show that in a DRM system, the content provider is always protected simultaneously by several means of protection. Each of these means is not 100% secure: technological protection can be circumvented, statutory prohibitions can be disobeyed, contracts can be breached. However, it is one of the most interesting features of DRM systems that these means of protection do not operate independently. If one of the means fails, another means steps in which sustains the overall protection level of the DRM system. The security of a DRM system is not accomplished by technology, law or market forces alone. Rather, it is a result of numerous different, but *intertwining* means of protection. This common feature of many DRM systems has often been underrepresented in the scholarly discussions. Regularly, critics of DRM assert that DRM ultimately will fail because it is impossible to create a technically secure DRM system. However, this criticism misses the point because it only regards one dimension of DRM protection.

5.1.2   Creation of a Privatized "Property Right"

The intertwining protection by technology, contracts, anti-circumvention regulations and technology licenses in a DRM system raises the question what the implications for traditional copyright protection are.

In a DRM system, it is possible to require that each consumer enters into a contract before accessing DRM-protected content (see above section 3.1). In principle, each of these contracts only binds the parties of the contract, i.e. the content provider and one consumer. However, if every consumer must enter into such a contract before accessing the content, no consumer exists who is not in privity with the content provider. In the U.S. legal literature, this has led many commentators to the conclusion that the contractual protection in a DRM system resembles a property right which is good against all the world.[8] The law has regularly already granted a property right to content providers: copyright law. As such, the copyright owner is entitled to exclude unauthorized persons from reproducing, distributing or performing his works. According to these commentators, the sum of consumer contracts in a DRM system leads to a similar level of protection because every consumer in a whole mass market is contractually bound to the usage terms set by the content provider.

However, this point of view captures only parts of the potential of DRM systems, as it underestimates the intertwining means of protection in a DRM system. If the content provider could only rely on a myriad of contracts to protect his digital content,

---

[8] This discussion has been fueled by a decision of the 7th Circuit Court of Appeals dating from 1996, [5].

this protection would have severe weaknesses. For instance, a consumer who obtained a pirated copy of the digital content would not be bound to any DRM contracts at all; the contractual protection would fail whereas copyright protection would still succeed. However, one has to keep in mind that in an idealized DRM system such a case would never arise: Normally, the DRM system grants access to protected content only after the consumer has agreed to a contractual agreement (*protection by technology*). If the consumer circumvents this procedure, he may violate anti-circumvention provisions (*legal protection of technology*). Furthermore, this procedure may be secured by appropriate *technology license* agreements. Through a combination of technological and legal protection a DRM system tries to ensure that a digital content can *never* be accessed or used without having agreed to the appropriate usage terms. The intertwining means of protection try to inextricably knit together content and usage terms.

Therefore, from a legal viewpoint the real innovation of DRM systems is not the protection of content by technology or unilateral contracts which bind every consumer. It is the combination of this protection with other supporting means that creates a level of protection commonly found only with traditional property rights. As with the protection by a property right, no consumer of DRM content exists who is not subject to the DRM protection. If one views this conglomerate of protection as a whole, the terms "privatized property right" and "private legislation" seem appropriate. Overall, a trend from protection by copyright law to protection by the intertwining means of technology, contracts, anti-circumvention regulations and technology licenses can be observed. This new conglomerate of protection has the potential to supplant copyright law as the primary means of protection in the digital environment.

5.2   Law and Economics Perspective

A law and economics analysis of the protection in DRM systems leads to similar results. Like any information, digital content is (to some extent) a public good characterized by its non-rivalry and non-exclusivity.[9] Because it is impossible to exclude non-paying consumers from the consumption of the content, no consumer will pay for using the content. Hiding his real preferences, every consumer hopes that another consumer will buy the content and that he can use this content as well due to its non-exclusive and non-rivalrous nature ("free rider" problem). As a result, nobody would create content in the first place, as the costs of creation could never be recouped (cf. [9]). To eliminate this market failure, the law grants the content producer a property right known as copyright. Through copyright law, the content producer is able to exclude non-paying consumers and copyists from using his content. Copyright law artificially raises the costs of copying content, thereby enabling the content producer to recover his costs of creation. To a certain extent, copyright law eliminates the non-exclusivity of content.

As was shown above, the intertwining means of protection in a DRM system enable the content provider to exclude unauthorized consumers from using protected content as well. Just as copyright law, the DRM protection eliminates the non-

---

[9]   A good is non-rivalrous when the consumption of this good by one consumer does not diminish its availability for others to use. A good is nonexclusive if it is (nearly) impossible to exclude consumers from consuming it.

exclusivity of content to a certain extent. This could have far-reaching implications for the necessity of copyright law: the market failure which copyright law was established to remedy does not seem to exist any more in DRM systems. Seen from a law and economics perspective, the protection by DRM systems could replace the protection by copyright law to a certain extent.

6   Necessity of Copyright Law

The analysis of the previous section seemingly leads to the result that copyright protection could become useless in DRM systems. However, such a proposition would ignore several objections, some of which will be depicted in this section. Firstly, copyright law could still be needed to limit the protection offered by DRM systems (see supra 6.1). Secondly, copyright protection could serve as a kind of safety net protection (see supra 6.2).

6.1   Limitations to DRM Protection

Copyright protection has never been unlimited. Some of the most noticeable limitations to copyright protection are the fair use defense and the limited duration of copyright protection. In contrast, the protection by DRM systems is potentially unlimited. DRM systems may protect digital content that is not copyrightable or restrict acts that are exempted from copyright protection. It is a complex question whether and to what extent copyright limitations should also apply to the different means of protection in a DRM system.

6.1.1   Law and Economics Perspective

From a law and economics perspective, one has to ask what the justifications for copyright limitations are and whether these justifications are valid also in the DRM context.

There is no single economic explanation of copyright limitations. One way of explaining is to view copyright as a sort of monopoly (which is a severe oversimplification, however). According to this view, copyright law – like any monopoly – allows the copyright owner to raise the price for his work above marginal costs.[10] Thereby, fewer consumers buy the work compared to a perfectly competitive market. This can lead to a social welfare loss due to the underutilization of the work (for a detailed explanation, see [10, chapter 10], [11, at 301-305]). From this perspective, it is the goal of copyright law and its limitations to reconcile two possible welfare losses: the welfare loss due to the underproduction of content (leading to copyright protection, see section 5.2) and the welfare loss due to the underutilization of the produced content (leading to copyright limitations). This analysis can be applied to DRM systems as well. Just like copyright law, DRM systems allow the content provider to charge prices above marginal costs. Therefore, DRM systems can lead to a socially wasteful

---

[10] Marginal costs are the costs to produce one additional unit of a good.

underuse of the protected content as well.[11] From this perspective, the protection by DRM systems should be limited just as copyright protection should be limited.[12]

Another way to look at copyright law – which in the last few years has continuously gained support – views copyright protection not so much as a tool to induce the creation of new works, but rather as an instrument to facilitate a market for the exchange of rights to creative works that can move to their highest socially valued uses. From this viewpoint, copyright law enables copyright owners to charge consumers for access not so much to give an incentive as to determine what creative works are worth and thus to create a guide for resource allocation (cf. [15, at 309-310]). For this line of thought, copyright limitations are far less important, as the allocation of rights should be left to the market to the largest extent possible. If one applies this theory to the protection by DRM systems, limitations could play only a minor role.

Another way of justifying copyright limitations is to view them mainly as an answer to high transaction costs. If the costs involved in forming and enforcing a contract between the copyright owner and the consumer are higher than the value of the transaction, the transaction will never occur and the consumer will not use the work. In such cases, it can be more efficient to limit copyright protection so that the consumer does not have to ask for permission to use the work. As DRM systems could lead to lower transaction costs (search engines could lower search and information costs, metadata could lower negotiation and enforcement costs, the latter of which could also be lowered significantly by technological protection measures), the necessity to limit DRM protection could diminish.

It is far beyond the scope of this article to analyze the conflicting economic theories concerning the necessary limitations to copyright and DRM protection in detail. The economic explanation of such limitations and their implications on the dynamic innovation process remain one of the great puzzles of the economic analysis of copyright law. For the purposes of this article it suffices to realize that even among the proponents of a very broad copyright and DRM protection, it is a widespread opinion that the protection should be limited at least in some respects (see, e.g., [16, at 135]). External effects and other factors still require the limitation of copyright and DRM protection (see [17, at 1056-1058]).

If one accepts the notion that the protection by DRM systems should be limited in some respects – whatever those respects may be – the question arises who should determine those limits. In principle, this can be accomplished either by market forces or by the law. According to one view, DRM systems whose technological or contractual protection is biased too much towards the interests of content providers and do not take appropriate limitations into account will not be successful on the market

---

[11] The reason for this parallelism lies in the fact that the welfare loss due to underproduction, which justifies both copyright and DRM protection, results from the non-rival nature of digital content. This is not changed by the way content is protected.

[12] Some commentators argue that the DRM protection should not be limited if the content provider can engage in nearly perfect price discrimination in a DRM system. Generally, the intertwining of technological and contractual protection in a DRM system offers numerous means to engage in price discrimination. However, it is a highly contested issue whether such price discrimination would really render limitations to the protection unnecessary; see [12-14].

because consumers simply will not buy them. Therefore, no action by the legislator or the courts has to be taken to limit DRM protection because it is the competition among vendors how consumers are protected in the DRM field (see [5, at 1453]).

However, this view assumes that well-functioning competition between different DRM systems or producers of DRM-protected content exists. This is questionable at least. Within DRM systems, information asymmetries, indirect network effects and lock-ins can occur, leading to market failures and thereby preventing well-functioning competition. Therefore, many commentators argue that it is the law that has to limit the protection of DRM systems in order to preserve fair use and other public values in the DRM field.

6.1.2   Legal Perspective

From a strictly legal perspective, the necessity to limit the protection by DRM systems becomes even more obvious. Copyright limitations such as the fair use defense in the U.S. or the more differentiated provisions in Continental Europe serve important societal goals. They preserve the free flow of information, freedom of speech and functioning competition. They induce the creation of new works, serve educational and cultural purposes, enable criticism, comment, parody, news reporting and other uses in the public interest and sometimes even protect privacy interests.

The justifications for these limitations are valid in DRM systems as well. Basically, DRM systems enable the content provider to create his own copyright law and determine the scope of protection by himself. Thereby, content providers tend to protect their own interests in DRM systems without paying adequate attention to interests of users or the society at large. And in fact, recent examples in the ebook sector demonstrate that DRM systems currently available prevent uses that would be permissible under traditional copyright limitations.

Nevertheless, some commentators argue that it is not necessary to limit the protection by DRM systems because the content is always available in other, less-protected formats: If it is impossible to extract a movie clip from a DRM-protected DVD for educational purposes, the consumer can still use a much-less protected VHS version for extraction. However, this argument is flawed in two ways. Firstly, there will be more and more content which is only available in a DRM-protected format. Secondly, in numerous jurisdictions it is highly questionable whether such a "fair use defense of inferior quality" could be legally constructed.

In summary, the intertwining means of protection in a DRM system have the potential to supplant copyright protection. However, no real reason seems to be in sight why the limitations to copyright protection may become obsolete as well. While the content provider is able to protect himself by the means of protection in a DRM system, the protection of the consumers and the society at large still depends on the law. Therefore, copyright law might transform itself from a body of law that protects creators to a consumer-protection statute. As Lawrence Lessig puts it: "The problem will center not on copy-right but on copy-duty – the duty of owners of protected property to make that property accessible" ([18, at 127]).

6.2   Copyright Law as a Safety Net

Besides limiting the protection offered by a DRM system, copyright law can have some other purposes as well in the DRM context. It is an oversimplification that a content provider can effectively protect himself by using technology and contracts. There will be numerous instances in a real-world DRM system where the technological and/or contractual protection fails: Contracts can be void or unenforceable. Technological protection can be defeated; the supporting circumvention prohibitions do not cover every attack and every person involved in an attack. In such situations, a right is useful that is effective against all the world: the protection of content providers by copyright law could fill protection gaps left open by the DRM protection. However, copyright law will not serve as the primary means of protection for content providers, but will only step in as a safety net when all other means of protection in a DRM system fail (see figure 2).

7   Law as a Limitation to the Paradigm Shift in Protection

As section 6 has shown, it seems to be necessary to limit the protection of DRM systems by law. As the different means of protection are interchangeable to a large extent (see above, section 5.1), this applies to all means of protection used in a DRM system. Overall, this analysis leads to the following completed interaction of different means of protection in a DRM system (see figure 2):

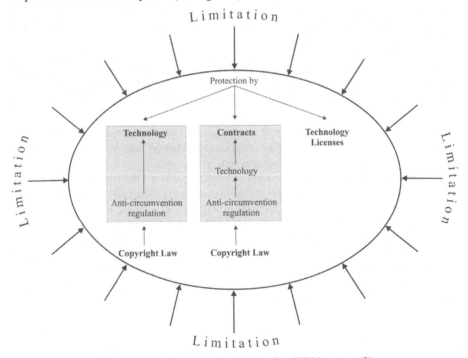

Fig. 2. Different means of protection in a DRM system (2)

In the following section, a short overview is given concerning whether and how legislators in the U.S. and Europe have responded to this need to restrict the different means of protection in a DRM system.

7.1   Limitation of the Protection by Contracts

In a DRM system, the content provider could in principle override copyright limitations such as the fair use defense by employing a contractual protection scheme. In the software sector, contractual terms forbidding the reverse engineering of software have been known for years. This raises the question whether the balance between the interests of copyright owners and the public as determined by copyright law can be altered by contractual arrangements. In the U.S., the tension between copyright and contract has attracted a significant amount of attention among legal scholars. The discussion reached its summit with an important decision by the 7th Circuit Court of Appeals ([5]) and the drafting of the public policy provision of the "Uniform Computer Information Transactions Act" (UCITA, see [6]). Under current U.S. law, DRM contract terms can be unenforceable if they are found to be unconscionable, in violation of public policy or of basics of the federal intellectual property scheme. Nevertheless, the scope of permissible DRM contract terms is still unclear under U.S. law and will probably remain so for some time.

In Europe, until now astonishingly the tension between copyright limitations and contractual arrangements has not been discussed a great deal. The European directives in the copyright area contain only very isolated provisions that prohibit the overriding of copyright limitations by contract. The recently adopted Copyright Directive of 2001 states explicitly that copyright limitations as defined in the directive should not prevent "contractual relations designed to ensure fair compensation for the rights holders" ([2, at 14]). In some member states of the European Union, blanket provisions of consumer protection statutes can limit the contractual freedom.

7.2   Limitation of the Protection by Technology Licenses

Copyright limitations can be invalidated by technology license agreements. If a hardware manufacturer is obliged by a technology license to manufacture only devices that do not allow the consumers to make personal copies of DRM-protected content, such a license term in fact abrogates copyright limitations. So far, this aspect of technology licenses has not been addressed at all in the legal discussion of DRM systems.[13]

7.3   Limitation of the Protection by Technology

Copyright limitations can be overridden by technological protection measures as well. In order to reconcile both in DRM systems, several regulatory options are available (see [19]).

---

[13] Only the U.S. Federal Communications Commission dealt with this aspect in its examination of the "POD Host Interface License Agreement", see [7, at 15, 19, and the separate statement of Commissioner Gloria Tristani].

7.3.1   Direct Influence on the Design of Technological Protection Measures

The first regulatory option for a legislator is to enact provisions that directly affect the design of technological protection measures. For instance, the legislator could mandate by law that technological measures must allow a certain number of copies for private or educational purposes without any additional permission by the content provider. Worldwide, the legislators only rarely take this approach. In Europe, article 3 (a) of the revised Television Directive of 1997 [20] requires that certain "events of major importance for society" (e.g. sports events such as the Olympic Games) be available not only on technologically protected pay TV channels. Whereas this statutory limitation of technological protection measures is not based on copyright considerations, it uses the same regulatory approach as described in this subsection.

7.3.2   Limiting the Anti-circumvention Protection

The second regulatory option to solve the tension between technological protection measures and necessary limitations to this protection is to restrict the legal protection of technological protection measures. The legislator could deny the protection by anti-circumvention provisions in certain cases. Without legal protection, there is no reason why the user should not be allowed to circumvent the technological protection. Basically, this approach gives the user a "right to hack" technological protection measures in certain cases specified by law.

This approach has been taken by the U.S. "Digital Millennium Copyright Act" (DMCA) of 1998. The very broad protection of technological access and usage control measures in 17 U.S.C. § 1201 (a) and (b) is limited by several very specific exceptions in § 1201 (d)-(j) (protecting libraries, law enforcement, reverse engineering, encryption research, privacy and security testing). Nevertheless, the DMCA has produced lots of legitimate criticism (see [21]). Firstly, several of the exceptions to the anti-circumvention provisions do not authorize the creation of tools necessary for benefiting from the exception. Essentially, this makes the exceptions meaningless. Secondly, there is no exception to the anti-circumvention protection that is as broad as the fair use defense to copyright law. There are numerous uses that are lawful under traditional copyright law but not under DMCA's anti-circumvention provisions. It is difficult to see a good reason for this differentiation. Finally, the relationship between the anti-circumvention provisions and the protection of free speech under the First Amendment to the U.S. Constitution remains a complex and unresolved problem. Basically, these are the issues that lie beneath many of the current legal quarrels concerning the DMCA, especially the DeCSS, Felten, Ferguson and Sklyarov cases.

7.3.3   "Key Escrow" Approach

A third regulatory option tries to evade some of the disadvantages of the approaches aforementioned. Under this approach, a consumer who benefits from a limitation to DRM protection would not be allowed to develop or distribute circumvention devices as it is the case under the precedingly described approach. Rather, he would be entitled to obtain appropriate means (circumvention devices, decryption keys etc.) from some instance in order to circumvent the technological protection (see [22, at 99-104], [19]). This approach resembles the "key escrow" approach taken in the crypto debate as in both cases encrypted communications can be decrypted with appropriate tools that are legally available under certain circumstances from a specified authority.[14]

In the DRM context, this authority could be placed in the hands of either the content providers themselves or a trusted third party. As was shown above, copyright limitations serve public interests that are very often not congruent with the content providers' interests. Therefore, it would be a much better idea to charge an independent trusted third party with the administration of such a key escrow system. Otherwise, the content providers could unjustifiably refuse access to circumvention tools when the circumvention ran contrary to their own interests.

In the European Union, the Copyright Directive of 2001 [2] basically employs a modified "key escrow" approach. According to the lengthy and hardly understandable article 6 (4) of the directive, under certain circumstances content providers can be required by law to make circumvention devices or services available to consumers who benefit from some copyright limitation.[15] However, the provision itself severely restricts the scope of this "key escrow" approach in several ways. The most important restriction is that the possibility for the legislator to establish a key escrow system depends on the business model the content provider chooses: If the content provider offers his DRM-protected content over the Internet and if he conditions the access to the content on the prior formation of a contract (e.g. by using click-wrap contracts), the legislator is not allowed to establish any "key escrow" system at all (see article 6 (4) (4) of the directive). By choosing a specific business model, content providers can dispose of all copyright limitations – a highly questionable development.

Moreover, the "key escrow" approach has some general flaws as well (see [19, at 16-17]). Before benefiting from a limitation, a consumer would have to contact a "key escrow agency" in order to obtain the appropriate circumvention devices. Due to considerable transaction costs, this could have chilling effects significantly diminishing the total number of fair uses made in a society. The "key escrow" approach could lead to a centralization of copyright limitations where only a few actors determine who benefits from such limitations for what purposes.

Ultimately, one will have to get used to the fact that no silver-bullet solution exists for reconciling technological protection measures with necessary limitations to this protection. Each approach has some drawbacks. The current regulations in the U.S. and the European Union each are overly complex and inconsistent. Unfortunately, we are far away from a coherent solution of the tension between technology and public interests in the DRM field.

8   Conclusion

Within DRM systems, content providers protect their interests by the combination of technology, contracts, anti-circumvention regulations and technology license agree-

---

[14] The idea of the "key escrow" or "key recovery" approach was to establish trusted third parties that keep copies of the users' private decryption keys (or at least of parts thereof). Thereby, the prosecution authorities and intelligence services would have the ability to intercept encrypted communications and decrypt them properly.

[15] However, this does not seem to be the only approach allowed under article 6 (4).

ments. The protection by traditional copyright law plays only a minor role as a safety net. Rather, the intertwining of the different means of protection mentioned could supplant copyright protection to a large extent. Legislators support this development by enacting anti-circumvention regulations that protect the content provider only indirectly and by treating shrink-wrap licenses as enforceable contracts. There are some dangers to this development, however. Firstly, it is far from clear that content providers really need the combination of five different means of protection (technology, contracts, technology licenses, anti-circumvention regulations and copyright law) instead of one (copyright law). Unfortunately, the assumption that such a "hyperprotection" is necessary is rarely challenged. Secondly, in DRM systems the control over the design of informational rights is shifted into the hands of private parties, who may or may not honor the interests of third persons or the society at large. It is the law that has to react to this "overprivatization" and limit the different means of protection in a DRM system.

These features of DRM regulation – an increasing protection by technology and contracts, an increasing privatization of protection, the statutory limitation of this privatization to preserve public values as well as the retreat of the legislators to mere indirect regulations – are common to many areas of Internet law. For instance, in the privacy field, discussions are going on as to whether consumers can protect their privacy interests by contractual licenses or privacy-enhancing technologies (*protection by contract or technology*). Concerning the tension between domain names and trademarks, the "Internet Corporation for Assigned Names and Numbers" (ICANN) has established a dispute resolution mechanism (Uniform Dispute Resolution Policy, UDRP). It enables trademark holders to challenge the registrant of a domain name and potentially gain control over the name. By a pyramid of contracts, ICANN – which is a private entity – obliges every domain name registrant to participate in such dispute resolutions. Some commentators have criticized this as the creation of a new body of international, but private trademark law (*privatization of protection*). Statistical analyses of the cases decided so far under the UDRP also suggest that public values (e.g. the use of domain names for criticism or parody purposes) might not be adequately preserved in this system (*tension between private ordering and public values*). Concerning the protection of minors on the Internet, private companies have developed filtering software that deny minors access to harmful content (*protection by technology*). It is no longer the state that provides this protection, but rather private software companies (*privatization of protection*). Many commentators have criticized such filtering software as means of "private censorship" (*tension between private ordering and public values*).

In such a context, it is no longer the role of the law alone to solve the regulatory problems at stake. Rather, the law has to provide a framework in which other regulators (e.g. technology or market forces) can evolve securely and effectively. The role of the law diminishes to a structural and backup responsibility. Questions of how to regulate self-regulation become vitally important.

Confronted with the myriad of problems in the DRM context, the solutions offered by the different disciplines appear disillusioning. The *technological* development of DRM systems is not yet complete. Large problems remain in the area of system security, interoperability and system integration. The *economic* analysis of DRM systems, e-commerce and the information society in general still poses numerous unresolved problems. From a *business* perspective, it is an open question which business model for distributing digital content will prevail and what level of security measures and usability restrictions the consumers will be willing to accept in a DRM system. In the *legal* area, the situation is no better by any means. Difficult legal questions remain unresolved. Legislators enact overly complex statutes the implications of which nobody can really foresee.

This article did not try to solve these problems. Instead, it tried to give an overview of some of them and to show that they can be grasped much better when one looks at them from a multidisciplinary perspective. Furthermore, this article did not cover all aspects of DRM. While it viewed DRM systems mainly as tools to prevent consumers from unauthorized copying and to control the use of digital content, DRM systems can be also viewed as instruments to enable digital distribution platforms where innovative business models can be implemented. A comprehensive analysis of DRM systems would need to take such business aspects as well as social implications into account and interweave the results with other parts of the analysis of Digital Rights Management.

References

1. Bechtold, Stefan: Vom Urheber- zum Informationsrecht – Implikationen des Digital Rights Management, Munich 2002
2. Directive 2001/29/EC of the European Parliament and of the Council of 22 May 2001 on the harmonization of certain aspects of copyright and related rights in the information society. Official Journal of the European Communities L 167, June 22, 2001, pp. 10-19
3. Directive 98/84/EC of the European Parliament and of the Council of 20 November 1998 on the legal protection of services based on, or consisting of, conditional access. Official Journal of the European Communities L 320, November 28, 1998, pp. 54-57
4. Universal Music Group/InterTrust Technologies Corporation: *Bluematter End User License Agreement*, http://offers.bluematter.com/sniffer/terms.htm (visited Dec. 11, 2001)
5. ProCD, Inc. v. Zeidenberg, 86 F.3d 1447-1455 (7th Cir. 1996)
6. UCITA online, http://www.ucitaonline.com (visited Dec. 11, 2001)
7. Federal Communications Commission: *In re Implementation of Section 304 of Telecommunications Act of 1996*, 15 F.C.C.R. 18,199 (Sep. 18, 2000)
8. OpenCable Initiative, http://www.opencable.com (visited Dec. 11, 2001)
9. Landes, William M./Posner, Richard A.: *An Economic Analysis of Copyright Law*, 18 Journal of Legal Studies 325-363 (1989)
10. Pindyck, Robert S./Rubinfeld, Daniel L.: *Microeconomics*, 5th edition, Upper Saddle River 2001
11. Posner, Richard A.: *Economic Analysis of Law*, 5th edition, New York 1998
12. Fisher, William W.: *Property and Contract on the Internet*, 73 Chicago-Kent Law Review 1203-1256 (1998)

13. Boyle, James: Cruel, Mean, or Lavish? Economic Analysis, Price Discrimination and Digital Intellectual Property, 53 Vanderbilt Law Review 2007-2039 (2000)

14. Gordon, Wendy J.: Intellectual Property as Price Discrimination: Implications for Contract, 73 Chicago-Kent Law Review 1367-1390 (1998)

15. Netanel, Neil Weinstock: *Copyright and a Democratic Civil Society*, 106 Yale Law Journal 283-387 (1996)

16. Merges, Robert P.: The End of Friction? Property Rights and Contract in the "Newtonian" World of On-Line Commerce, 12 Berkeley Technology Law Journal 115-136 (1997)

17. Lemley, Mark A.: *The Economics of Improvement in Intellectual Property Law*, 75 Texas Law Review 989-1084 (1997)

18. Lessig, Lawrence: *Code and Other Laws of Cyberspace*, New York 1999

19. Burk, Dan L./Cohen, Julie E.: *Fair Use Infrastructure for Copyright Management Systems*, 2000, http://papers.ssrn.com/abstract_id=239731 (visited Dec. 11, 2001)

20. Directive 97/36/EC of the European Parliament and of the Council of 30 June 1997 amending Council Directive 89/552/EEC on the coordination of certain provisions laid down by law, regulation or administrative action in Member States concerning the pursuit of television broadcasting activities. Official Journal of the European Communities L 202, July 30, 1997, pp. 60-71

21. Samuelson, Pamela: Intellectual Property and the Digital Economy: Why the Anti-Circumvention Regulations Need to Be Revised, 14 Berkeley Technology Law Journal 504-566 (1999)

22. Stefik, Mark: The Internet Edge. Social, Legal, and Technological Challenges for a Networked World, Cambridge 1999

Taking the Copy Out of Copyright

Ernest Miller[1] and Joan Feigenbaum[2]*

[1] Information Society Project, Yale Law School, PO Box 207286, New Haven, CT,
USA 06520
ernest.miller@aya.yale.edu
[2] Computer Science, Yale University, PO Box 208285, New Haven, CT, USA
06520
joan.feigenbaum@yale.edu

Abstract. Under current U.S. law and common understanding, the
fundamental right granted by copyright is the right of reproduction – of
making copies. Indeed, the very word "copyright" appears to signify
that the right to control copying must be a fundamental part of any
system of copyright. Nonetheless, we claim that this assumption is
incorrect. The advent of digital documents has illuminated this issue: In
the digital realm, copying is not a good predictor of intent to infringe;
moreover, copying of digital works is necessary for normal use of those
works. We argue that the right to control copying should be eliminated
as an organizing principle of copyright law. In its place, we propose as
an organizing principle the right to control public distribution of the
copyrighted work.

1   Copyright Is Not About Copying

Under current U.S. law and common understanding, the fundamental right granted by
copyright is the right of reproduction – of making copies. Certainly, the first
"exclusive right" granted to the owner of a copyright under Section 106 of the
Copyright Act[1] is the right to reproduce the copyrighted work "in copies or
phonorecords" or to authorize such reproduction. Indeed, the very word "copyright"
appears to signify that the right to make copies must be a fundamental part of any
system of copyright. Nevertheless, we believe that the primacy given to the right of
copying, while seemingly intuitive, is both illogical and counterproductive,
particularly when one considers its application to digital documents. We base our
analysis on both the nature and characteristics of the digital realm and on a historical
and instrumental understanding of the law of copyright.

  Our examination of whether reproduction should play a central role in copyright
law is motivated in part by the question of security in digital rights management

---

*   Supported in part by ONR grants N00014-01-1-0795 and N00014-01-1-0447 and NSF grant
    CCR-0105337
[1]   17 U.S.C. §106.

T. Sander (Ed.): DRM 2001, LNCS 2320, pp. 233–244, 2002.

(DRM). Many designers of DRM technology seek to enforce copyright by controlling copying. Consequently, there is careful attention paid in the security and cryptology literature to the question of whether such control is technologically feasible and, if so, at what cost to our computing and networking environments. Experience to date with fielded DRM systems is limited, but it seems to indicate that copy control is at best quite difficult in a world of networked general-purpose PCs. We believe that it would be far more productive to organize copyright law around something other than the right to control copying than it would be to change the fundamental designs of PCs and networks.

The purpose of copyright is instrumental. In the United States, copyright is not a right of the author by reason of his creation. Copyright is not a Lockean "natural right" but is a limited right granted to authors in order to further the public interest. This principle is explicitly expressed in the U.S. Constitution, which grants the power to create a system of copyright to Congress in order to further the public interest in "promoting progress in science and the useful arts."[2] This point cannot be overemphasized: Copyright has a purpose – to further the public good by promoting the creation and dissemination of knowledge. Thus, copyright is structured to create incentives for authors to create and publishers to distribute new works – that authors and publishers benefit from these rights is the means and not the end of copyright.

By granting certain exclusive rights to authors, copyright seeks to ensure that authors will be able to recoup the costs associated with their ingenuity and publishers the costs of distribution. The paradigmatic example of this is the book publishing industry, where an author grants a publisher the right to print and vend a work in return for payment. The payment from publisher to author is recompense for the author's creativity. The publisher then sells instances of the work instantiated in a physical medium (copies) to recoup not only the author's payment but manufacturing and distribution costs (plus profit). Obviously, if a pirate press is able to publish its own edition of the work with impunity, the (legitimate) publisher will suffer economically, and authors will not be properly compensated for their creativity. Thus, as the conventional history would have it, was born the right of reproduction.

Unfortunately for the conventional history, in the Copyright Act of 1790, reproduction was not one of the rights granted to the author. This first federal copyright statute did not mention copying at all. Instead, the statute spoke of "publishing, printing, and vending." All three of these terms mean something other than the simple reproduction of a work – they imply distribution.[3] After all, it is the *distribution of copies to the public* that cause the publisher to suffer economically. The publisher cannot be harmed by copies that are never distributed and, for example, sit moldering in a warehouse.[4] Conversely, one cannot distribute what one does not

---

[2] U.S.C.A. Const. Art. 1, § 8, cl. 8.

[3] While it may seem that "printing" does not necessarily entail distribution, the "right to print" was subordinate to the right to publish. Although the right to print might be held by a party other than the one that held the right to publish, the right to print did not exist without a corresponding right to publish.

[4] This is not to say that an individual found with hundreds of unauthorized copies of Microsoft Windows XP in a warehouse should be free of liability. Certainly, the creation of such a large number of copies of a commercially valuable copyrighted work would be a strong indication

have. Distribution to the public is the necessary condition for harm to the publishers' economic interests.[5] Distribution, in the broad sense, can occur with or without copying. Thus, it is not surprising that the original Copyright Act failed to mentioning "copying" *per se* as an exclusive right.

Furthermore, since the purpose of copyright is to provide the opportunity for exploitation as an incentive to innovation, presumably the rights in copyright should be capable of exploitation independently. This is not the case for reproduction, which cannot be exploited independently of the right to distribute. What value does the right of reproduction have absent the right of distribution?[6]

Historically, the fundamental object of copyright law was not a copy or copies of a work but rather publication of the work. The meaning of "copy," as used in the word copyright, was a reference to the manuscript. The "copyright" was certain exclusive rights with regard to the manuscript, in particular the right to publish – not an exclusive right of reproduction. The etymology of the term "copy" (from the Oxford English Dictionary) as used within the copyright is clear:

IV.   That which is copied
8. a.   The original writing, work of art, etc. from which a copy is made.
      ...

9. a.   *Printing.* Manuscript (or printed) matter prepared for printing. (Now always without *a* and *pl.*)
      Formerly used in a sense nearer to 8: a MS. [Manuscript] or other exemplar which is printed from, or serves as 'copy', though not specially prepared for that purpose.
   b.   Property in 'copy'; = COPYRIGHT. *Obs.*
      In its beginnings, only contextually differing from 9: the registration and licensing of the 'copy' or 'copies' proposed to be printed, conferred the 'right'.[7]

Copyright is not about the right of reproduction *per se* but rather the licensing and registration of the "*copy,*" in other words, the work (or, as the U.S. Constitution refers to it, "writings") for publication. Indeed, it is unlikely that the idea of an independent right of reproduction would have been conceivable when the term copyright was developed. Although early copyright did distinguish between the right "to publish" and the right "to print," printing was clearly subordinate to the publishing right, which

---

of *intent* to distribute. Harm to Microsoft, however, would not occur until the copies actually were distributed.

[5] Comm. on Intellectual Property Rights and the Emerging Information Infrastructure, National Research Council, *The Digital Dilemma: Intellectual Property in the Information Age* 141 (National Academy Press 2000) [hereinafter *The Digital Dilemma*].

[6] Of course, one might claim that the right of reproduction governs the making of copies for personal use (where there is no distribution) and that personal uses may thus be economically exploited. For example, a publisher might charge a higher price for an e-book from which text could be cut-and-pasted than an e-book from which text could only be manually copied. This, however, would turn copyright into a mandatory licensing scheme. Either a right would be explicitly granted or it would only exist within the vagaries of implied license or fair use. Such a result is unsatisfactory for reasons explained below.

[7] Oxford English Dictionary (2nd ed. 1989) (italics in original)

was the right to have the copy reproduced for distribution to the public. The idea of a right to print without an associated right to publish would have been inconceivable at the time.

As a matter of fact, the term "copying" did not enter the copyright statutes until the Copyright Act of 1909. The term was used as a generic addition to the original "publishing, printing, and vending" in order to take into account the various new forms of mechanical reproduction that were proliferating at the turn of the century. After all, it does not necessarily seem appropriate to speak of "printing" or "publishing" statuary. The addition of the term "copying," then, was not the creation of a new right but an extension of the existing regime to ensure coverage of the new technologies of the era.

Once the term "copying" entered the statute, it is easy to see how it could eventually come to be interpreted as granting a right to reproduction. In the first decades of the twentieth century, this was actually sensible. After all, prior to the advent of electronics, making copies of a work was difficult and rather expensive. It is not simple to set hot lead for a printing press or to transfer a motion picture to negative in order to develop new positives. Accordingly, reproduction was a good predictor of an intention to distribute as well. There are few legitimate reasons, for example, to set lead type in order to make one or two copies of a book for personal use.[8] In a world in which works are embodied in difficult-to-reproduce physical objects, it is reasonable to assume that, if someone goes to the trouble of making multiple copies, he intends to distribute them.

Indeed, under current law, the fixation requirement for copying requires that a "copy" be "sufficiently permanent or stable to permit it to be perceived, reproduced, or otherwise communicated for a period of more than transitory duration."[9] One of the reasons for the fixation requirement is that transitory "copies" will not last long enough to be distributed, certainly not long enough to be distributed to the public in such a way as to undermine the incentive structure of copyright. If copying alone were harm to the incentive structure of copyright, it would be hard to justify the fixation requirement. The fear, then, is not of reproduction itself, but of subsequent distribution of the resulting copies. Undeniably, the statutory exceptions to the right of reproduction are numerous (making of ephemeral copies,[10] backups and runtime copies of computer software,[11] and some digital sound recordings[12]). One has to wonder when the exceptions are so numerous whether the underlying rule is the appropriate one.

However, in the networked, general-purpose computer world, digital documents are not hard to copy at all, whether fixed or transitory. Reproduction, then, is not a good predictor of whether there will be distribution to the public in the digital world. For example, web pages are copied into temporary caches so that browsers can display them quickly, programs are copied from hard drive to RAM so that they can be run, and entire file systems are copied onto back-up stores to ensure that they are

---

[8] We cannot think of any plausible reasons for such an action.

[9] 17 U.S.C. § 101

[10] 17 U.S.C. § 112

[11] 17 U.S.C. § 117

[12] 17 U.S.C. § 1008

protected from user errors, software bugs, and malicious intruders. Digital music may be among the most versatile media. Music on CD is copied from disk to hard drive in order to be used by jukebox software, transported to school or office via laptop, or copied into an MP3 player to listen to while jogging. In these and numerous other ordinary circumstances, digital files are "copied" in the literal sense, but in none of them is there an intention to distribute to the public that would undercut the publisher's ability to benefit from the work.

The point is that, in computers and networks, copies are made *constantly*, often without explicit instruction by or even knowledge of a particular user. Surely there is a better conceptual starting point for the development of copyright law than to define each of the copies as presumptively infringing.

More important is the fact that copies are not only frequently and continuously made in the computer world but moreover are *necessary* in order to make use of a work -- any use. This is something entirely new in the realm of copyright. Reproduction is not necessary to access a work embodied in a physical artifact. No copying is required to read a book or watch a movie. However, copying is necessary in order to read an e-book or watch a DVD. In the digital world, the right to control copying becomes tantamount to a right to control *access* to a work for purposes of normal use, such as reading, viewing, and listening.[13] In the digital world, the right to control copying means that actually reading an e-book is presumptively a violation of the copyright owner's rights.

Of course, it is very unlikely that a court would decide that reading was not a right granted by purchase of a digital book. However, the decision in such a case would have to rest on some other aspect of copyright law, such as fair use or implied license. Such reliance on alternative doctrines is less than satisfactory. For example, it would be strange indeed for a court to conclude that reading an e-book is only justified by the affirmative defense of fair use or that reading is permissible as an implied license and thus occurs at the sufferance of the copyright owner, who may disavow such a use.

Our proposed approach to this problem of the right to reproduce in the digital age is a radical one: Eliminate the right to control copying as a fundamental aspect of copyright and as an organizing principle of intellectual-property law. We believe that efforts to accommodate the right of reproduction in copyright of digital works will fail. For example, attempts to distinguish between "permanent" and "transient" copies will fail because of the truly vast number of circumstances in which computers and networks makes copies. Attempting to make such fine technological distinctions would cause the resulting law to be far too complex, even by the Byzantine standards of copyright law. Furthermore, the rapidity of technological evolution would seem to counsel strongly against adopting a decision-making process so dependent upon technologically specific circumstances.[14]

Our solution lies in a return to the original understanding of and principles behind copyright, principles that are more appropriate in the digital realm than the "copy-centric" view of current copyright law. In our view, copyright should return to its

---

[13] *The Digital Dilemma*, 141-4.

[14] For example, in the case of "permanent" and "transient" copies, how would law adapt to a major shift in technology, for example, from volatile to non-volatile RAM?

focus on *distribution to the public*. The rights of distribution, public performance, and display are all examples of distribution (broadly defined) to the public and reflect early copyright law's focus on publishing, printing, and vending. We do not address the issue of derivative works. Copying, absent distribution to the public, should not be considered a violation of copyright at all.[15]

We now analyze two key doctrines of copyright law in light of our position.

1.1   First Sale Doctrine – Physical Property Only

The history of the first sale doctrine is coterminous with the history of copyright itself and developed as case law[16] prior to statutory codification. Formalized by legislation in 1976 as Section 109 of the Copyright Act, the doctrine is framed as a limitation on the copyright owner's exclusive right to distribute works; it entitles the owner of *a particular copy* of a work to "sell or otherwise dispose of" that particular copy *without the permission of the copyright holder*. The first sale doctrine does not restrict the copyright owner's exclusive right to *make* copies or to authorize the making of copies. The first sale doctrine also incorporates certain other restrictions; for example, it only applies to lawfully made (authorized) copies and only to the "owner" of such copies. In other words, one cannot sell or loan what one does not own. It is this doctrine that enables the existence of libraries, used book stores, and video rental stores.[17]

With regard to works in digital format, the first sale doctrine is an anachronism; it is essentially concerned with copyrighted works embodied in physical objects. Indeed, the doctrine is actually an element of property law that prevents copyright from running roughshod over other areas of law. Without the first sale doctrine, a copyright owner might claim, for example, that you were not permitted to resell a book for less than its original value or could not throw it away without the publisher's permission. If this "right" were accepted, imagine the consequences that would result if all items of manufacture had copyrighted material embodied in them, such as a haiku poem stamped on the bottom of a lamp. Suddenly, questions of personal property and normal trade would become questions of copyright.[18] Such control would be at

---

[15] Others have also advocated jettisoning the focus on the right of reproduction. See Jessica Litman, *Digital Copyright* 177-80 (Prometheus Books, 2001) [hereinafter, *Digital Copyright*]. Litman has offered, as an alternative organizing and fundamental principle, the right of the copyright owner to prevent others from commercially exploiting the work. Our alternative organizing principle is simply to emphasize the right of public distribution.

[16] Bobbs-Merrill Co. v. Straus, 210 U.S. 339, 350-51 (1908).

[17] Note, however, that lending, leasing, and rental have certain limitations with regard to phonorecords (or sound recordings) and computer software in the statute.

[18] Nimmer on Copyright. Sec. 8.12[A] (p. 8-150.4): [T]he right to prevent unauthorized distribution at that point [after first sale] (although no doubt still desired by the copyright owner) is no longer a necessary supplement [to fully protect the owner]. In such circumstances, continued control over the distribution of copies is not so much a supplement to the intangible copyright, but is rather a device for controlling the disposition of the tangible personal property that embodies the copyrighted work. Therefore, at this point, the policy favoring a copyright monopoly for authors gives way to the policy opposing restraint of trade and restraints on alienation.

variance with common law, which disfavors restrictions on the free alienation of property.

Similar reasoning appears to apply to other areas of copyright law. For example, owners of a copy of a protected work are permitted "to display that copy publicly, either directly or by the projection of no more than one image at a time, to viewers present at the place where the copy is located."[19] Thus, for example, one may place lawfully purchased statuary (such as a garden gnome) on the front lawn where it will be displayed to the public. However, one may not broadcast the image of the gnome via television. Again, the focus seems to be on permitting an owner of physical goods to dispose of the physical property as desired without overly many restrictions.

Of course, while the first sale doctrine expresses elements of property law, it does point out some fundamental characteristics of copyright law. First, it shows that maximizing the return to authors and publishers is not, in fact, the ultimate aim of copyright. Through the first sale doctrine, among other things, individuals can gain access to copyrighted works through a number of means, many of which create no direct financial benefit for the copyright owner. After all, if you borrow a book from a friend, you are potentially depriving the publisher of a sale. Second, it shows that copyright owners do not have the right to regulate use (other than uses explicitly governed by copyright law itself) once the work is released into public channels. Once a member of the public acquires a particular copy of a work, he can use it in any legal manner he desires. If a reader desires to read the last chapter of the mystery novel first, he can do it, regardless of the copyright owner's desires. This shows that, traditionally, use-control has not been an exclusive right of the copyright owner.

The first sale doctrine applies to *particular copies* embodied in physical objects. Books, CDs, and videotapes are all examples of such physical embodiment. Such copies can only be possessed by one individual at a time, and transferring such an instance of the work does not involve reproduction. These characteristics are not shared by digital works on a computer or network. In the digital realm, there is no technologically sensible way to give a buyer of a particular instance of a digital work the right to redistribute that instance but withhold from him the right to copy it.

Our conclusion then is a radical one. The first sale doctrine simply does not apply in the realm of digital objects, though it remains applicable with regard to free alienation of physical copies. The values of more open access embodied in the rule are attainable but only by avoiding the copy-centrism of current law. In our argument, a violation occurs only if there is public distribution of a work not granted by the copyright owner.

Alternative proposals with regard to the first sale doctrine are even more radical. Some copyright absolutists argue that, because no one but the copyright owner has the right to make copies under existing law, no one but the copyright owner should be permitted to lend, trade, or sell digital objects at all, because doing so always entails making copies. Since, in the future, many forms of information will be available only in digital form, the alternate means of access to works that the first sale doctrine enabled would be virtually eliminated. Others propose systems that would force digital objects to behave like physical objects. One example of this "trusted-systems" vision is described in *The Digital Dilemma*:

---

[19] 17 U.S.C. § 109(c)

In these systems, when a merchant sells a digital object, the bits encoding the object would be deposited on the buyer's computer and erased from the merchant's computer. If the purchaser subsequently "loaned" this digital object, the access control and rights management systems on the lender's computer would temporarily disable the object's use on that computer while enabling use on the borrower's computer. These changes would be reversed when the object is returned by the borrower to the lender.[20]

We share the skepticism of the authors of *The Digital Dilemma* that such systems will enjoy successful technical development and market adoption in the near future.[21] Moreover, we reject the trusted-systems vision on the grounds that it vitiates the nature of digital documents. Transformative social benefits of the switch from analog to digital publication, if they are to occur at all, will derive in part from the fact that digital documents have fundamentally different characteristics from analog physical documents. If we were to try to ensure that digital documents behave like physical ones, we would eliminate the incentive to innovate. Finally, it is unlikely that such trusted systems would be acceptable to copyright holders themselves. If such a trusted system were both effective and economical, it would likely have devastating consequences for copyright owners, because lending of digital objects would become extremely efficient. In this scenario, large groups of like-minded individuals, neighborhoods, entire dorms, or apartment complexes would be able to share one digital object, such as a song, because all they would need to do in order to be in compliance with the law is use the trust-systems technology to ensure that no two people use the object at exactly the same time.

1.2   Fair Use

Prior to its codification in the Copyright Act of 1976, fair use was a judicially created doctrine governing the use of one work in the work of another.[22] It was analogous to fair competition law. There were fair uses (uses by one author, such as a reviewer, of another author's work, the subject of the review), and there were unfair uses, such as out-and-out plagiarism. But there was another category of use, use that was not competitive at all and thus not subject to fair use analysis. This might be called "normal use," use by the consumer.

This makes sense. When a consumer obtains access to a copy of a work, *i.e.*, a copy embodied in a physical medium such as a book or CD, the consumer is actually obtaining the ability to make use of the work (an intangible object). The physical medium itself is largely irrelevant.[23] This ability to make use of the work accrues

---

[20] *The Digital Dilemma*, 167-8.

[21] However, we do agree that such a system, if effective, should protect its users under both current law and our proposal from conviction for copyright infringement.

[22] Sony Computer Entertainment America, Inc. v. Bleem, LLC, 214 F.3d 1022, 1025-26 (9th Cir. 2000).

[23] It is possible for a publisher to create physical obstacles to certain uses – but that does not mitigate this right. For example, a publisher might print a book on paper that disintegrates in sunlight, hoping to prevent individuals from reading outside for some unfathomable reason.

simply through gaining access to the work. It is not an implied license from the publisher. For example, if one borrows a book from a library, one has the ability to read the work regardless of the desires of the publisher (who may be opposed to the loss of a potential sale). What the individual obtains is the ability to use the intangible work itself. Thus, when an individual accesses (by whatever means) the work by making personal use of it, no issue of competition is raised.

The very concept underlying fair use, the rules governing the use of one work in the work of another, does not apply to personal uses. After all, if an individual merely transfers a work to which she already has legitimate access from one physical medium to another physical medium, in what way is that using one work in the work of another? By photocopying a page from a book, does one suddenly become the author of a new work – one which incorporates the work of another? Mere copying for personal use should not raise a question of either fair or unfair use. Moreover, one of the early tests of fair use was whether the questionable use supplanted the market for the original. Personal uses do not supplant the market for the original. After all, if a user already has legitimately obtained a copy of the work, how can any copying supplant that copy absent distribution? The user may have altered the physical characteristics of the particular embodiment, but that has not supplanted the user's need for access to the work in the first place.

Unfortunately, the law of copyright has been transformed so that normal use by the consumer is not always permissible; rather, the permissibility of any use that incorporates copying must be decided on a case-by-case basis, usually under the rubric of fair use. While it is unlikely that a court would hold a single personal-use copy of a work to be infringing (even granting a plaintiff would bring such a case), the court would still have to apply fair use analysis to the copy, because fair use is an affirmative defense. Under current law, every copy is presumptively infringing, and copying may only be justified under the fair use doctrine. This is the case even when the original question underlying fair use analysis, whether or not the use is one that competes with the copyright owner, is not relevant.

This is important, because, in the transition to the digital world, copying has become much easier. When copying is difficult, it is likely that only commercial entities and those similarly situated would be making copies. Thus, copying *per se* could be enough to trigger a fair use analysis, because the relevant presumption was that copying would only take place in a commercial context with intent to distribute the work publicly. However, in the digital world, copying becomes necessary to make normal use of works. In order to watch a (lawfully-acquired) *Shrek* DVD on the video equivalent of an MP3 player, the movie must be copied from the DVD. This act of copying should not require, should the consumer be challenged, the mounting of an affirmative defense of fair use in which the copying is presumptively unfair. This act of copying should not be actionable at all.

Of course, the current state of affairs is that any copying is presumptively illicit. This being the case, it is lawful for copyright owners to inhibit all copying of their works. Unfortunately, because it is necessary to copy a digital work in order to make use of it, the prohibition against copying means that the copyright owner may

---

However, while the right of distribution allows the publisher to make such choices of printing materials, it would not prevent a clever reader from circumventing such limitations.

determine which uses are permissible and which are not. The doctrine of fair use, as it is now codified, completely undermines its own purpose in the context of digital works.

1.3   The Right of Public Distribution

To this point, we have been making the case that the idea that the right of reproduction as an exclusive right granted to the copyright owner is illogical and improper as applied to digital works. What, then, should the alternative principle be? We argue that the alternative principle is already part of existing law; it is *public distribution of instantiations of a work* that is the key right granted to a copyright holder. As we stated above, what harm to the copyright holder can come from copies that sit moldering in a warehouse? Harm can only occur if there is distribution to the public.

Indeed, Section 106 of the Copyright Act already limits the exclusive right of distribution to distributions made "to the public."[24] The right to make *private* distributions is not an exclusive right of the copyright owner. Furthermore, the concept of a public/private distinction is reinforced by the fact that it is only *public* performance and display of works that is a right of the copyright owner. In our analysis, both performance and display are forms of instantiation of a work. Performance is an instantiation of the work in action, and display is an exhibition of a physical instantiation of a work. Thus, performance and display imply forms of distribution. If it is *public distribution* that is the exclusive right, then performance, which is a form of distribution, only infringes when the performance is to the public. Both the rights of performance and display are unlike the right of reproduction, which, although an instantiation of a work, does not necessarily entail distribution.

This private/public distinction is very familiar in the realm of performance and display. After all, anyone who has ever invited friends over in order to watch a videotape or DVD has engaged in a private performance of a work. Playing a copyrighted song on the piano for friends, if anyone still does that, is also a private performance. An exclusive right to private distribution with regard to performance would be absurd. It would imply, for example, that it is presumptively infringing for a parent to read a copyrighted book to a child.

Some have argued that the right distinction in such cases is not private vs. public distribution but rather distribution that has limited effects on the commercial market (which would not be infringing) vs. distribution that has major effects on the commercial market (which would be infringing).[25] Indeed, it is argued that this distinction would be useful even in situations in which one person's acting on his own did not have major commercial effects, but the widespread and similar activities of

---

[24] Under current law, this right is odd in light of the prior right of reproduction, which makes the right of distribution redundant. After all, how can one distribute works to which this third exclusive right applies without first making copies? If making copies is a violation of the copyright owner's first exclusive right, there is no need for a right of public distribution, because any such distribution presupposes that copies have been made.

[25] *Digital Copyright* 180.

others would have commercially devastating effects.[26] In other words, posting a copyrighted song to a website would be permissible, as long as there were not too many downloads. According to this theory, there would be no problem if the practice was widespread, as long as each individual site did not have too many downloads. Such a result seems odd. Yet it is required unless one accepts the alternative economic test that certain forms of distribution are permissible unless the widespread practice of such forms of distribution would be commercially significant. This, of course, would be no test at all, because nearly every type of distribution would have commercially significant effects if practiced widely enough.

Moreover, the distinction between public and private fits very well with what is actually enforceable. After all, one of the major elements of private distribution is that it is *private*; it takes place where copyright owners will not be able to police it. Public distribution, on the other hand, takes place in *public*, where copyright owners will be able to monitor and patrol. For example, if a teenaged girl emails an MP3 to her father, this is a private distribution and one that the recording industry will likely never find about. The law might give the recording industry the right to prohibit this, but this law would be essentially unenforceable. However, if the teenage girl posts the MP3 on a website, it is possible for the recording industry to take appropriate action either against the girl or, ultimately, her ISP. There are any number of technical options to track, subvert, or otherwise interfere with public distributions of copyrighted works.

Fundamentally, it is extremely difficult for copyright owners to determine when the right of reproduction has been violated, unlike theft of physical property. Furthermore, the fact that the right of reproduction is very difficult to enforce is likely to lead to disrespect for the law. Of course, no law is perfectly enforced, but a law that can almost never be enforced independently is of questionable benefit.

Finally, reliance on public distribution will not substantially change the existing balance of economic incentives. To the extent that the right of reproduction is essentially unenforceable, copyright owners will be able to achieve the same amount of economic incentive through enforcement of the distribution right – which is essentially the status quo.

2   Conclusion

Today, it is commonly assumed that the right of reproduction, the right to control copying, is and always has been a fundamental element of copyright law. However, that assumption is incorrect.

Historically, the right of reproduction is of relatively recent provenance. Prior to the Copyright Act of 1909, there was no exclusive right to control copying. Indeed, even in the Copyright Act of 1909, which first mentioned the word "copy," it is more than arguable whether there was any intention to create a right of reproduction, rather than merely to extend existing rights of distribution to new subject matter.

Logically and theoretically, the right of reproduction is not fundamentally required to be part of a system of copyright. After all, copies *per se* do not harm any of the

---

[26] *Id.,* nn. 32.

interests that copyright is intended to support. The fact that the right to make copies is considered to be an essential element of copyright is the result of both misinterpretation of the origin of the word "copyright" and the fact that, for many years, the making of copies was a good predictor of intent to infringe.

However, digital technology has illuminated the issue and demonstrated that the traditional assumptions about the right of reproduction are false. In the digital age, copying is not a good predictor of intent to infringe. Moreover, copying is necessary for normal use of a work. Allowing normal use is a principle that copyright is supposed to support. To that extent, digital technology has revealed the illogic and inconsistency of the traditional view of the right of reproduction.

Of course, it is possible to attempt to write and interpret laws that uphold two inherently contradictory principles at once. Unfortunately, the results will be confusing and incoherent. The Digital Millennium Copyright Act is a good example of this. The DMCA purports to support the right of reproduction while maintaining existing rights of fair use. First, the concept of fair use codified in the Copyright Act of 1976 is itself incoherent as shown above. Second, the DMCA as interpreted by the courts does not protect fair use at all, except for those with a high level of technical skills. Third, the DMCA is confusing even by the standards of previous copyright laws.

Because the DMCA attempts to uphold two contradictory interests at once, it has numerous exceptions and exceptions to the exceptions.[27] Such messiness will always be necessary in order to harmonize, at least partially, two fundamentally opposed principles. This is not unlike the case of Ptolemaic cosmology, in which Ptolemy attempted to reconcile two opposing principles: the assumption that planets moved in perfect circles and the observed motion of the planets. Current copyright law, with its exceptions and exceptions to exceptions, is not very different from Ptolemy's epicycles and epicycles within epicycles.

In order for progress to occur, Copernicus abandoned the principle of circular motion in favor of observed motion – despite the widely and strongly held assumption that celestial motion must be "perfect." Just so, copy-centrism should be abandoned in favor of the right of public distribution.

---

[27] For example, a library may circumvent digital-rights-management software (which is otherwise prohibited) in order to determine whether to purchase access to a work, but not if an identical copy of the work is available in another format. 17 U.S.C. §1201.

Author Index

Lecture Notes in Computer Science

For information about Vols. 1–2252
please contact your bookseller or Springer-Verlag